Speedbird: Echoes of Yesteryear

Speedbird:Echoes of Yesteryear

The 8 Pillars of Wisdom: Airline Computing and my Role in its Development.

Don Hill

AuthorHouse™
1663 Liberty Drive
Bloomington, IN 47403
www.authorhouse.com
Phone: 1-800-839-8640

First published by AuthorHouse 01/25/2012

ISBN: 978-1-4567-8036-4 (sc)

Printed in the United States of America

This book is printed on acid-free paper.

In Loving Memory
'Don Hill: 1/6/23 to 3/4/11'
"Ciao Papa'!
(Photograph provided by Chris Hill)

Synopsis of the '8th Pillar' (chapters 1-3)

Unlike the television series Airport or Airline, this book covers an airline operation from the viewpoint of one individual over the last 60 years.

The current series of television programs tend to focus on a single Airport and the activities in episodic form of a few airlines at these airports.

The episodes in this book describe the scenes starting in 1941, when Airlines had barely changed from short into long pants, to the modern day activities of the same Airline, using all the modern technology advances made available to it over the 60years of growth.

In 1941 when this narrative starts any travel away from the UK especially during the war was an adventure. Living conditions at stations to which staff were sent, particularly in Africa, were very primitive to say the least.

The experiences recounted are all true, even though in time the facts may have become slightly distorted. Memory and time do play tricks to one's recollections. What has been recounted is only as good as that extracted from my memory bank and no additional research has been done for, if it had, it would ring less true.

The first 3 parts of this book cover my personal experiences whilst on overseas service with one of the world's great airlines. The period in question is from 1941 until the latter half of 1960.

Part 4 describes the writer's return to the UK and initial frustrations whilst being integrated into a whole new world. It also sets out in some detail the writer's experiences, and his part in the use of advancing technology to support that airline's entry into the post war years as one of the dominant players in the airline scene.

During this period other parts of the world, (not covered in the first 3 parts) were visited. These describe in short, cameo episodes, some of these places.

The visits in question covered all five continents, many of which involved some extended stays, others only a matter of days.

If some readers are interested enough to want, more substance about these visits then it is possible to provide this. I will not do so unless asked.

The original version known as 'The 8th Pillar' forms the quintessence of the fuller revised 'oeuvre'.

Dedication

This book is dedicated to my wife Carmelina, who has stood by me over the last 56 years of our marriage even though on occasions due to my frequent absences from home, her patience has been sorely tried.

'edited by Lewis Hill'

(with contributions from brothers, Paul and Anthony).

Preface

I have finally hung up my boots in my late seventies, after a lifetime with the same employer.

My family and erstwhile colleagues have asked me to put down on paper my experiences throughout my working life. To outsiders this may appear to be a mundane request of no significance whatever.

Once having set these down on paper, it seems to me that this book represents a part of modern history, both because of the times in which the events described have occurred and also due to the history of the airline which employed me from 1941 to 1981 and again from 1986 to 2002.

The book is written as a series of remarkable episodes experienced by the writer throughout his working life. It contains no dialogue.

I have entitled this book the 8th Pillar, as it is not based on such a stable platform as 'The Seven Pillars of Wisdom'.

In the same way that T.E Lawrence's books were written around his exploits in the Middle East during the First World War, (and showed how he developed his philosophy of Life), this book represents a series of episodes in mine, including those in the Second World War and subsequent years that shaped me, linked, 'synoptically', through the eyes of one person.

As will be seen in later parts of this book, it represents a walk through the writer's adult life, but these are incidental to the narrative. In the main, this book describes a series of episodes during this walk, which are of interest to my immediate family, and on reflection maybe to others as well.

The stories are not intended as a personal biography, but a series of distinctly linked episodes. It uses the writer to bridge all these together. Without such a link the story would not provide any continuity, but remain a series of single incidents, without a central theme.

Any elements in the first three parts of this book which appear to have a biographical content, are only included so that the various incidents which are told, can have some continuity based on the writer's travels around the world, and through whose eyes and memories these are reflected in the narrative.

Unlike Col Lawrence, who actually was involved in the episodes he recounted, only some of those experienced by myself, include the writer in the narrative. It just so happens that I was present at the time to recount these, with only partial personal involvement.

It could be stated that in some parts, the writer is like Dr. Watson: always present but only intermittently involved.

The writer of 'The Seven Pillars of Wisdom', developed his own philosophical views of life, based on his personal experiences, including the trials and tortures he endured in the Middle East, in the First World War.

It was not only his enemies in the field who tried to thwart the completion of his mission, but ironically also those in the UK, (through their vicissitude and disapproval) and who had initially set out his objectives. It appears he felt betrayed and these experiences dictated how he lived the rest of his life in partial seclusion, very much as a loner.

The period of imprisonment he endured under the Turks must have affected deeply, surmised by the way he spent his life after that war and his subsequent desire for anonymity.

In the same way that T.E. Lawrence developed a philosophy based on his life experiences; so this book attempts to describe how this writer matured by the episodes related, and as a result developed views, which may be different to others in today's materialistic society.

The whole of my working life has been devoted to service in the civil aviation industry, and as a result, have been an observer of its development over the years. I also believe that I have played a significant part in this development, by espousing new technology as it evolved, and its use for the benefit of the industry as a whole. These, and the overseas travel connected with such developments are told in Part 4 of this book.

The latter aspect of the book also includes a cameo of various places of interest around the world, which have been visited, and from the writer's point of view are worth relating.

Any views expressed in this book are purely those of the writer and have not been influenced by anyone else. Some may consider the references to British Airways' current failings, and future course of action to be naïve and immature.

Any such persons, who do criticise these opinions, should ask themselves, upon which basis are they making such judgements? Would they have developed any different perspectives, faced with the experiences described in this book?

If the critics of this book had not grown up and matured during this period of history, can they in all honesty evaluate the thoughts and hopes expressed by the writer and take these into consideration, when formulating their opinions about its contents?

The age of the writer, and location at the start of his career are fundamental to the development of these thoughts. Critics would have to imagine that they are walking alongside me throughout the episodes described. Only then can the effects on the writer's character be truly evaluated.

There cannot be many persons in this world that can meet these conditions.

The philosophies and codes of living, expressed later in this book, have evolved directly from this personal walk through life. Anyone else could write down their thoughts, and experiences, and produce their own views on life, but these recollections are unique to me.

All lives and characters evolve in different ways, and as a consequence, life patterns differ. Furthermore decisions taken, and courses of action followed will differ based on the evolution of that person's character.

Can I suggest that this book be read with these concepts in mind, before any judgement is made?

As a final point, the writer does not claim to be a literary expert, and some of the grammar and punctuation may be incorrect. However in my view this makes the narrative more readable, as it tells a story in the words that the author would use, and not how the literary world would expect it to be written.

Introduction

This narrative is not a biography, but a series of episodes over the last 61 years of my career, connected with the Airline Industry.

Strangely enough, this period covers the developing history of BOAC, from its inception, shortly after being created by the merger of Imperial Airways and other UK airlines, through the days when the airline became British Airways (Overseas Division), into the British Airways of today in the year 2002.

Although I retired provisionally in 1981, I was reintroduced in 1986, as a Consultant for a period of about 6 months. The temporary advisory role terminated in June of 2002, at the age of 79. The book was started 2 months later at the insistence of my family. Thus the consultancy task which was to last a mere 6 months, continued for a further 16years after my retirement.

There cannot be many people alive today, who can state, that they have been present throughout the life of this airline, both in an overseas capacity, and a development role. The development role coincided also with the introduction of new technology.

In part 4 of this narrative, the descriptions become a little more biographical, as they have been introduced, to show the influence my life has had on the well-being of the airline up to the time I retired for the first time.

Apart from my temporary retirement for about 5 years, my attachment to the airline has been constant throughout. I have never worked for anyone else during this period, except under the cover of a consultancy company used by the airline, for the employment of its ex personnel.

Apart from Part 4, which is mainly biographical, other parts of the text may also appear at times to be semi-biographical, but this is only so that the various unrelated episodes can be linked, through the eyes of one person,(synoptically).

I have only included those parts of my life, which are relevant to the development of my character, or would explain the reasons for any courses of action taken as a result of these.

Throughout the earlier parts of this narrative, there are frequent references to incidents in the Second World War, and in particular the North African campaign. This is so that the episodes can be placed in the correct time frame

It should be realised that I have tried to narrate these 'episodes' using the thoughts appropriate to the circumstances of that era. Many of the developments today, which make up the civil aviation scene, were not present when these situations occurred. Should the events narrated have been introduced in the context of today's working environment, the steps taken, and solutions offered would be quite different.

Throughout the period of this narrative the author has developed from an immature youngster joining an Airline for the first time, into a very mature adult who until his retirement had always been associated with the same Employer.

Before the start of this life with BOAC, my family protected me from life outside the home environment. This perhaps was the main reason for the immaturity displayed in the earlier parts of this book.

This walk through life has allowed me to develop with a flexible approach to innovation, and has allowed me to espouse with zeal, new concepts which have evolved with the passage of time, to the benefit of the airline industry as a whole.

The part played by the writer in this evolution is narrated in Part 4 of this book, after I left overseas service and returned to the UK for the first time in my career.

The book, from time to time expresses personal views of today's problems which beset the airline, and give rise to concerns about the direction in which British Airways long-term strategies are being formulated, and progressed.

The basis of any criticisms directed at the airline in this book, are meant to be constructive. The loyalty of the writer to the airline cannot be questioned.

The stories recounted, and the hopes, and aspirations for the future of British Airways, are reflected through the eyes of the author whilst associated with this airline.

Beginning in the late 1940s, BOAC became a world force in the civil aviation scene, and took a prominent part in the evolution of the industry, both in the political and operational fields.

Wherever one went around the world in the last century BOAC, and later BA was always respected for the role it played to simplify cross border movement of people both within Europe, and further afield.

The airline also became a world leader in recognising the need for changes in the industry with the advent of newer and larger aircraft. The carriage of larger loads needed to make these new aircraft to operate profitably necessitated the design and development of new ground equipment, and changes to operating procedures to meet this growing demand for air travel.

BOAC's role in the facilitation process automatically carried with it an element of airport design, so that the reduction in controls could be linked to the simplification of the interior design of airport terminal buildings

Architects around the world, commissioned to design new airport terminals, frequently consulted BA on the interior designs of terminal buildings. Among these were those responsible for the development of London's Heathrow airport.

After the war, ICAO, the International Civil Aviation Organisation, a part of the United Nations, were asked to identify what had to be done to facilitate cross border International Air Travel, both in Europe and further afield. BOAC became an advisor member of this International Body.

Throughout the writer's life it was never anticipated that he would one day be asked to commit these experiences to paper. My family has requested that this be done for their benefit, and having agreed to this, some of these experiences are worth recounting to others. In fact my erstwhile colleagues at work have often asked me to do just that.

Unfortunately no diary was kept of the events, which follow. It is because of this that some of the earlier episodes may be both slightly coloured, and perhaps a little inaccurate. However, they do make for a good yarn, and in all cases are broadly true.

The only fanciful bits are those, which surround the description of the environment in which the episodes are described. Even then these are only fanciful insofar as my memory can recall them. All the episodes described are real in my mind.

To a large extent memory is fashioned by time. The Mind does not recall with great accuracy any events that are hurtful and rather tends to embroider and dwell on those which were most pleasant. As a result memory leans towards the making of one into an optimist rather than a pessimist. Such has been my belief.

A true biography would be very dull. Apart from the episodes described, the writer's life would have been no different from the large majority of other people's lives, proceeding to and from their places of work on the 8 to 6 transport runs. As such I can well see that these would not interest anyone.

However, the life of the writer has taken him around the world, starting during infancy and continuing throughout his development years and subsequent career. The many episodes that have occurred should make this book of sufficient interest to other potential readers.

Also those persons who are interested in recent history may appreciate the contents of this book. All the episodes and scenes described are told through the eyes of someone who has been present throughout these changing times, both politically, and in a more restricted way through the growth of civil aviation.

To some extent the above two factors, have helped the different world cultures to get together on a larger scale than hitherto. Mass air travel has taken away the mystique provided by the explorers and expatriates of yesteryear. In the early part of the last century these persons narrated their experiences to their home audiences by means of slides and lectures. Moving pictures only became the vogue in the latter part of the nineteenth century.

The speed, at which travel was undertaken before mass air travel developed, did not provide the range of options about the countries and nations with whom these persons had been associated. Travel throughout was mainly on foot, and in consequence was limited by this factor. This is not the case with the writer who used more up to date means of transport to explore the countries visited.

Today the audiences can see for themselves without the need for such travelogues or lectures. They can gather all this by going there and seeing for themselves how people in different parts of the world live. However, what they see today is not as it was yesterday. This they can only learn from books such as these

The ease with which different peoples can move from one country to another, makes it a lot easier today for the intermingling of cultures.

The start of this book describes the life of a young expatriate abroad, during the remaining days of Empire, and the war years spent in and out of the services. All these war years were spent away from the UK.

The views expressed therefore, are completely unbiased, as these have not been coloured by the ravages of wartime Britain, and the effect this would have had on one's views of any foreigners responsible for this.

In the later episodes of this book, I describe the conversion from a person fully involved in the Commercial aspects of the Airline, into one whose work becomes much more closely aligned, first with the operational needs of the airline, and subsequently with the use of Computers to assist and control the tremendous growth in passenger numbers, coupled with the introduction of ever larger aircraft to carry these around the world.

In particular, this book should be of interest to others, whose life and career has also followed a similar path to the remote parts of the world, especially those who have worked for any airline, British or Foreign.

Throughout these episodes I have met and became friendly with other airline personnel working with the larger European and American Airlines, and in the more recent episodes, many people working for Airlines from other parts of the world. In many cases through these links, my name is still recognised to many of these, particularly those in the development of computer solutions to solve the growth problem.

The views on the British Airways corporate strategy expressed in this book are based on the knowledge gained in the growth years, and from a close association with the Airline from the age of 18 up to the age of 78, in the Commercial, Operational, and Information Handling departments. This association includes the not insignificant role played in the introduction, and advancement of new equipment and technologies, to maintain the Airline at the forefront of the Worlds' Airlines.

It is with a tinge of regret that I see this role being usurped by others. British Airways appears to be submitting meekly to its new world role.

The large numbers of airlines, which are linking their future with other similar airlines, have taken over the dominant role in the advancement of the industry. BA is fast being left behind, and in fact in doing so it is also giving up its birthright, to many of the facilities and systems, which it has fathered.

THE WESTERN DESERT
(copied from p351 of WINSTON CHURCHILL'S 'The Hinge of Fate')
Derna
Martaba
Imimi
Mechili
Ain el Gazala
Tobruk
Bardia
Sollum
Sidi Rezegh
Bir Hacheim
Sidi Omar
Fort Maddalena
Sidi Barrani
Mersa Matruh
Fuka
Alamein
Alexandria
Minqa Qaim
CYRENAICA
(modern Libya)
Giarabub
FRONTIER
E G Y P T
QATTARA DEPRESSION
* VOLUME IV of The History of the SECOND WORLD WAR

Sir Winston Churchill's map

Contents

Speedbird Logo

Chapter 1

From Khartoum to Malakal

Part 1

The Start of the Walk through Life

My working life started in earnest in 1941, on the banks of the River Nile in the Anglo Egyptian Sudan.

My father, who at the time this narrative begins, was a Lieutenant Colonel in the wartime British Army. He had been placed in charge of the Prisoner of War camps housing Italian POWs from the ongoing Abyssinian campaign. This posting took us to Khartoum in the Sudan.

The events, which led up to this scenario, could well be the subject of another book, and would include my father's experiences, as seen through my eyes. This story, from the First World War into, and including his Second World War exploits are in themselves worth recounting.

Before the posting to the Sudan, he was indirectly involved in the original battle in the Western Desert, which *involved Field Marshal Wavell, and General Wilson (Jumbo)* in the star roles. He was given the responsibility to govern a large part of Cyrenaica after this campaign was over, and before the Erwin Rommel saga deprived him of this post.

My father, mother, brother and sister were with me at the time of enrolment, as a complete family unit., and were being accommodated at the Grand Hotel in Khartoum, until such time as suitable private accommodation could be found.

My brother, Robert, and I being overseas at this time were too young to be enlisted in the armed services, and by the time I was old enough, I was in a reserved occupation, being part of the Merchant Air Service as BOAC was then identified.

During the war the airline had its own pennant. This would be flown at all ground establishments and on its aircraft. The pennant was the same as that flown by the Merchant Navy but had an RAF blue background instead of white.

Later in this book I was seconded from BOAC to the RAF, and given the rank of Pilot Officer, a rank that stayed with me until I was formally de-mobbed in July 1946. This was by a gentleman who identified himself by the name of *Street,* on the piece of paper indicating my release from active service. The service number I was given as a *Pilot Officer*, I remember well as **71919.**

The Grand Hotel in Khartoum was situated on the banks of the river Nile; a river that flows through Khartoum even to this day. The river at this point is the product of the Blue Nile, which originates in the highlands of Ethiopia, and the White Nile, originating much further to the South in the Kenya/ Uganda area of Africa. Both rivers join at a point some 15 to 20 miles to the south of Khartoum. I have no reason to believe that this has changed in the last 60 years.

It was early May in 1941; while my father was at the bar of the Hotel, when, to the best of my knowledge he met the Regional Manager of BOAC (British Overseas Airways Corporation).

BOAC had recently been set up from the Merger of 2 or 3 other pre-war Airlines, of which Imperial Airways was one. Because of the war situation in North Africa at the time, BOAC had moved part of its headquarters' staff from Cairo to Khartoum.

The History of BOAC and its expansion and growth have already been fully documented and it is not the intention, in this book to expand on this historical event, except insofar as the writer had some influence on this.

A passing remark between my father, to his drinking companion resulted in me being introduced to the life of an Airline employee, albeit a very lowly one as a Mapping Clerk, This work involved preparing Map sections of the routes North and South, and West of Khartoum. These map sections provided the navigation details by which the pilots would fly these routes.

The map sections were to be placed on board the *C Class Flying Boats* operating from South, and West Africa, to Cairo and beyond. My duties in this operation were to release the maps, relevant to the current operation in Africa, for the use of pilots in transit through Khartoum.

Before the fall of France, and Italy's entry into the war in 1940, the Empire routes flown by the C Class flying boats, operated from the UK via the Mediterranean to Egypt, then to the East and South from Cairo.

After 1940, the direct UK link with the Empire had been cut by these events, until after the whole of North Africa, had been reclaimed, starting with the successful outcome of the battle of El Alamein, and operation Torch.

Operation Torch was the name given to the allied plans to reclaim North Africa from the Atlantic Ocean to Tunis. This operation involved the landings in North Africa by US and the British forces in Morocco and Algeria, with the aim of linking these armies with the advancing 8th Army from El Alamein.

Until the battle of **El Alamein** had been concluded successfully, and the Allied forces had reclaimed the whole of North Africa, the ascendancy of the Italian, and German armies would not allow these flying boats to operate to and from the UK. This was due to the aircraft's height and, range limitations. Those aircraft that found themselves to the East of the conflict when it began would terminate their operations at Cairo.

The above period covers the years, from 1940, to late 1943/early 1944.

During this period, direct operations to and from the UK by BOAC had ceased to exist, and the only links were via the circuitous routes from West Africa.

Flights across French North Africa were not possible after the fall of France, until the whole of this territory had either been regained, or had moved its allegiance from the axis powers.

The link between the UK and West Africa, was primarily by sea to either the Gold Coast (Ghana), or Lagos in Nigeria.

The whole of BOAC's route structure to the south and east of Europe had to be revised and a new headquarters set up in Cairo, under a Regional Director, to control and administer this operation. Strangely this Director's name was *Robert Maxwell* but he was in no way connected with the other person of the same name.

A number of landplanes had also been trapped by these events. These also came under the jurisdiction of this new Middle East Headquarters.

The above helps to set the scenario for my induction into the ranks of BOAC's overseas establishment.

The real start of my Career

After about a fortnight carrying out the boring job as a mapping clerk, a gentleman by the name of *Keith Granville* interviewed me, and as a result I was soon on my way to Cairo, to start my true career in the civil aviation industry.

Keith Granville, who at that time was based in Durban in South Africa was the Establishment Manager of BOAC. Among his responsibilities was the recruitment of potential airline management staff.

The above gentleman met me while he was proceeding on a duty visit to the new headquarters in Cairo, and had to stay over in **Khartoum** for a few days.

After the war Keith Granville became a Director of BOAC, initially in the Commercial field of the Airline.

The result of this successful interview allowed me to start my career as a Commercial Trainee with BOAC. This appointment required me to undertake a two-year Trainee Course starting in Cairo, before I could graduate. The course was to provide me with the basis for eventual promotion to Station Officer and Station Management.

There is a hint of the 'Midshipman' about all this.

I was provided with a uniform and had to wear Cadet 'Flashes' on my lapels to indicate my Trainee status. The uniform provided was still that of the now defunct Imperial Airways since BOAC had not yet finalised its true livery.

At the tender age of eighteen, these flashes were worn proudly, as they distinguished me from locally employed staff carrying out tasks similar to mine regardless of the station to which I was posted.

In order to complete my cadetship, I was moved on a regular basis, from one department to another over about six months. This covered short spells in Accounts, Supplies, Catering, and Engineering, and Operations Control as it was known then. For the final eighteen months, I was to complete this training at various outpost stations in that region.

The region based on Cairo covered all points in Africa to the north of the equator, as well as points East, as far as India.

After a three month stint at *Rod el Farag*, the flying boat base on the Nile just outside Cairo in Egypt, (in order to get operational experience), I was sent up-river to my first outpost station. *Malakal* was the capital of the Upper Nile Province in the Anglo Egyptian Sudan and there I was to remain for the next fifteen months or so.

Some Information about Malakal and its Residents

Malakal is located some three to four hundred miles south of *Khartoum*, and in 1941/2 was accessible only by River Steamer, or by Air. There was talk of building a Cape to Cairo road, but at that time there were many broken sections of this enterprise, and the Khartoum to Malakal section, both to the south and north had not yet been completed

Due to the presence of cataracts,(on the Nile flowing north to Khartoum from *Kosti),* the steamer that came to Malakal, originated south of *Kosti.* It could not negotiate the cataracts between Kosti and Khartoum. Kosti became the railhead from Khartoum to all points in the southern Sudan.

The above chapters hopefully set the scene for the episodes, which appear in Part 1 of this book. It also helps to explain how an immature eighteen year old started a career in such a remote part of the British Empire, as the Sudan was at that time, albeit only as a Protectorate and no longer a 'colony'.

The protectorate was under the joint mandates of Egypt and Britain.

Britain administered the country and population outside the capital Khartoum, and the Egyptians controlled both the Civil Service and the water flow of the River Nile.

At that time, 1941, Britain was at war with both Germany and Italy; Japan did not enter the fray until later that year. These were desperate days:' . . . the tide had not yet turned . . .' as Winston Churchill had indicated in his memoirs.

In that part of Africa, to which I had been sent, the war had touched only remotely the region. Life continued normally, no doubt in the same manner that the residents in Singapore had continued their lifestyle, until rudely interrupted by the Japanese invasion of that territory.

The war on our doorstep between the Italian and British armies in Abyssinia, had little effect on the day to day life of the expatriate residents in this part of the world, even though the fighting in that area was ongoing and in some cases only about a hundred to two hundred miles to the east. There were no defensive positions between them and us, had the Italian army decided to advance to the west from Ethiopia.

The real start of my walk through life began when I first left the family environment, and ventured forth on my own. At each stage of this walk I became more mature and worldly wise.

Once my overseas service had been completed and transferred to a head office appointment, I was able to bring with me the invaluable experience gained through some sixteen years of overseas life, some of which were in the war years, spent in various war zones, albeit not on front line duties.

I was one of the '*Bastards Overseas Avoiding Conscription*' as servicemen, some of whom had never seen a gun fired in anger, identified BOAC staff generally.

At least I was able to contribute even indirectly to the actions taken in North Africa, and Italy by the true heroes of these campaigns.

My contribution to these operations can be read later in this book.

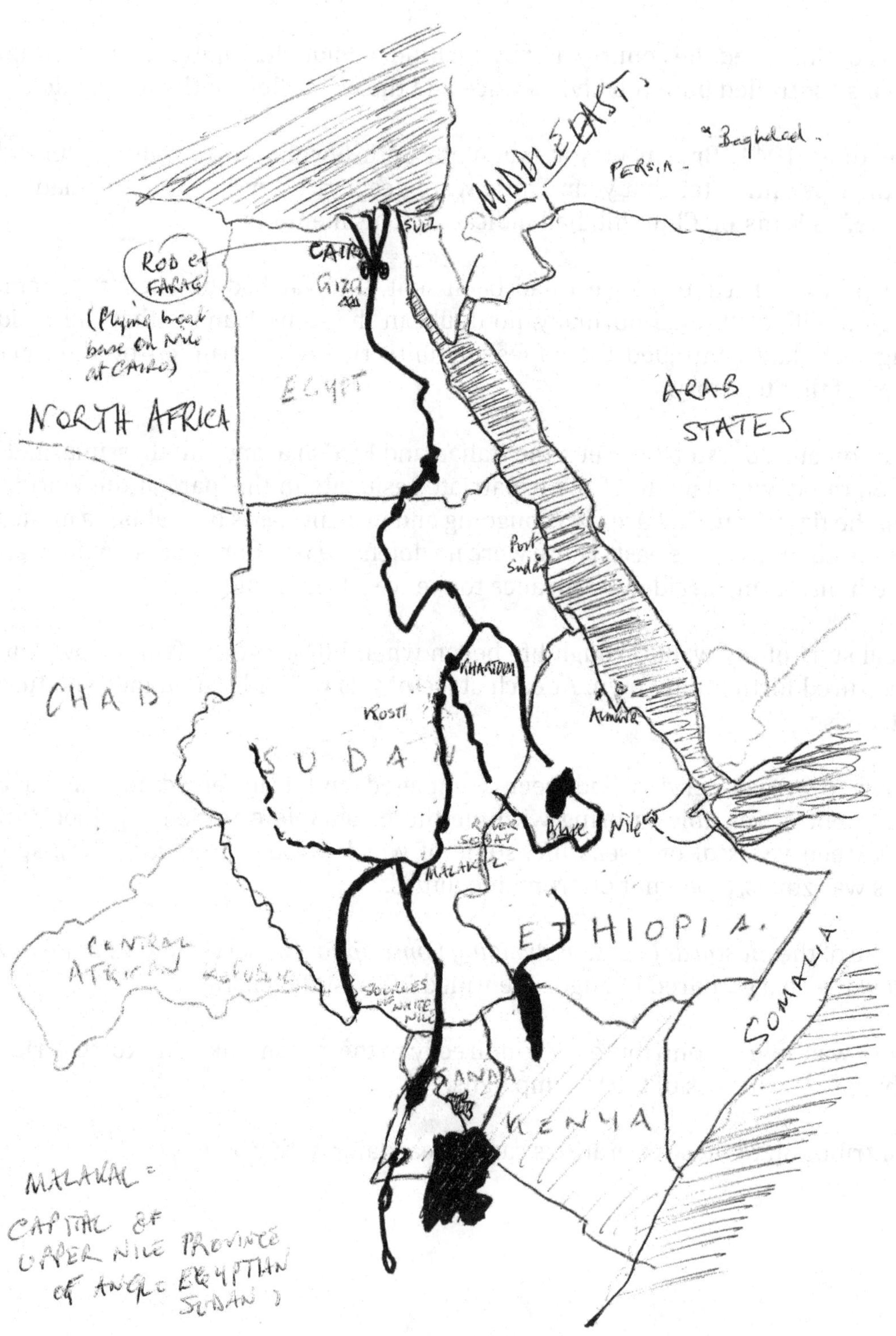

map 1—flow of River Nile through Egypt and Sudan

The Start of my Maturation in Life

My departure from the closeted family environment at a tender age, and far away from England this was a quite traumatic event. I had to learn about life and its pitfalls very quickly if I was not to be damaged both mentally and physically by the events which followed. I matured fast under the influence of those with whom I came into contact after leaving home.

Family values to a large extent were replaced by experience gained from the day-to-day life of these times. For many others, called away from home at an early age, maturity developed in a similar way.

However, for many of those, maturity developed in an operational war environment, mostly under direct command from their superiors. We were not afforded such luxuries, we had to define our own personal battles and fight these alone.

My growing up, and thus my maturity, would take a different course to those who passed through the same period, but mostly under the direction of a superior ranking individual.

Maturity grew with each year of my life from the time the 'walk' started. It derived from the influences of the period, and lifestyle of the times in which the incidents occurred.

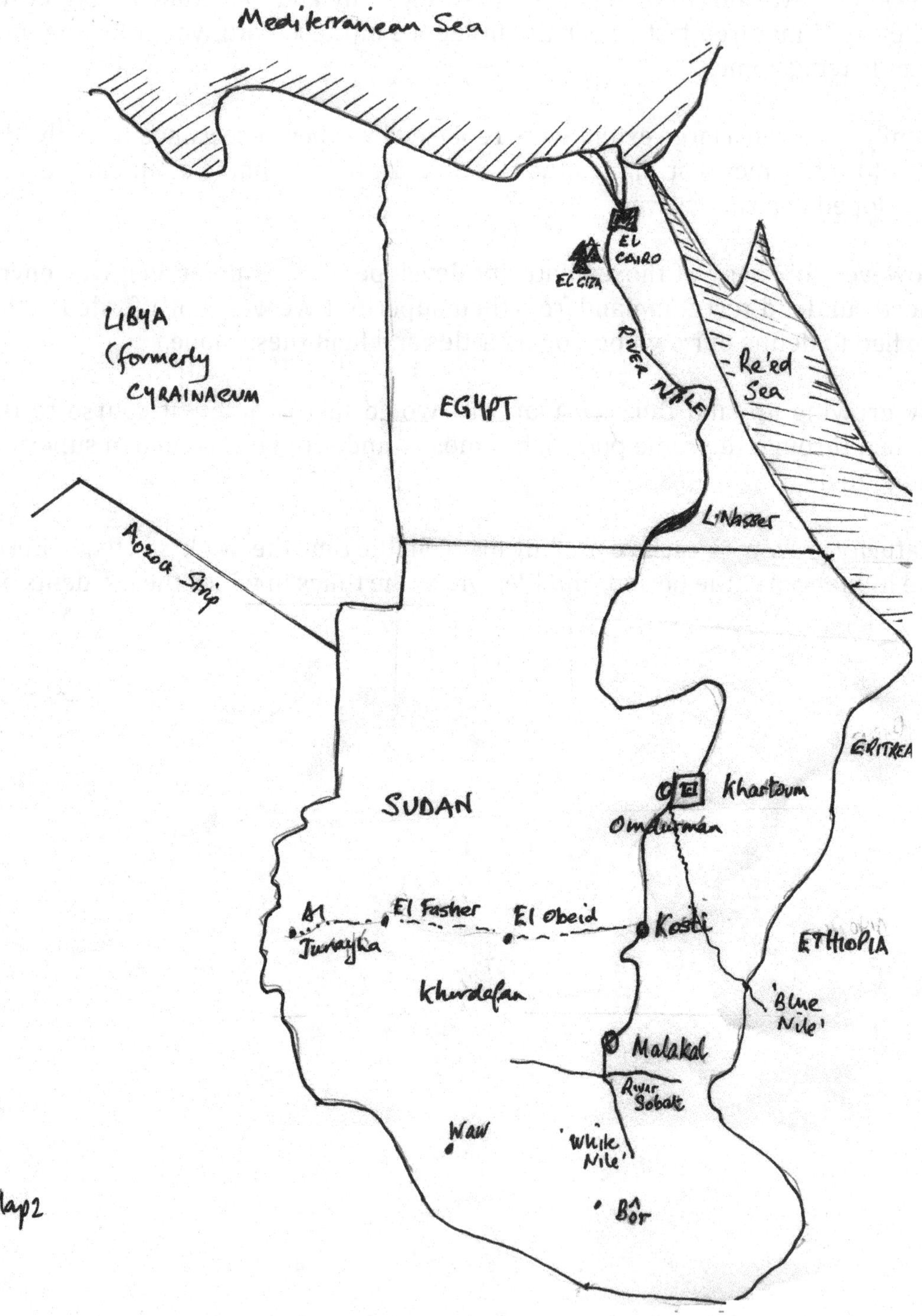

Map 2 showing details of towns and cities in the Sudan

Part 1—My first posting to a land forgotten by time—or Malakal as I knew it in the years 1941/2

In the last part I described the events, which preceded my arrival in Malakal.

In this book my description of Malakal is, as I remembered Malakal in the year 1941/2. What and how it has developed since 1941, is not relevant to this narrative.

In 1941, Malakal was the chief city of the Upper Nile Province in the Anglo Egyptian Sudan. A Governor ruled it with a Deputy Governor appointed by the then Colonial Office. Even though it was the chief city of the province, not one building was more than one storey high, and of a ramshackle construction, apart from the Governor's residence. By one storey, I mean the ground floor plus one.

The local Greek and Arab traders owned the higher buildings in the town. Even the rest house, near the flying boat landing site, described later was a ground floor building, with the outsides mainly covered with wire netting, to allow air circulation, in the tropical climate, but also to keep out the numerous marauding insects, lizards, and snakes.

The town sits astride the White Nile some 300 hundred miles south of Khartoum, (the capital city of the Anglo Egyptian Sudan), and only about 150 miles west of the Ethiopian border.

The river Nile around the town was some 500 to 700 yards wide, and in some areas became much wider during the rainy season.

The fast flowing river coupled with the heavy rains to the south, would bring with it large and small floating islands from the southern swamplands. These islands would have become detached from the riverbanks at source, together with all their resident wildlife. The islands would be teeming with snakes and other dangerous species of wildlife and insects.

The islands, when they reached Malakal, would be free flowing, as they were not attached to the mainland, neither at the bottom, nor on either bank. They were deemed to be 'islands' because they were dense enough to walk on if one dared.

Any attempt to land on these 'islands' would be fraught with danger.

In 1941/42, the Allied armies were engaged in a war to liberate Ethiopia, from its domination by Italy.

The objectives of this campaign were unclear, other than that the Italian forces occupied the land, and that we were at war with Italy. It could be that we as a country were altruistic enough to wish to return the government of this country to its indigenous population.

By the time I left Malakal, the occupation of Ethiopia and Eritrea by the British and Commonwealth armies was complete, and the Italian army in that part of Africa was no longer a threat.

The above diversion is relevant to this story as will be seen later.

Malakal, and the Upper Nile province was the principal habitat of the Shilluk tribe, but was also inhabited by a considerable number of Dinkha tribesmen, who moved East and North to this town from the Southern and Eastern part of the Sudan. Whilst the Shilluk tribe were relatively passive, the Dinkhas were of a more aggressive nature.

The great majority of these two tribes were illiterate, and the only work available was either farming or manual labour.

More about the resident Tribes

At this point it is worth describing in general terms, the cultural background and habits of the indigenous population. The Shilluk race formed the dominant tribe in this region.

The Shilluk females that we came across wandering around the town were dressed only in skimpy 10 inch flaps around their lower body, both fore and aft, and suspended from a sort of belt hung loosely below the waistline. Apart from this they wore little other clothing. Only those females, who had come under the influence of the Christian Missionaries, would be clothed in a more modest way.

The women in this part of the world aged very quickly. They would marry in their early teens, would become very old in their late twenties, and positively wizened in their later years around the age of forty!

The Shilluk male would take considerable care about the appearance of both the upper and mid sections of his body. Apart from this the only clothing worn would be a type of orange coloured toga slung from his left shoulder, which reached only to mid-thigh.

The younger mainly adolescent men would attach stones to their genitals, to extend their length. For those who carried on this culture, the stones would be visible at all times as they would hang below the toga line.

The adult males had no need for such antics, and resorted to other methods to attract the other sex, the appropriate length of their genitals having been achieved by the above adolescent habit.

After the extensions to their manhood, the young men would introduce pebbles or other such objects, in a straight line around their temples. To do this they would puncture the skin, and allow the skin to grow over these. Many others would do the same around their upper arms. I presume they used pebbles for this operation. However this was done, the end result was as stated below.

After a while these would appear as raised scar tissue around their head below the hairline, and also on their upper arms. I can only assume that the females of the tribe, regarded these as symbols of their manhood. If not, why go through this painful and dangerous process?

Presumably this habit would indicate the status of the individual in the Shilluk society, in the same way that Indians identify their status in the Indian society, by the dots, which they attach to their foreheads.

The dressing of the hair of the adult Shilluk male was a very strange custom and warrants a separate description.

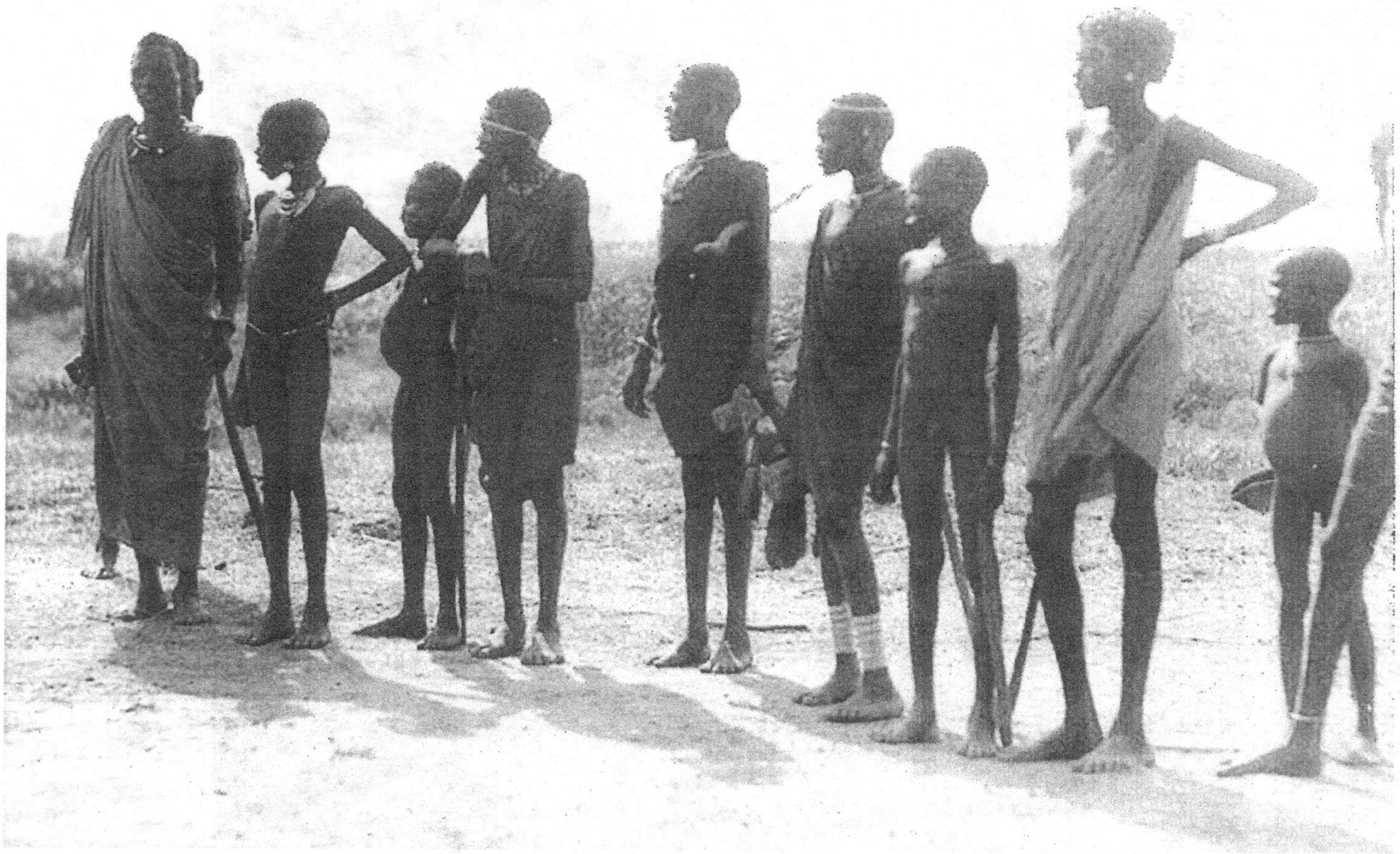

photo of Dinkha/Shilluk tribe fullpage here

The majority of the young Shilluk males would use a mixture of cow dung and mud to rub into their hair. When partially dry, they would fashion this hair into elaborate shapes. Once dried, the hair would become a reddish brown, and conform stiffly to the shape fashioned by the individual.

No doubt the shapes and sizes of these hairstyles would also be used to attract the young women of the tribes, in the same way that a peacock attracts the female of the species by the extension of its plumage.

The creation of each hair masterpiece was so intricate and took so long to complete, that the male could not rest his head on the ground directly, for fear of upsetting this hairstyle. To preserve this across each day, he would use a forked twig, and rest the back of his neck on this so that the elaborate coiffeur was not disturbed whilst asleep. The setting of the hairstyle was not a daily occurrence. Any change of hairstyle would have involved around a three day cycle.

It must be remembered that this narrative relates these episodes to the years 1941 and 1942. I cannot state with certainty that this habit exists today.

I have digressed from the narrative for a while, as I feel that this description is worthy of elaboration, if only to show the level of civilisation reached in 1942, by the local inhabitants of Malakal.

The reason for most of the movement of the other tribe, the Dinkhas tribesman from their homelands to the south was to find employment. This fact was bitterly resented by the resident Shilluk tribe. The enmity came to a head when a land airport was to be built and a number of Dinkha tribesmen were employed alongside the Shilluks as manual construction workers. This fact is the subject of an episode described later.

Both the Shilluk and Dinkha tribes resided in village compounds. The compounds comprised of many huts, each made of rounded walls fashioned with mud and perhaps cow dung, strengthened with reed like grasses, and allowed to dry. When dry, each hut was topped with conical shaped roofs also made of mud but with additional straw to add extra strength, and provide extra waterproofing. The term used to identify this type of construction was *'a Tukl hut'*. The whole terrain around the villages abounded with reed like grasses to provide the necessary building material.

Most of these grew to a height of around 4 feet, or waist high, except in those areas surrounding the river. The grasses there would be over 5 to 6 feet high.

It was because of the presence of these tall grasses that we were required to wear Suede Boots as standard issue; these ended just below the knee, and were designed to protect us from snake and scorpion bites during any off path walks.

Day and night Activity in the Compounds

The compounds around the town were all located away from the town centre, but near enough to form part of the town itself. All were located a short distance away from the river.

Each village was presumably under the control of a Headman, who in most cases was an elder of one of the related family groups.

The huts in each village were constructed around a centre, which had been cleared of the foliage and grasses. These centres would become the social meeting place of the village, as well as for food preparation. The women of the village would beat the vegetables into a pulp prior to cooking. Food was cooked in large pots over open fires outside the various huts.

The great majority of these village compounds were without electricity or lighting. At night wood fires would be lit in the centre of the compound, and by smaller fires outside the various huts.

In the tropics, night follows day with a very brief period of twilight. After dark, village-to-village movement was non-existent. Only Malakal and the compounds immediately surrounding the town would be alive and active, but only to the extent that any social activity could take place in the mosquito-infested areas of this part of Africa.

To walk about after dark was not recommended, due to the insect life and darkness that pervaded the area. Street lighting was non-existent, as was any form of entertainment normally associated with a provincial capital.

A feature of the landscape around Malakal was the tall, reed-like grass, sometimes waist high and above that flourished here by the banks of the Nile. There was little soil preparation for the growing and harvesting of crops in any great numbers only that which was needed for personal consumption.

This landscape abounded with insects and large birds, which feed on carrion; these were vultures of a sort. I am no expert on the subject of birds, except to know that these were birds both ugly and unpleasant.

The most repulsive of these large birds was the Marabou Stork. This bird would also live in the long grass and its long spindly legs would allow the head and beak to be above the grasses

The beak and neck of this bird were about the most ugly I have ever come across in my travels. The beak itself has a long reddish pink extrusion, similar to that of the male turkey, but much more ugly because of its size. This extended from the upper end of its lower beak for about two feet down the front of its scraggy neck. It would resemble an ugly growth to us humans, but no doubt a thing of beauty to the female Marabou stork.

The Marabou stork, like the vultures would also prey on dead wildlife. Both were not averse to feeding on dead humans, whenever the opportunity arose.

These birds were not hunters and did not kill their prey; other circumstances were allowed to do this, before they intervened in the kill.

The development of the Cape to Cairo road, did not affect the Malakal region at this time. Part of the plan, required a bridge to be built to span the river Sobat some 20 miles to the south of Malakal, This river had its source in southern Ethiopia, and meandered to the west, linking with the Nile, south of Malakal. This bridge construction was completed before the roads linking the two banks of the 'River Sobat' were ready.

To the south of the above mentioned river was lion country, and as they would not swim across the river, the prowling lions searching for food did not affect the villages surrounding Malakal. Once the bridge was complete, these lions would use it as a means of establishing new territory.

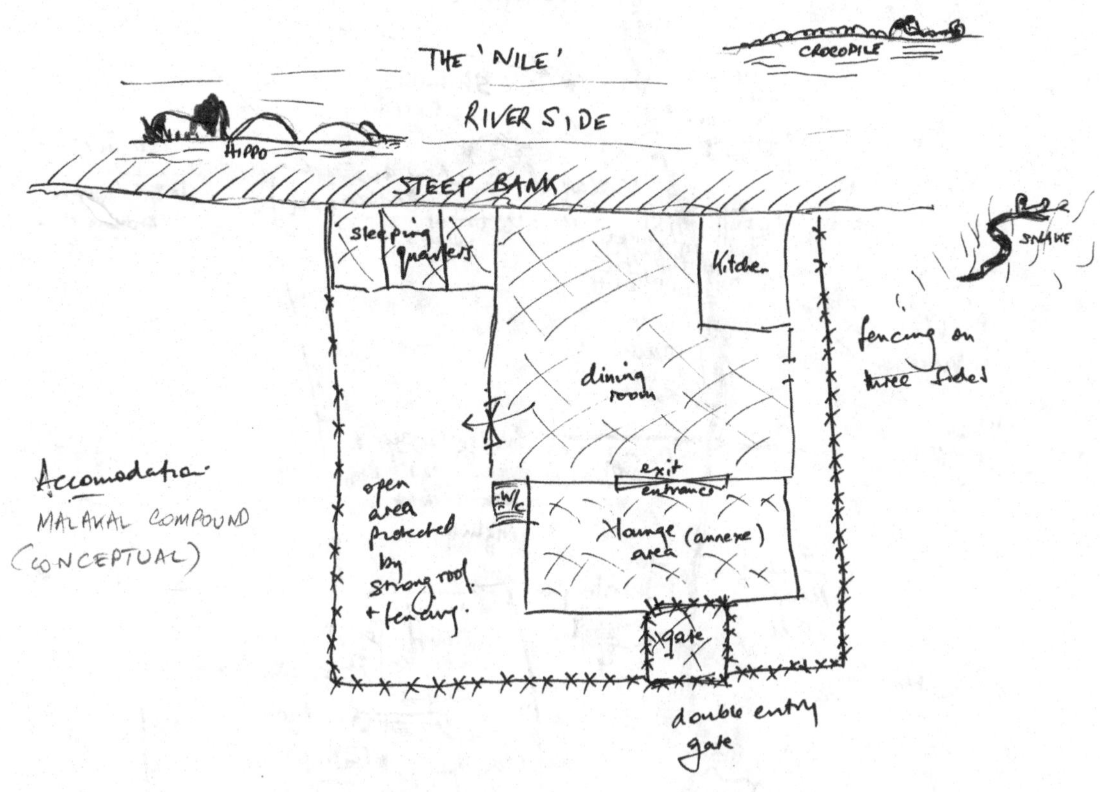

map 3 of E I D compound

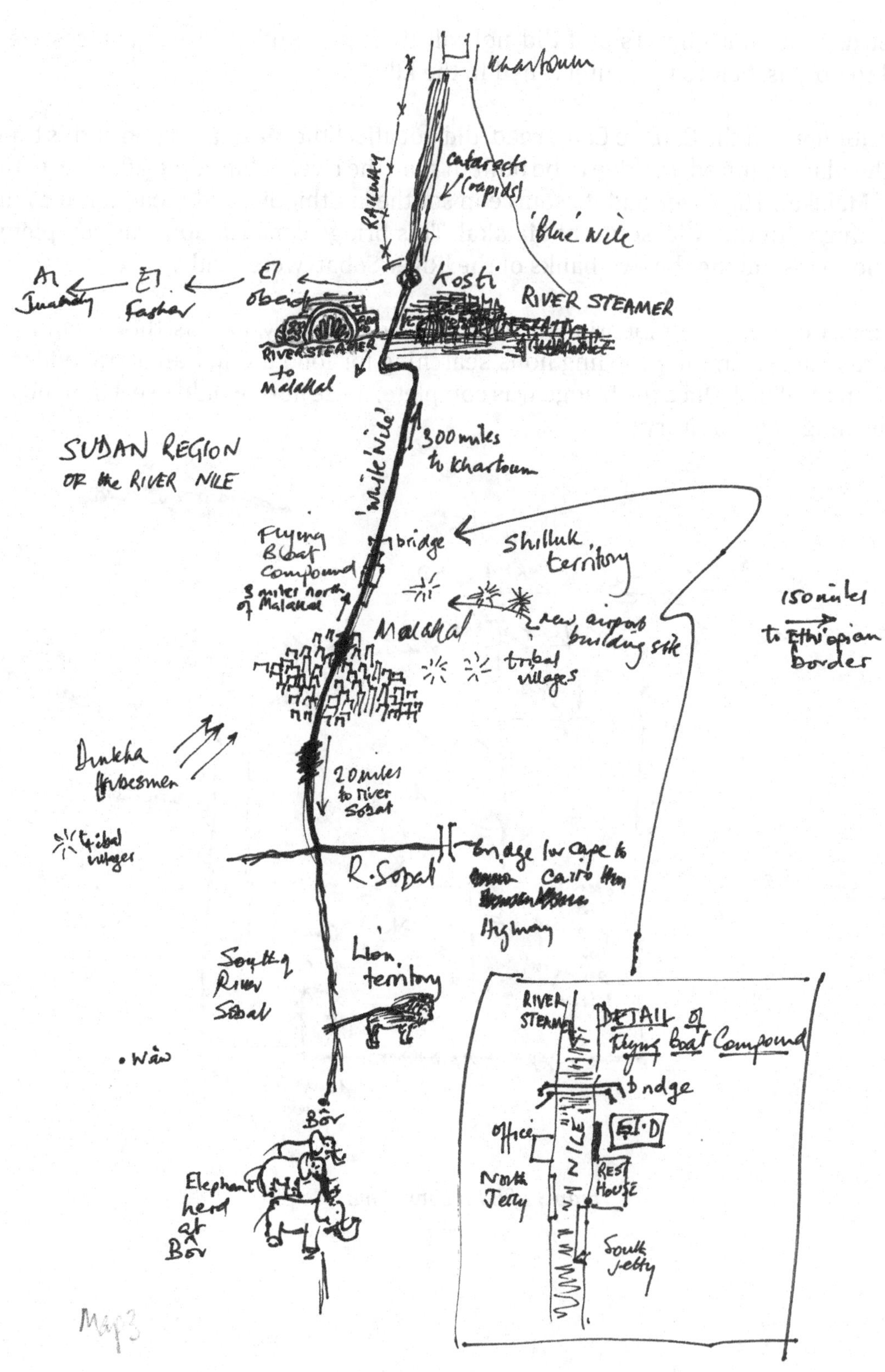

map 4 showing riverside compound

The effect of this was to increase the dangers to villagers, on nocturnal visits, either for food or for social reasons. In addition food for the Vultures and Marabou Storks became more plentiful, as they would consume whatever the lions could not consume of their captured prey.

As time progressed, these birds became more plentiful, as others migrated from where carrion was scarcer.

Having endured the life in Malakal for a year and a half, I could easily identify with life in England as it must have been in the pre Edwardian era, and could sympathise with the environment in which country folk in the UK must have lived in the nineteenth century. The Bronte, Austen, and Dickens novels describe these times in great detail.

Most country people during that period were house bound after dark, and so for the educated minority, a 'Music and Writing' culture prevailed. This could not happen in this part of Africa, due to the poor level of literacy of its population.

In this atmosphere, each evening the air would be filled with the sound of beating drums from the outlying compounds. Each village group would collect around their campfires to while away the time and perhaps discuss local gossip against this background of the African Drum beat music. These sounds would continue late into the night, until bedtime called a halt. Presumably this music would also be used to keep away prowling animals.

Each compound would generate a distinctly separate series of drum beats. Perhaps this sound was a means of communicating between the various compounds to reassure the residents of each, that all was well. It could well have been that these would also serve as a means of communication from compound to compound, just like the Town Criers of old in our society.

I never discovered if this was the reason for the night-time sounds, but the explanation seems plausible.

We ourselves also lived in compounds, but in buildings, built and equipped to a much higher standard, with stone or brick walls, solid roofs, cold running water and electricity.

The different sounds from the compounds would pervade all our evening hours, and intrude on the music we would play after dinner to pass the time. None of my companions were card players, so music was the only entertainment available.

After a while we would come to recognise each distinctive sound from the various compounds around, and in some cases its village origin.

Our living room was an extension from the main building, with wire netting on three sides, and a solid roof. This was an annexe, attached to the dining room entrance. The dining room and kitchen was part of the main building, as well as the bathroom such as it was. All the bedrooms led from the dining room along a wide corridor one side of which was netted.

The entrance to the living room, and the principal way into the house, had two netted door sections, about a yard apart. The first would allow us to open one, and only open the second when the outside door was shut. This prevented access to the millions of insects, which flew around outside, attracted by the inside lights.

Sitting in the lounge after dark, we could see that the netting was covered in both lizards and other insect life all-attempting, to gain entrance from the outside, to the lighted room visible to them from beyond the net.

It was because the lounges was open on three sides that the drumbeats from the villages could be heard more loudly, and to a great extent drown the sounds of our own music played on an old fashioned gramophone. This gramophone was similar to those seen in the HMV advertisements of today and yesteryear. I believe the dog in those advertisements was called Toby.

HMV dog and Gramophone horn

The records, which were available to us, were played over and over again. These were well-worn 78s, the choice of these being dependent upon their owner. I recall Joseph Schmidt being played frequently as it was the favourite of my manager at the time.

Radio reception was particularly bad for the primitive radios available (Transistors were a thing of the future), and apart from the occasional news bulletin, we were totally unaware of what was happening outside our world, which was Malakal and its environs.

The Role of the Egyptian Irrigation Department, (EID) at Malakal.

An essential part of the agreement to run the affairs of the Sudan jointly by both Britain and Egypt was the control of the river flow from the White, and Blue Nile.

The responsibilities of the Egyptian Irrigation Department, was to ensure that Egypt controlled the amount of water reaching the river Nile in Egypt. At the time this was considered necessary to prevent too much water being extracted from the river before it reached Egyptian territory.

The water from the river Nile was the lifeblood of the Egyptian economy. This meant that the EID authorities at Malakal would need to monitor closely the amount of water and the river levels in both the wet and dry seasons. They would also control the amount extracted during its course through the Sudan to Egypt.

The Engineers employed by the Egyptian authorities would agree the water flow and river levels. The Manager and Engineer of the EID, was invariably an expatriate from the UK supported by Egyptian and other nationals. These were the technicians who provided the necessary expertise.

I cannot guarantee that the same applies today, as this is now a matter to be resolved, by the Egyptian and Sudanese authorities. The UK has no say in this situation any longer.

The EID had many more such groups located at various other sites on the banks of the Nile, both Blue and White; However, my only contact with this department was the Malakal EID organisation, which provided the necessary housing to accommodate us. It so happened also that the Manager and his wife were part of our social group. The EID squash Court was regularly used for our daily social gathering.

Egypt's dependency on the River Nile has been well documented throughout the history of Egypt. Without an adequate supply of water Egypt as a country would die. Most villages and towns along the thin strip of land on either side of the river were dependent on the water flow, to irrigate their crops, and feed both their inhabitants and livestock.

The house allotted to BOAC, was one of the properties built by the Egyptian Irrigation Department, for its employees.

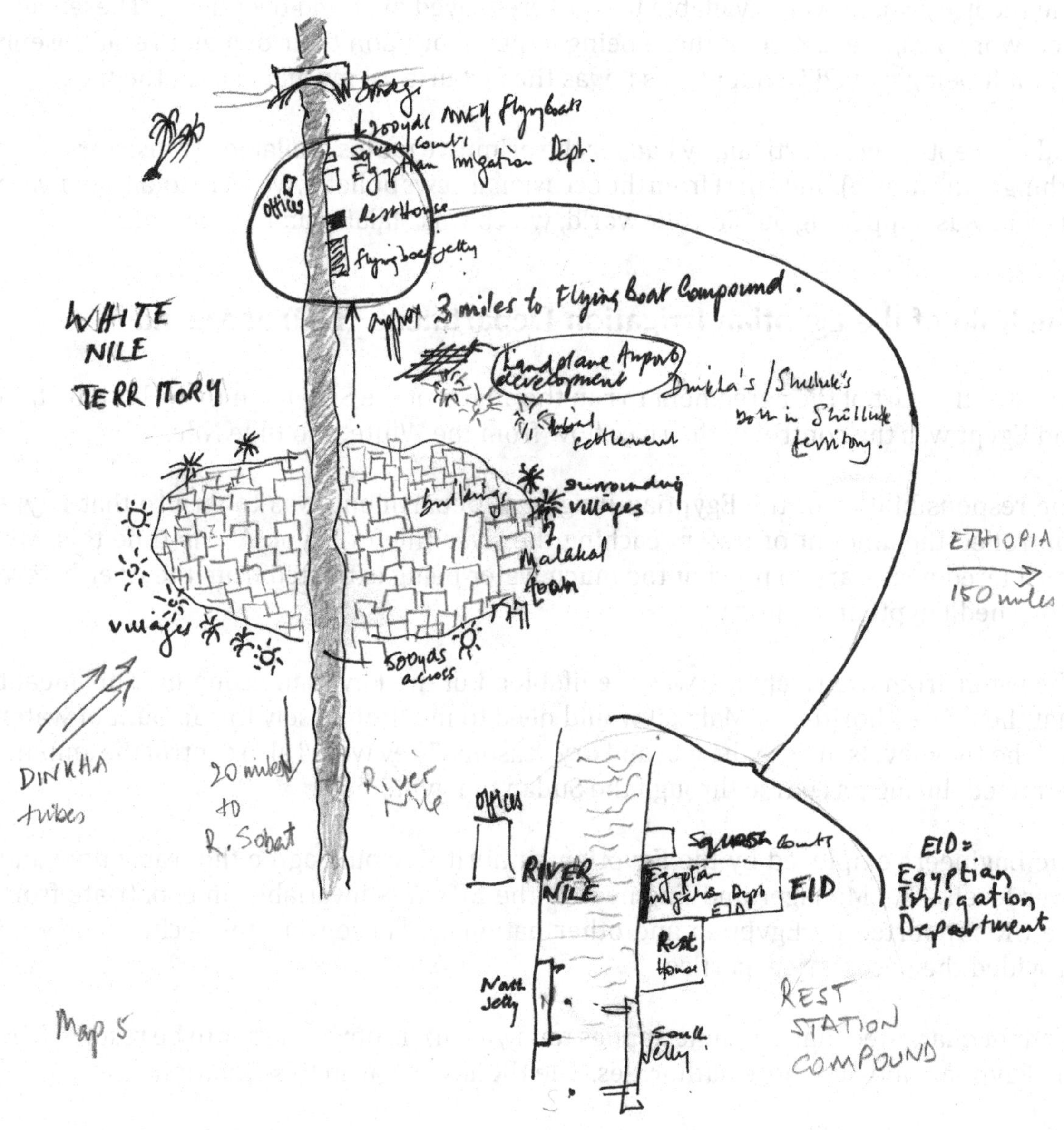

Map 5 showing flying boat compound north of Malakal

The Flying Boat Operation through Malakal.

Malakal was a fuelling stop on the flying boat route from Cairo in the North to South and West Africa.

This stop although not commercially viable, was a necessity due to the lack of range of the C Class flying boats operated by BOAC at the time.

The route south took the aircraft to Juba, (later Larope), then to a lake near Nairobi (Lake Naivasha), and then via further intermediate stops to a lake near Johannesburg. (Vaal Dam)

The original BOAC staff comprised a Station Manager, a Coxswain, and myself, all unmarried. To this should be added a Sudanese émigré from Khartoum, strangely enough by the name of Elton John, and a couple of local men used by the coxswain.

As this was 1941, the current day Elton John had not yet been born, so this can only have been a strange coincidence.

The duties of the expatriate staff were clear and I as the most junior had the responsibility for carrying out my duties as instructed, by both the manager and the coxswain.

The coxswains duties together with his staff, was to ensure the serviceability and safe operation of the watercraft under his control, and also to act as the Air Traffic Controller for each landing on the river.

These boats comprised one large Control Launch used to assist the landing and takeoff of the aircraft, and two 'Cris'-craft whose principal function was to keep the landing area clear of obstructions, especially the floating islands referred to earlier, before each landing, take off, and during re-fuelling.

While the aircraft was on the river those floating islands that were capable of causing damage to the moored aircraft, had to be forced away prior to their arrival in the operational zone. The two 'Cris 'craft, each with their hundred horsepower engines were used for this purpose. The Control launch was fitted with two such engines, and occasionally, in order to achieve their objective, the two craft had to be supported by the control launch, due to the size of the oncoming obstruction.

The landing area, which had to be kept clear, was around one mile in the direction of the wind and at least two thirds of the river width, which at that point varied between four hundred and six hundred yards.

The landing area was about three miles to the North of the town, and surrounding villages. This was to minimise the threat of Malaria and Yellow Fever from the resident mosquitoes, whose range at the time was estimated to be about 800 to 900 yards. This restricted area was sprayed regularly to kill off any of these, and any foreign ones which strayed into the area. No village compounds were allowed within this 1000-yard radius, the extra 100yards was to provide an additional buffer zone.

In 1941, DDT* (the wonder spray which keeps insects at bay) was used in abundance, whereas today this insecticide is banned, because of the long-term effects of the spray on the resident human population via the food chain.

The Upper Nile province is situated within the Yellow Fever belt in Africa; this being between latitudes 15degrees north and south of the Equator. It is not therefore, only Malaria, which affected the region.

Later, when the landing strip was to be developed, the location and extension to this airstrip required that some of the nearby villages on the borders of this malaria free zone had to be moved. The Medical authorities had by this time revised the range of the existing mosquito population by some 400 yards, to a safer 1200 yards.

The new breed of mosquito was called the Mark 2 mosquito, in the vernacular used to describe more advanced models of current aircraft (not the Mosquito at that time).

Once the flying boat had landed, it would have to taxi on the river to a mooring buoy anchored in the river at a location near to a wooden jetty, which had seen better days.

The station at Malakal had two such mooring buoys to allow simultaneous aircraft arrivals from the south and the north. Dual operations were very much the exception rather than the rule.

The jetty would be used to land the passengers out of reach of the waiting crocodiles below. Such passengers after disembarking from the launch would have a short walk to the Rest House, where they would be given refreshments while the aircraft was re-fuelled.

Passengers would disembark from the launch about 3 feet above water level, and climb up about 8 steps to the pier. Only when these were at the higher level were they safe from the resident crocodile and serpent population. However, the approach of the launch with its engine noise would deter any incursion by these beasts until all was quiet again.

Occasionally during this operation, the noise of the launches would disturb the resident crocodiles from their slumber, and 2 or 3 of these would emerge from their resting place and hurriedly enter the water with a great splash, to escape from the noise and activity around the jetty, and find peace and quiet in the fast flowing river. Some of these reptiles would measure around 15 feet from snout to tail.

**DDT is abbreviation of di-chlor,di-phenyl,tri-chloro ethane*

G AHIR during refueling showing crew and staff clambering over wings

The Mooring Process

In order to moor the aircraft, the Radio Officer an essential member of the crew of all aircraft in 1941, had the task of grabbing, with a grapnel carried on the aircraft, a ring attached to the top of the buoy, Once attached, the aircraft would be drawn closer to the buoy, and a rope looped through this ring top. The rope would then be safely attached to the aircraft around a bollard situated below the front hatch. This fixing was an integral part of the aircraft.

The passenger launch could not approach the aircraft, until it was safely anchored, and the aircraft stabilised at its moorings. Until this was the case the aircraft's engines would not be shut off.

If the first mooring attempt failed, the aircraft would have to taxi around and return to the mooring buoy for a second attempt. Only the engines would be used for these manoeuvres. The radio officer would take great pride in the first time connection. The launches could not assist with the mooring process, unlike tugboats with ships.

Once moored, the aircraft would turn to face into the direction of the current and any wind, which was present. Until this manoeuvre was complete, the Control/Passenger launch could not approach the moored aircraft for fear that the launch would damage, the hull or, the floats attached by struts to the underside of each wing near the wing tip section.

The launch had to approach the aircraft on the port side where the passenger door was located. The location of this door was between the hull and the float, with very little space between. This meant that the coxswain was obliged to manoeuvre the launch with both engines using these both in reverse and forward drive mode to position this craft gently alongside the passenger door.

The same procedure had to be followed twice during each transit operation, to disembark and re-board these passengers.

Before I left Malakal, under the guidance of the coxswain I was able to carry out these manoeuvres, but never felt comfortable and in charge when doing so.

Once the passengers had disembarked, the short walk to the nearby rest house would take them past a local Shilluk or Dinkha man. He was employed to add flavour to the transit stop, and would be dressed as a warrior, complete with spear. He had to stand stock-still on one leg, with the other resting on that knee. This was common practice with both the tribes in question.

The story of one of these is recounted later in this narrative as his life and background was of considerable interest to us.

The next phase of the transit operation was the transport of fuel to the aircraft by the local re-fuelling contractor. This was achieved by bringing the contractor's launch alongside, but on the opposite side from where the passenger door was located,

This launch was loaded with a large number of 4-gallon 'aluminium' or 'tin' receptacles, containing highly flammable, high-octane aviation fuel. Each of these containers had to be passed up from the launch to a bearer on the top of the wing, opened and emptied into the requisite tanks.

The flight engineer, a member of the crew, had the task of ensuring that sufficient fuel was loaded into each tank, and was not adulterated during this process He also had to check the various oil and hydraulic levels, and other such duties.

Standing on the wings of a high winged aircraft, in a fast flowing river was a hazardous task, and the engineer and re-fuelling agents, were always in danger of falling into the river during this process. This would be even more hazardous if work had to be done to the engines, as these projected forward of the wing.

I have described the aircraft and the peculiar handling problems associated with this type of aircraft, so that today's ground handling units at airports throughout the world will recognise the primitive nature of the operation in the middle of the last century.

It should also be remembered that the C Class Flying Boat was the pride of the BOAC fleet during that period, in much the same way that the Concorde is for British Airways today.

The river Nile around Malakal abounded with very large crocodiles. These would sun themselves in the rushes on the riverbank around the jetty, and would be ready to launch out if anyone should fall into the river during the re-fuelling process.

More about the environment

During the wet season the area surrounding Malakal, was full of lush vegetation, in which lived millions of insects. These insects would be disturbed if anyone walked through their habitat. These insects would attack anyone so inclined causing considerable distress to that individual.

In the dry season the brush would turn to a light arid yellow, but would still be teeming with insects, ready to fly up in the event of any intrusion into their territory.

In both the dry and wet season the land on both sides of the river banks remained very green for about hundred yards inland. The bulrush—like plants at the river's edge would be around five to six feet tall. To walk through this also would be extremely dangerous because of the presence of large and small crocodiles, and venomous snakes, all invisible to the walker.

The Shilluk population greatly feared the snakes. If bitten, they would lie down and await death. Little did they know that very few venomous snakes in that area are fatal to the human race, provided remedial action is taken immediately? In many cases it was the death wish rather than the snakebite to which they would succumb . . .

The 'C' Class Empire Flying Boat.

If the reader wishes to have a more technical description of the C Class Flying Boat, may I refer the reader to the book published by by New Burlington Books and written by Robert Wall entitled 'Airliners'.

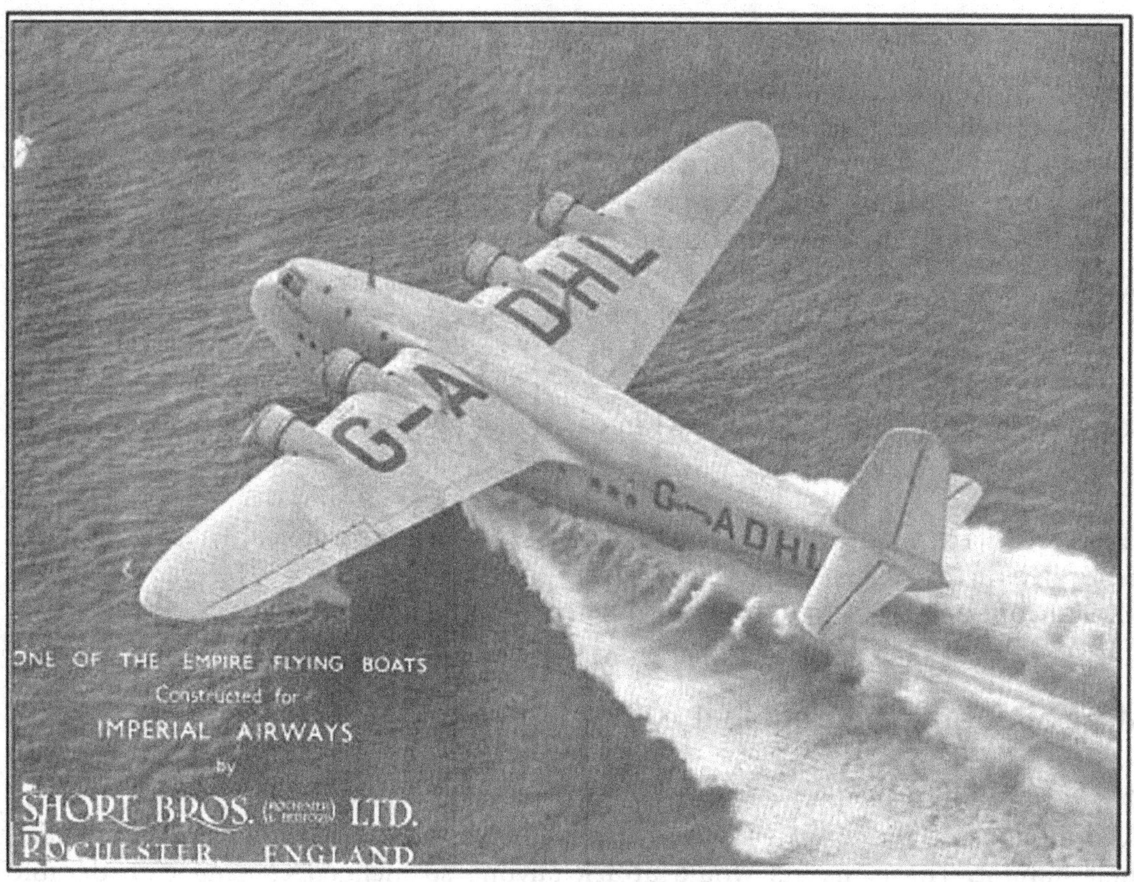

picture of GADHL taking off from water

The description in this book is geared around an understanding of the operation of this aircraft, particularly from my viewpoint, knowing very little of the technical aspects of any aircraft at the time. After all, this was my very first posting.

The C Class Flying Boat dominated our lives at this time. It is worth a description in layman's terms to indicate the feelings we had when one of the giant aircraft of that era presented themselves to us in our operating environment. This operational description includes a passenger's eye view of the take-off, and landing of such aircraft.

A landing strip on the water had to be selected carefully, and cleared of obstacles before the aircraft was allowed to land or take off.

A green 'VEREY' light signal fired into the air by the coxswain would confirm to the pilot that the area was clear. The control launch had to position itself at the point of landing, to identify the cleared area and the direction of landing. A windsock located over the launch cabin would indicate the wind direction.

Unlike today's operations from fixed landing zones and runways, the flying boat had no need for such pre-ordained landing areas. This was even more relevant at Malakal, when the landing area was governed not only by the prevailing weather conditions but also by the river conditions.

The river flow at Malakal was never less than 5 knots and in the rainy season this could reach 7 to 8 knots.

The presence of large floating islands and their proximity to the landing area often determined where the aircraft would land; Occasionally this would be far to the North to await the passing of these large island obstructions, around the true landing zone near the moorings.

Any obstacles on the water, even the smallest object, could seriously damage the aircraft should any of these come into contact with the hull. This was particularly so when the aircraft was moving through the water at the higher speeds associated with the landing and takeoff.

When the landing was to the North of Malakal, it would become necessary to take off and land again, after the obstruction had cleared the landing zone. If it waited too long, the obstruction would eventually reach the aircraft, and it would then become an even greater hazard.

Sometimes after landing, if the hazard was only a small island, the aircraft could taxi to the normal landing area bypassing 'en route' the floating island obstacle. In order to do so, it would seek the advice of the station personnel by radio.

The responsibility for preparing the landing area, and clearance for landing fell upon the coxswain in consultation with the station manager. In many cases the pilot would make such a decision, following personal observation of the landing zone. Ground to air communication in those days, was almost non-existent.

The ground staff acted as Air Traffic Controllers, but with none of the aids available to these today. Most of the communication was by light signals, despatched from the Control Launch or the Aircraft.

All the coxswains employed by BOAC were trained to use Morse code. Morse Code was the principal means of communication at the time, and the launches were equipped to provide this communication link with the aircraft.

The fact that so many operations were completed safely is to some extent due to the infrequency of operation, and the cooperation and faith in each other's ability that existed between pilots and ground staff, together with the use of the communication devices indicated.

Even more about the 'C' Class Empire Flying Boat.

The C Class Flying Boat carried around twenty-four passengers, all in one luxury standard, seated in three cabins. Each cabin was, literally, a step up from the others. This was due to the shape of the hull.

At the rear of the last cabin, was the area designated for the carriage of baggage and any cargo. Between the first and second cabins, in line with the wing floats, was an observation cabin from which passengers could observe the terrain below.

Passenger seating arrangements on this aircraft were quite luxurious, a far cry from the wicker chairs provided in the 1920s. The seats were of the reclining variety; however the metal frames of the seat structure and arm rests were clearly visible, and formed part of the cabin décor.

In general the décor comprised various shades of green, not the ideal colour for those inclined to airsickness, to which I was at the time

Other passengers in addition to myself, used the *'cuspidors' supplied to all passengers, with great frequency.

It cannot be said in all honesty, that air travel for the likes of myself, was a pleasant adventure, except in the very early morning, or just before dusk, when the heat of the day had not affected the flying conditions.

Having experienced the turbulent conditions on the flight out from Cairo to Malakal, I was not looking forward to my transfer from Malakal, as this would involve further air travel.

It is necessary to put air travel in the early 1940s into perspective. Today's air travellers prone to air sickness have no idea how uncomfortable flying was in those days.

In those days, pilots and passengers would get to know each other over the four days or so it would take for the travellers to reach their destination. Pilots were briefed to provide a level of passenger service to make the flight unforgettable for the small number of passengers carried on each trip.

Passengers when flying south from Malakal particularly the seasoned travellers, frequently used the observation platform to view the landscape over which they were flying just as Balloonists do today.

During such flights the pilot would try to locate the 'Bor' elephant herd, and fly as low as possible over them so that these could be observed from a position of safety only a hundred or so feet above the herd.

The Bor elephant herd consisted of a large number of African Elephants,('Loxodontor Africanus'), who moved around constantly searching for food but always near to a water source, in this case the Nile:(see maps 2 and 3).

The herd was named after the town in the southern Sudan located between Malakal, and Juba, where this herd would normally be found.

For any worldly wise traveller, to see this migrating group of elephants in their natural habitat became a must during any journey which might take them near this area of Africa.

Again, I have digressed, but can now return to a description of the aircraft. Hopefully this diversion takes away some of the boredom from aircraft description.

**a 'cuspidor' is a receptacle to contain phlegm or vomitus*

A purser's cabin was located in front of the first passenger cabin, and immediately aft of the galley. This was also used to de—plane the passengers.

Other load was carried above the Purser's cabin, behind the flight deck, which was at a higher level. In addition a further compartment for load was situated immediately aft of the section used by the Radio Officer for his mooring responsibilities.

The front passenger cabin was separated from the purser's compartment by a galley designed for food preparation. On the African route many of the shorter flights would not carry a steward At each stop rest houses were available for passenger use, and flight sectors were short due to the re-fuelling needs of this aircraft. For many passengers they preferred to eat on the ground rather than in the turbulence experienced in flight.

When these aircraft started pre-war operations across the North Atlantic, and further east to Australia, the galley may have been used to provide the passengers with more substantial sustenance in flight. This was not the case on the African routes.

Night operations were an exception rather than the rule, and all flights would overnight before nightfall. Most flight sectors were of only 3 to 4 hours duration. The start time, and flight day were planned around good overnight accommodation, and Malakal was not one of these.

Malakal was a transit port only, except in emergencies. The aircraft would overnight either in Khartoum to the north, or near Nairobi to the south, and two stops away from Malakal.

In the later years of the C Class operation, the role of purser was abolished, and the presence of Cabin stewards was introduced for all flights. They would also carry out the remaining on board duties of the purser.

The duties of the purser had become superfluous, as the staff on the ground took over more of the responsibilities for load acceptance and safe distribution on the aircraft. The number of crew on these aircraft represented about 40% of the persons on board and the role of purser was an unnecessary overhead.

Passengers seated in the front cabin were close to the waterline, and their windows would be covered with spray, as the aircraft settled down after landing, or as the aircraft began its take-off run. This was quite an exhilarating cabin to be in during these operations, and before airsickness took its toll.

The takeoff operation was quite an experience as the four engines roared at maximum power. The spray visible from the lower passenger cabin at this stage of takeoff gradually eased as the aircraft gathered speed and began to raise itself, first on to the first step of the hull, then to the second. As the aircraft continued to gather speed, the drag from the water was reduced, and by this time was barely in contact with any water, only the lowest mid rear section of the hull was touching and barely skimming the surface. Only once this point had been reached, could the aircraft gain enough speed for lift off.

As soon as the aircraft was airborne a stream of water appeared from the lowest part of the hull. The aircraft lumbered into the air, gaining altitude slowly, unlike the sleek take off of today's aircraft. Its cruising speed was barely over 120 knots.

Up to now this narrative has concentrated on the flying boat as the principal aircraft operating into and out of Malakal. I may have dwelt on this overlong, but it was the first aircraft of note during my full life with the airline, and despite its shortcomings I still hold fond memories for this aircraft.

Malakal and its Social Side

My induction to the social life of the expatriate community, and the development of a land airport at Malakal, forms the basis of the next section of this book.

After about six months of my stay in Malakal, an existing unused airstrip had to be developed to support air links between South Africa and Egypt. This airstrip was also to be used to open up a new route for military aircraft landed in West Africa, bound for the North African battlefront. Until this new route was opened, all short-range aircraft had to be transported by sea around the Cape of Good Hope in South Africa.

By the time this part of the story starts, the war in Ethiopia was over and it was safe to deploy landplanes to open the north/south links from South Africa to Egypt.

The runway, which was already present, would have to be extended and strengthened to support the land plane operations planned for this airfield. This new runway was only a short distance from our office and the rest house. Its location will be the subject of an interesting episode later.

The airfield did not have a Terminal building to accommodate passengers in transit. These would be ferried to the rest house whilst the aircraft would be re-fuelled.

Apart from the local population, Malakal was under the commercial control of Greek and Egyptian, and Lebanese traders who ran most of the commercial enterprises, including the provision of fuel to replenish the fuel tanks of both Flying Boats and eventually the landplanes, which would operate from the landplane base.

A river steamer from the North transported the aviation fuel, in 4-gallon tin containers. This steamer arrived twice weekly at the river port near the centre of the town. A local Greek trader who had the commercial monopoly to provide fuel for both flying boats and landplanes brought in the fuel

The arrival of the river steamer was a great social occasion, both for the local inhabitants and us, everyone trooped down to the pier on the river bank to welcome the arrival of this multi deck leviathan!

While the steamer was moored, the whole area was a blaze of light; the steamer being well lit during the hours of darkness with electricity generated by its own electricity source. This was independent of the town's limited lighting resources.

Along the river bank between the flying boat base, the rest house and the town, was the Egyptian Irrigation Departments' (EID) compound, comprising a number of Bungalows. A narrow paved unlit road separated the compound from the river.

This road led from the River Steamer port, to a narrow bridge about two hundred yards to the north of the bungalow in which we lived.

We had available to us a three ton lorry to take us from the EID accommodation, to the office. This vehicle was also used to move passengers between the landplane base and the rest house.

The journey to our office from where we lived, required us to negotiate this narrow bridge. There was only about an 8-inch clearance on both sides as the lorry crossed the bridge, and it was my wont, after a while to traverse this bridge at about 30 miles an hour.

Throughout my stay I never touched either side of the bridge greatly to my satisfaction, and also my companions, who would have been seriously embarrassed had I done so, and put the vehicle out of action. Repair facilities were practically non-existent.

I was young and carefree, and could not judge the folly of such behaviour. On reflection later, I realise how this attitude demonstrates how stupid and immature I was at this time.

Beyond this bridge, was a tortuous badly paved road, which led through two or three villages to the land and seaplane bases. These villages sat astride this road, and people would cross it ignoring any approaching traffic and the hooting of horns.

There was very little road traffic in Malakal, and the local inhabitants had never before come across this level of activity on the highway. At least five vehicles a day passed down this road. To the local population roads were there to ease their journeys between villages and town, not for vehicles to move on.

On the other side of the road from the EID compound was a steep bank, which led down to the river. It was covered, in lush vegetation, so much so that the edges of the riverbank could not be seen because of this.

In the river below this area, there were a number of resident crocodiles and an even larger number of Hippopotami. These could not be seen from the road, but could be heard.

Our bungalow was no more than 15 yards from this riverbank, just across the road from the entrance to our front garden.

The Hippopotami were most vociferous during the night hours, making it difficult to sleep. The grunting noises they made were both loud and continuous.

The EID compound covered a large area from the river, and included a Squash Court. This became the Social meeting place for all the British expatriates.

Squash was the order of the day each afternoon after 4 o'clock.

After the usual round of games, this group would gather to one of the houses to continue the social occasion. This activity was most circumspect, and consisted either of sessions of bridge, or purely social drinking and conversation.

I had been taught to play bridge by my mother and father whilst we were in residence in pre-war Malta. My brother, my parents and I would make up the bridge four. My sister was too young at the time.

The Social group, apart from the 3 BOAC incumbents, would consist of the EID manager and his wife, the local Civil Engineer and wife. To the group was added the Area Doctor and his wife. He was also the head of the local hospital. All except the EID manager were British Colonial officers.

Dad's Army?

Occasionally the Deputy Governor of the province, an Army Lieutenant Colonel, would join the group. He was also the Commander of the local defence force to which all the BOAC incumbents were automatically enlisted.

One of our responsibilities in the early days at Malakal was to defend the territory around the town in the event of any incursion by the Italian Army. For this task we were ill equipped. Each of us was provided with a '.303' rifle and a considerable number of rounds of ammunition. However we were given no training in the use of these firearms.

In the event of a conflict we would have the support of a half trained number of local inhabitants, and the local police under the jurisdiction of the local District Commissioner.

Thus the area was to be defended by a rabble similar to the Home Guard of Dad's Army fame. An impossible task regardless of the confidence we exuded at the time: but then we were young and immature.

The level of responsibility granted to us by our masters in Cairo, far exceeded the levels of our combined 'common sense'. On reflection, who knows how we would have reacted in a real military emergency?

The Saga Continues

Apart from those persons identified in this book so far, the only other expatriate was the Governor of the Upper Nile province. His residence was at the other end of town. The Deputy Governor was also a resident of Government House (as it was named).

In the grounds of the Governor's residence was a twenty yard long swimming pool, filled with water from the river, which we were assured, had been filtered, but still appeared a dirty greyish brown colour.

Next to the swimming pool there was Tennis Court with a Hard Court surface, which was not very 'true'. The main challenge on this court was not the tennis, but trying to judge where the ball would bounce after hitting the surface!

This also became a venue for other social gatherings, as and when agreed with the Governor. As an eighteen year old trainee, I was in awe at the ease by which I had been introduced and accepted by this group. We were all friends and on first name terms, even with the Governor and his Deputy. In fact many were the days when, to attract our attention at around 4 o'clock, the Deputy Governor would throw pebbles at the windows of our bungalow, to indicate that it was time for the afternoon squash court social.

We would be resting at this time, after our morning exertions at the airport, which usually started before 6 am.

The squash court was only about 50yards from our bungalow, through the EID compound. Our bungalow was the nearest to the river, the others being situated further in. A non-paved path, leading to the squash court, linked all the bungalows in the compound.

Members, who did not live in the compound would make their own way to the social venue.

I have deliberately omitted names from the descriptions in this narrative, but those who were there at the time will know to whom I refer, and to others they do not need to know.

The above shows how isolation can bring individuals together, from the youngest to the oldest, and from the lowliest to the highest. The only bonds were ones of origin and language; age and status appeared not to be relevant.

The group I have indicated were the only Europeans throughout the Upper Nile province; an area comprising some thousands of square miles, and under the jurisdiction of the District Commissioner. The area under his control covered an area far to the East near to the borders with Ethiopia,

About twenty miles to the south was an American Missionary compound, which comprised husband and wife and one or two children. The exact number I cannot be sure as our contacts with them were very infrequent, perhaps one or two occasions in the year and a quarter I was in Malakal, mainly at Easter and Christmas at the Governor's party.

I think it necessary to outline the environment in which I started my apprenticeship, so that events, which follow, can be put into perspective.

Episodes of Note at Malakal—circa 1941/2.

During my stay in the Upper Nile Province, five situations come readily to mind which may be of interest to the reader:

> **the life history of our head manservant,(a Dinkha by the name of 'Millwall'),**

the local fight between the Shilluk and Dinkha tribes;

the start of North-South Landplane flights by the South African Air Force;

the arrival of the RAF;

and my departure from Malakal, and posting to *'El Fasher'*.

The first of these occurred immediately after the start of the reconstruction of the landplane airfield: the cause of the fight was a matter of pay.

The workforce set up to prepare and build the runway extension, comprised a mixture of Shilluk and Dinkhas tribesmen. All of these were young men of fighting age. On the first payday, the Shilluks objected to the Dinkhas being paid before all of the Shilluk tribe had been given their wages,(just in case the money ran out before all were paid).

The reasoning behind this altercation was that the landplane base was being developed in Shilluk territory. Any shortages in the money supply should come out of the wages for the Dinkhas.

'O ye of little faith'

The Dinkhas, who were a more aggressive tribe than their compatriots, did not accept that they should be at the rear of the pay queue and took umbrage at this discrimination. A fight started between these two groups using whatever weapons they had readily available.

At the start, although less numerous but more aggressive, the Dinkhas gained the upper hand, and drove the Shilluks towards their villages, down the road towards the town of Malakal.

The Shilluks retaliated, drawing many other local fellow Shilluks from the surrounding villages, not initially involved in this dispute, They were now able to overwhelm the opposition, by sheer force of numbers.

As indicated earlier in this book our work-place on the outskirts of the town was midway between the Flying Boat base and the site of the new airport. This quickly became the site for the conflict. Although not targeted we became involved because of the location of our workplace.

As a result of this we were isolated from the local forces of law and order by the warring hordes. The Law Enforcers were slow to arrive even though a phone call to the District Commissioner received an acknowledgement.

The battle between these two warring factions, moved back and forth around our workplace, with the distinct possibility that this would be overrun during this conflict, with grave risk to our persons.

Fortunately we had in our possession the rifles and ammunition, provided for the defence of the region. The three of us, the Station Manager, the Coxswain and myself, collected the rifles, (with some ammunition), and came out of the office firing rifle shots in the air, in an attempt to stem the advance of these warring factions towards the river!

The action we took was successful as none of the insurgents were armed with guns. Our action did not harm anyone; they just stood back at this show of aggression, and continued throwing the odd stone at each other, until the local security force appeared in trucks.

The forces of Law and Order together with the District Commissioner were fully armed, and had more right to use force than us. Their arrival in large open sided 3ton trucks, with mounted machine guns ready for use, calmed the situation. Shortly after, pay was distributed and work recommenced.

The Start of Landplane Operations at Malakal.

In due course the airport was completed, albeit ill equipped with neither control tower nor terminal buildings. In addition neither were there Navigational aids to assist the flight operations. However the presence of this new airfield resulted in the start of daily flights by the South African Air Force to and from South Africa. These flights were identified, as the HP and PH flights, (Heliopolis to Pretoria, and *vice versa*).

Heliopolis at that time was the main Cairo Airport.

These daily flights were operated by Lockheed Lodestars, which were the principal transport plane in this part of the world at this time.

During this period, General Smuts was the prime political force in South Africa,(South Africa was still part of the British Empire, although self—governing).Since General Smuts was a firm friend of Winston Churchill, South Africa had sent forces to North Africa in support of the desert campaign. Presumably this air link was set up to reinforce, and supply its own forces, with Air Mail, and some luxuries. In addition it was also a means by which some of these forces could return to their homeland . . .

The start of these flights brought some welcome social relief, as the passengers from these planes would overnight at the local rest house, a stone's throw from our place of work. Many of the passengers were young women, as also were some of the South African Air Force pilots.

We were given the task of providing all the necessary ground facilities for these passengers and crew. We used our three ton Army truck to transport them to and from the rest house.

For the first time during my stay it was possible to entertain young unattached women. This provided a welcome relief from the loneliness experienced by three young men in the far outposts of the Colonies.

The Pilots, both men and women became good friends, as they plied up and down this route on a regular basis. Most of them recognised that we lacked luxury items, and they frequently arrived with presents from South Africa. These were unsolicited gifts, for which we very grateful.

Many were the times the crew and I sat in the aircraft cabin after the passengers had departed for the rest house, and shared a bottle of South African rum!

After the war some of these wartime pilots became Captains on the South African Airways flights, and I was able to re-establish my friendship with them. SAA had no women pilots so I never saw these again after the war.

My re-acquaintance with these SAA pilots was in Rome, to which I was posted many years later. These senior pilots and myself would reminisce about those days over a glass of wine and plate of pasta.

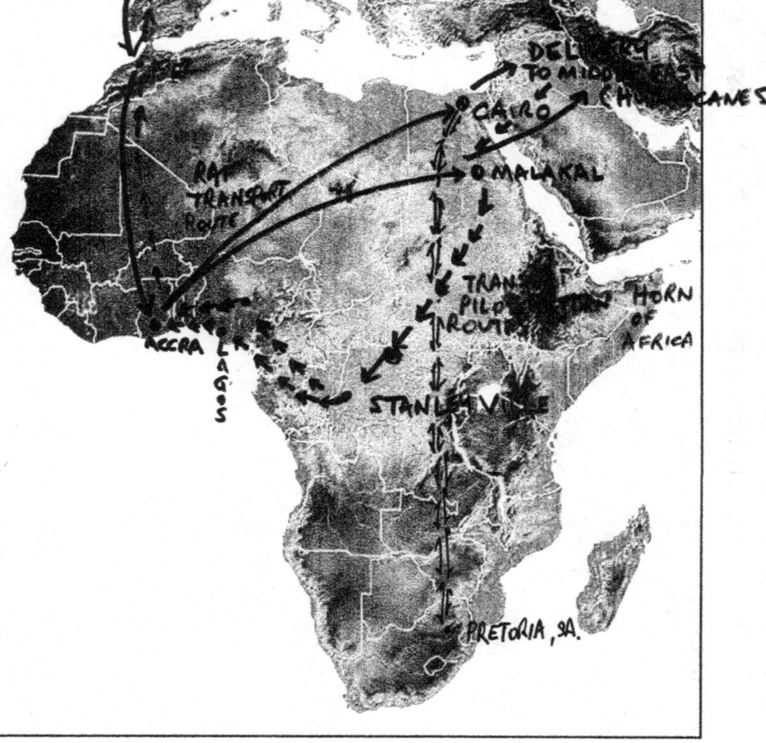

↗ FAST DIRECT ROUTE TO MIDDLEEAST (VIA AFRICAN CONTINENT)

↙ SLOW RETURN ROUTE OF RAF TRANSPORT PILOTS (VIA STANLEYVILLE AND LAGOS)

⇅ CAIRO-PRETORIA FLIGHTS (RSAAF) so called Heliopolis-Pretoria Highway.

map 6 showing pilot routes across Africa

The Arrival of the Royal Air Force at Malakal.

With the completion of the runway, the powers that be in the UK, decided that the best way to re-supply the RAF in the Middle East was by shipping new warplanes from the UK to West Africa, then ferrying these aircraft, from West Africa via Malakal to the Middle East war zone. This route was quicker than shipping them by sea via South Africa.

The aircraft would be ferried by special crews, who would deliver their aircraft, and return to West Africa, to pick up the next consignment of aircraft.

This plan enabled new short-range aircraft to be sent to reinforce and strengthen the older types of aircraft, (mainly Hurricanes), which formed the basis for the desert air force at that time.

Many of these new aircraft were of American origin, and provided this force for the first time with light bombers specifically designed for support purposes. It was also the first time that I saw aircraft with a tricycle undercarriage, fitted with a nose wheel and its tail off the ground while at rest.

The return of these crews to West Africa, (as passengers), would be by whatever means were available at the time. The Flying Boat operation to West Africa would be used frequently. The route took the aircraft from Malakal, to StanleyVille in the Belgian Congo, then to landing sites on the Congo River, and on to Nigeria and further west to the Gold Coast, the name for Ghana at this time.

This development meant that the Flying Boat route to and from West Africa became more important. The increased frequency of operations at Malakal substantially increased our daily workload.

The arrival of the RAF team caused an upset to the local expatriate community, who were ill prepared for the sudden influx of servicemen, 'unused' to the social niceties of the Colonial way of doing things. It took a while for the RAF to be accepted; hence they were initially restricted to their living quarters around the Airport.

We had no such inhibitions, and in any case, our brief was different to the others and our social life increased accordingly.

The RAF, to which I was later to be transferred, brought with them habits to which we had not been subjected to in the stiff colonial environment. This new element in our social upbringing, in its own way, became quite pleasant for the young men that we were. I refer to the habit of getting seriously drunk whenever we were invited to a social evening with the RAF.

This new habit was to rest with me for a few years more. It was not until I was married, that I toned down these drinking excesses.

As the western desert war changed for the better, so the supply route via West Africa became irrelevant, and the presence of the RAF at Malakal was no longer required. As quickly as they came so they departed, all in a matter of months.

All the facilities built for the RAF were abandoned and quickly became an eyesore. No one was left behind after their departure to tend to the buildings. In the tropical conditions at Malakal, with frequent heavy rains, the wooden elements of the buildings rotted, eaten by the termites which infested the region.

When I left Malakal, these buildings, remained as an eyesore on the landscape.

The story of Millwall Our Head Houseboy.

'Millwall' was the name someone had given to our Head Houseboy.

I don't know how he was given this name, unless one of our predecessors was a football fan, and oddly enough, supported the team from 'the Den'.

Millwall was not his real name: this we never knew. He always answered to the name our predecessors had given him.

He was a Dinkha tribesman from *Wau,* a village to the south east of Malakal. Access to his place of birth, was extremely difficult for those unaccustomed to travel in this part of Africa, but he regularly went to his village and his brother, and cousins also visited Malakal every now and again, to take his earnings back to his village in the form of cattle or goats.

The story goes, that at early age he had asked the village chief for the hand of his daughter, and was told that the chief would only give his consent, when he had become an important man in the village. Importance in '*Wau*' was based on the material possessions and stock owned by the would-be suitor. Thirty head of cattle was the minimum required.

To achieve this objective he trekked to Malakal and looked for employment.

All this is hearsay. By the time I met him he had already achieved the position of head houseboy, and ruled over the chef and cleaner, who were also employed by us.

When he first arrived in Malakal, he was a very personable young man, barely in his teens. He stood well over six feet in height and well built. He was also a very black Sudanese, as were most of the Dinkhas and Shilluks.

Even when we first came across him as head houseboy, he was in his late twenties, and still had this imposing appearance.

The lighter hued Sudanese came from further North, in fact North of Khartoum. Regular interbreeding with lighter skinned, mainly Sudanese of Arabic origin, caused the Sudanese to be a nation of light and dark skin-colour individuals. Those originating from the Deep South had less opportunity to interbreed and thus were in the great majority the darkest of that nation's race.

Population migration was mainly from the poor south towards the river Nile and northwards, where most employment was to be found, albeit for very little reward.

We were given to understand by other residents, that Millwall's first job was to stand on the pier where the flying boat passengers would land on their way to the rest house for refreshments, while refuelling took place. The method of refuelling has already been described.

Refuelling would take around 30 to 40 minutes, during which time Millwall would be the centre of attention both for his physique, and his warlike stance,(whilst at rest) and for his manner of dress, (or rather lack of it).

Millwall's 'apparel', was the same as all other locals in this area, and comprised an orange toga-like piece of cloth, linked over the left shoulder. While at rest this toga—like cloth barely covered his manhood. Any small movement on his part would cause excitement to the women passengers. Under garments was not the norm for the local population.

Normally he would remain stock-still on one leg whilst maintaining his balance by means of a spear resting on the ground, the point of the spear being at the top. The other leg would be placed just below the knee of the leg on which he stood.

I have no doubt his income was significantly increased by the tips offered to him by the passengers.

Even while he was earning in this job, by wage and tips he would buy up cattle from the Malakal market, and get his brother or cousin, to take these back to his home village, about 5 to 7 days walk from Malakal. Each trip would build up his prestige in *Wau*, his native village, as his wealth increased.

From 'modelling' on the pier, over the years he became an employee of BOAC, and moved into our residence as houseboy/ cleaner, responsible for the cleaning and maintenance of the property.

Once he had been promoted to head houseboy, (like Jeeves in the P.G Wodehouse novels), he, Millwall, would rule his charges. Let us be clear, we were his charges and he expected us to behave in the way that would maintain his standing with his own neighbours' houseboys, and the life style expected of us as colonials and ex-patriates.

He was always impeccably turned out, wearing a starched and un-creased long flowing white gown from shoulder to ankle, with a black sash, and a white sort of turban, loosely wrapped around his head.

Whereas we would have preferred to take our meals in informal dress, he used to prepare our baths, and lay out our dress, comprising white shirt and trousers, black cummerbund, and black bow tie, and would be very upset if we did not dress formally for dinner., even when we were not entertaining.

Dinner was always after the evening games of squash. We would return from these exertions, hot and sticky with perspiration from the tropical climate and, Malakal being reasonably close to the Equator, all of us would be much in need of a bath.

Even though there was no running hot water in the bungalow, Millwall would always have this available, for each of us to bathe twice a day, once in the morning, and later in the evening. This must have been a Herculean task, which he performed daily without complaint.

In the morning we had to be in uniform for breakfast and in the evening in formal attire. If we did not conform, to these rules, he would lose face with his counterparts occupying similar positions to himself in other houses in the compound. No doubt, he learnt these ways by mixing with them.

Millwall brought this level of discipline into our lives. It was good for us, as without his presence, our standards would have lapsed.

His purchases in the Malakal cattle market continued on a regular basis, with his brother or uncles, collecting, and taking this stock back to his village.

The day arrived when he called us together in the evening and tearfully gave in his notice. He indicated that he was now a person of great importance in his village, and had been advised by his brother, on his last visit to Malakal, that the village head, was ready to accept him as a son, His vow had been fulfilled, and he had to return to *Wau,* his native village.

It was with a sorrowful heart that he left the *'metropolis'* of Malakal, to return to *Wau*. Shortly after his departure I was also posted away from Malakal, but then this is another saga in my African adventures.

Chapter 2

North Africa after Malakal—
Postings to the Western Desert-

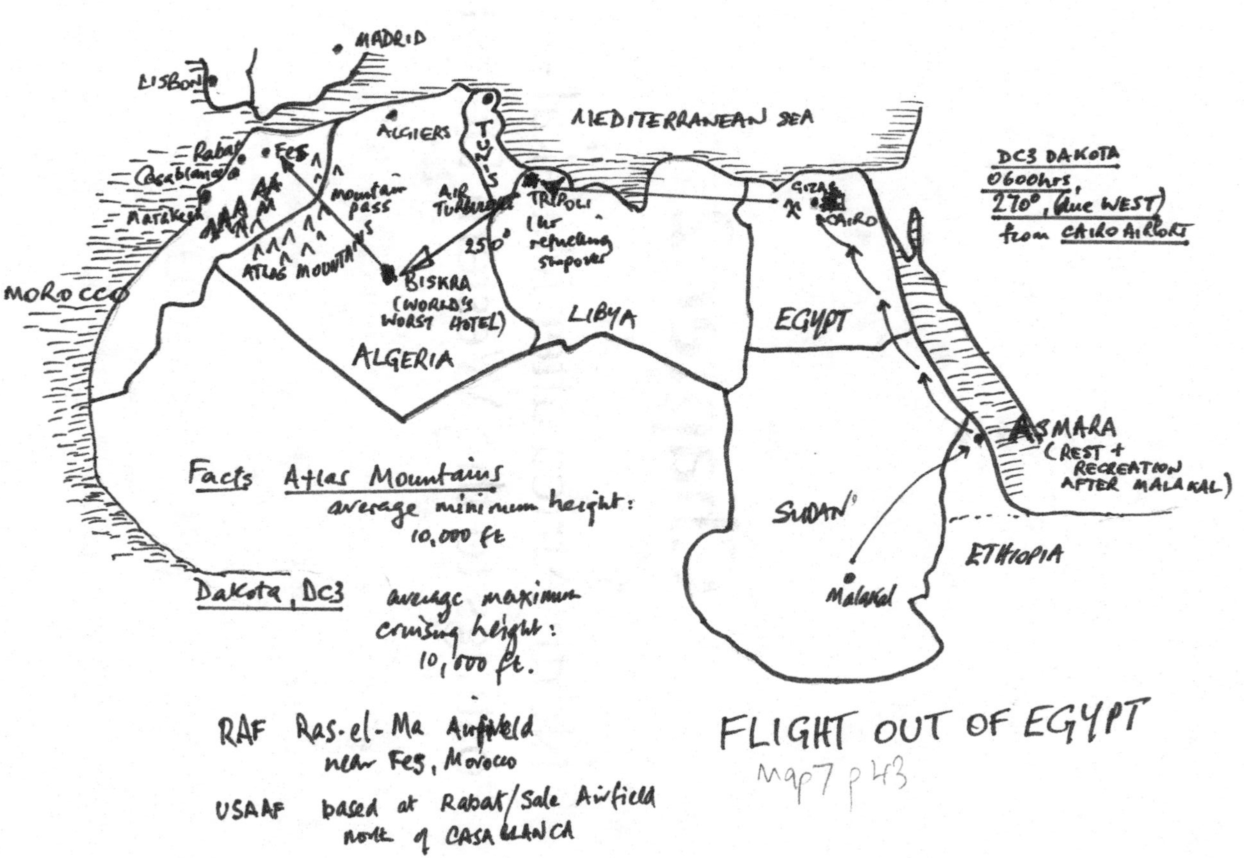
"GO WEST, YOUNG MAN (c. 1943)"
MADRID
LISBON
MEDITERRANEAN SEA
ALGIERS
TUNIS
Rabat
Fes
Casablanca
Marakesh
mountain pass
AIR TURBULENCE
TRIPOLI (1hr refuelling stopover)
250°
ATLAS MOUNTAINS
BISKRA (WORLD'S WORST HOTEL)
MOROCCO
ALGERIA
LIBYA
EGYPT
GIZA
CAIRO
DC3 DAKOTA
0600hrs,
270°, due WEST)
from CAIRO AIRPORT
ASMARA (REST + RECREATION AFTER MALAKAL)
SUDAN
Malakal
ETHIOPIA
Facts Atlas Mountains
average minimum height: 10,000 ft
Dakota, DC3 average maximum cruising height: 10,000 ft.
RAF Ras-el-Ma Airfield near Fes, Morocco
USAAF based at Rabat/Sale Airfield north of CASABLANCA
FLIGHT OUT OF EGYPT
map7 p43

map 7 showing route to Morocco via Tripoli,Biskra

I left Malakal with deep regret, this having been my first major experience away from the family environment.

The periods spent away from home after leaving Khartoum, and my arrival at Malakal, were spent in relative luxury in Cairo, in a flat rented for us by BOAC. The flat was located in Zamalek, the most desirable location in Cairo at the time. It was also close to the Gezireh Sporting Club, to which we became automatic members.

The flat was shared with four other expatriates, all much older and experienced than me. The majority of these eventually became very senior executives of BOAC, and British European Airways in the post war years.

British European Airways was only formed in 1946 as an offshoot of BOAC. The purpose for the formation of this Airline was to meet the air transport shortages of post war Europe

Many of the senior staff of BEA came from BOAC, together with ex-service members of the RAF. In fact two of the ex BOAC staff, (now with BEA) were those with whom I shared the apartment in Cairo.

There is very little to recount about this period of my life, although in later years my association with some of the residents of the flat did become useful in the furtherance of my long-term ambitions in BOAC, and subsequently British Airways. They became good sounding boards to advance the concepts, which I formulated later in my career. These concepts are described in later episodes of this book.

My next move after leaving Malakal took a number of strange and somewhat fortunate twists, before I arrived at my next overseas station. Cairo was still my home base at this time, and all overseas movements were dictated from there rather than the UK.

After leaving Malakal I was to proceed to another station in the Sudan, a town by the name of *El Fasher*. This place was some 150 miles west of Khartoum, and I understand from a climatic viewpoint was as different to Malakal, as chalk is to cheese. Malakal was semi jungle territory with daily monsoon rains, whereas *El Fasher* was located in the desert regions of the Sudan, not dissimilar to the North African scenario which follows. However, before I was to proceed there, I was due some leave.

Asmara in Eritrea is where I decided to take this vacation in order to recuperate from my tropical sojourn in Malakal. The climate in Asmara was more tolerable than Cairo.

By this time in 1942, Asmara had become the principal landplane maintenance base for BOAC. The Cairo base had moved to Asmara due to the war conditions, which at the time were threatening that city. I was able to use this threat plus the climatic benefits of Asmara as the excuse for not wanting to spend my holiday in Cairo.

The town of Asmara is about 6 to 7000 feet above sea level, and its climate was almost temperate. Most days the town was above the cloud level for the area. The atmosphere was very rarefied and for the first few days one became quite breathless after even the minimum exertion. In fact the air was so thin, that the FIAT cars, which were available as a legacy of the Italian occupation, (mainly the 'Ballillas',) were so underpowered, that in some hilly parts of the town, when fully loaded, these had to be navigated up the hill in reverse. Any attempt to drive up in first gear would cause the car to stall halfway up.

On arrival at Khartoum from Malakal, I had to travel to Asmara by the first available landplane aircraft. There were few scheduled services between Khartoum and Asmara, most flights were from Cairo, and routed via the Red Sea to Asmara.

The aircraft I travelled in was an 'Ensign', which had to proceed to Asmara for its usual maintenance. The Armstrong Whitworth Ensign was a very large aircraft for its time, but greatly underpowered. How it ever took off and landed at Asmara remains a mystery to this day. It certainly could not have done so with any worthwhile payload.

Being naïve and inexperienced in the operation of aircraft, I was blissfully unaware of the operational difficulties and boarded the aircraft. I was the only passenger.

picture of Armstrong Whitworth 'Ensign'

The flight in this aircraft was my first experience of flying in an aircraft other than a flying boat, even though, towards the end of my stay in Malakal, I was processing more landplanes than flying-boats, through that station.

Anyway this is an interesting digression from the facts to be related.

The flight time to Asmara was relatively short and uneventful, and we landed around mid-morning in Asmara.

On arrival, a message from Cairo awaited me, in this I was informed that instead of proceeding to *El Fasher* as originally planned, I was to return to Cairo after my holiday, for reallocation to another station. This station was *El Obeid* another outpost station in the desert region to the west of Khartoum, similar in climate to *El Fasher*.

I have to state that of all the stations under the control of the Cairo region, these two stations ranked as two of the worst locations. However any protest would be ill considered. Perhaps this was a test of my durability and loyalty.

It so happens that this is not the end of this movement saga, and I never experienced the joys of living either in *El Fasher* or *El Obeid.* These stations were however, only land plane bases, and my work experience with this type of aircraft, was very limited.

On completion of my vacation, I returned to Cairo as requested, on a scheduled Lockheed aircraft operating the Asmara to Cairo schedule. We landed at Port Sudan on the way.

Port Sudan was then a smallish town on the shores of the Red Sea and served as the main seaport for the Sudan.

When I reported in to Head Office to advise them of my return, I was advised that my posting to *El Obeid* was no longer an issue, and I was to be transferred to *Habanniyeh* the airport for Baghdad in Iraq. *Habanniyeh* was a flying boat station on the lake of that name, serving the route from Cairo to the East.

At the time I was thankful that I would still be handling flying boats and I was not to lose my 'webbed feet', and the *verdigris* of my cap badge. I was also more comfortable handling the aircraft I knew well. At the time the sign of *verdi*gris on one's cap badge distinguished those who had been at flying boat stations, as distinct from those with only landplane experience. The Flying Boats were the pride of the BOAC operation. I was glad that my brief experience with them meant my career would continue to evolve around my association with water instead of the sandy surfaces of landplane bases.

In those days there was a marked difference between staff that serviced flying boat operations, to those handling landplanes. Those with flying boat experience considered themselves a superior member of staff, even though bearing the same badges of rank.

As the post war future of the Civil Aviation scene developed, this was a naïve and erroneous view of what was to be.

The period now is around the end of 1942, and early 1943. The North African war had taken a turn for the better, and the 8th Army had broken through the German and Italian lines and was advancing to the West.

It was because of this situation that I was posted temporarily back to *Rod el Farag*, and *Heliopolis*, until the move to could take effect.

By now I was about to complete my two year apprenticeship. This would see me promoted to the rank of Traffic Assistant. I could then remove the flashes on my lapels, and replace these with a one-quarter inch gold band against a white background. This was to be worn either on the sleeve or on the epaulettes of the summer uniform.

Secondment to 216 Group

Whilst I was passing the time between the two Cairo airports, Air Commodore Whitney-Straight was given the task of forming for the RAF in the Middle East, an air transport Command wing. This was to be identified as **216 Group**.

The RAF had no personnel with the requisite air transport expertise in this sphere of operation. BOAC were asked to provide this necessary expertise to form the nucleus of this group.

The group's task was to provide a support service for the Armies advancing to the west from El Alamein. By this time the advance had taken the army far to the west of Tobruk, and it was necessary to provide forward air support to return injured soldiers to the base hospitals in Cairo and Alexandria, and also to move mail, and supplies as well as replacement troops to the forward positions.

Incidentally after the war Air Commodore Whitney-Straight became the Deputy Chairman of BOAC.

I was one of the BOAC personnel selected to provide this expertise to the RAF transport group, and my posting to Baghdad was cancelled.

The cancellation of my posting to Baghdad was a fortunate occurrence, as subsequently, history shows, a gentleman by the name of Rashid Ali had overthrown the pro-western regime in Iraq, and all the BOAC staff at Habanniyeh, were imprisoned by this 'so-called' General.

Genera Rashid Ali was himself subsequently overthrown with the help of the British forces located to the East of Egypt, without the need to move troops from the 8th Army.

It took around 3 months to my knowledge before the release of the BOAC staff held prisoner. During this period they suffered great hardships, and their lives frequently threatened. I learned this later from one of these prisoners, a person with whom I had shared accommodation at the flat in Zamalek, in Cairo.

My part in the North African campaign after El Alamein

My 'secondment' to **216 Group** did not entail absorption directly to the RAF; this came about later. I remained on the BOAC overseas establishment, and BOAC continued to pay my salary. Thus I was somewhat wealthier than my counterparts in this Group, even though annual salaries for my rank were of the order of £200-£300 per annum.

To put the above salary in perspective; a made to measure suit made up with quality cloth, and manufactured in Cairo by a quality tailor, would cost around £5. I had such a suit made and the quality was so good that it lasted me until well after the war was over.

When we joined the Group, the RAF granted us Officer Status. However, we continued to wear our BOAC livery, presumably our 'officer status' related to the wearing of gold bands on our uniforms, (its 'livery').

Initially all the aircraft used by this group belonged to BOAC, and were Lockheed Lodestars. The pilots who flew these aircraft on the North African route were also all from BOAC and continued to wear the BOAC livery.

My first posting for **216 Group** took me to *El-Adem*, an RAF station near Tobruk on the North African coast of Cyrenaica. *El Adem* was near the railhead for trains from Egypt.

The railhead serving *El Adem* was about midway between Tobruk the seaport in that area, and *El Adem* the military airfield. The distance between Tobruk and *El Adem* was about 10miles. An inspection of any map of this area for 1942/3 will show this.

I boarded one of the Lodestar aircraft early one day in early 1943 at Heliopolis airport, and arrived some two hours later at *El Adem*. I was met on arrival by the other BOAC staff already in position.

The three BOAC staff members, including myself were accommodated around the Officer's Mess located within the aerodrome precinct. All this accommodation had been built previously by the Italian Air Force, and was the worse for wear. This was as a result of the recent action to capture this airfield. El Adem was one of the main airfields in use during the desert war by both sides.

My assignment to *El Adem* required me to report to the RAF Station Commander (a Wing Commander, who as it later transpired, knew my father well). The RAF unit at *El Adem* was identified as either 70, or 72 Staging Post.

During my period with the **216 Group**, I was sent to both 70, and 72 staging posts, one being at *El Adem*, and the other in Morocco. All this was so long ago that my memory fails me on this point.

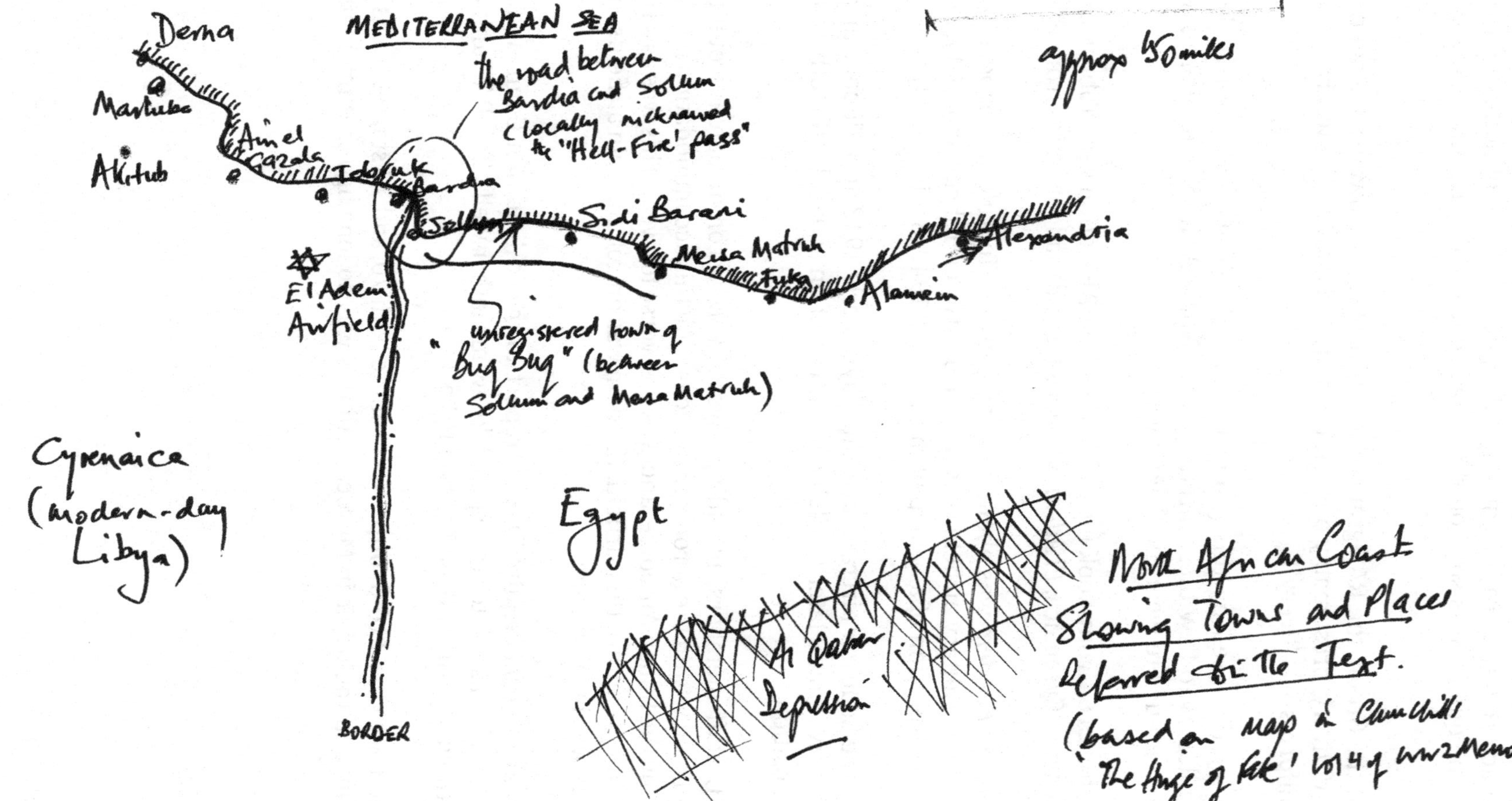

map 8. coastal towns of Cyrenaica(Libya) and Egypt +'hellfire pass'

Our brief was to set up an **Air Despatch and Reception Unit,** identified in short as an **ADRU**. This expression is used throughout, to describe the other stations to which I was posted whilst attached to **216 Group**.

A dispassionate view of El Adem

El Adem was an airfield built in the desert, I can only assume by the prewar Italian Air Force. Even the runway surface was constructed of hard packed sand.

The terrain surrounding the airfield, consisted of a mixture of sand and small rocks, but mainly sand. Everything around was a dirty yellow, with a blend of grey wherever the rocks were exposed. This scenery provided a very depressing outlook to which I never became accustomed. There was no hint of greenery apart from a few twiggy bushes.

This dreary outlook surrounded the accommodation assigned to us.

The only construction of note on one side, about 30yards away was the open-air toilets, which were for the use of the inhabitants of our hut and others around this location.

Each hut was separated from the other by a safe distance of desert sand and rock. Our particular hut was on the outskirts of the airfield precinct, and about 5 minutes' walk to the Control tower where our duties were to be performed.

The walk to the office would take us past other billets, various administrative locations, and the Officer's mess. The going underfoot was sand and small rocks. The small rocks would get into our shoes, even though we wore the typical 8th Army officer's high backed suede shoes.

The toilets are worth a mention. These comprised a series of 4-gallon fuel cans, filled with sand and stacked on three sides to a height of around 5 feet, but open to the elements on the fourth side. Fortunately for our privacy the open side was not visible from our accommodation or any other dispersed personnel around the area.

The toilet seat comprised a unit similar to the 'thunder boxes'. Thunder boxes were the name given to these 'ablutions', in those parts of Africa, where there was no running water to flush the toilets, or carry away the sewage.

The contents from these boxes in Malakal were taken away on a daily basis by municipal staff dedicated to this function. In the El Adem environment the contents had to be physically removed on a regular basis by those on latrine duties, and taken to more remote parts of the desert, where the contents was allowed to decompose naturally. However it seems that at no time was there sufficient decomposed matter, to turn the desert green.

The accommodation, to which we were allotted, consisted of four concrete walls with one door and one window with no glass. The walls were somewhat pock marked by the fighting and shelling which had just recently taken place, The 'bedroom' which slept the three BOAC staff had a roof of sorts, but which leaked in parts. The three bed locations were spread out strategically to avoid the floor areas susceptible to these leaks. Fortunately it did not rain very often.

The beds were superior types of camp beds, but even so not very comfortable. The only other bits of furniture were broken bits of bedroom units, which we were able to salvage from other surrounding unoccupied buildings in a similar state of disrepair. There was no seating accommodation in this luxury establishment. It was bed or nothing.

These dormitories were on the outskirts of the aerodrome. On three sides of our building was open desert, sand interspersed with the odd rock and stone. The other billets were between the officer's mess and us. We therefore were constantly presented with the beauty of the toilet construction, which gleamed in the sun.

The Officers' mess was a building similar to the accommodation in which we were housed, but it had a leak proof roof, and, therefore in a better state of repair than ours. Apart from this the officers' mess had little else to commend it, and certainly not the cuisine, which at its best was never 'haute'. It consisted mainly of corned beef made up in various ways, but with little sense of adventure in its presentation.

The one saving grace about this station was that the supply of bottled beer was not rationed. Beer was transported by rail from Cairo and all stops to the west, to the railhead between Tobruk and El Adem Supplies were so plentiful that we could shave with it, whenever this became necessary.

The beer originated in Australia, and was stronger than the normal brew. As I recall the names on these bottles were Frontenac, and Dows, with proof values in excess of 6.

Water was in desperately short supply. It had to be transported by water tanker over the rough road surfaces from wells near *Derna*. The town of *Derna*, another town in Cyrenaica, was situated on the coastline some 150 miles to the north west of Tobruk.

The water, which reached us, was undrinkable as it was slightly brackish. Even when it was used for tea making, the tea tasted foul.

The catering personnel would dry the used tealeaves in the sun, and package it up for barter with the nomadic tribes who occasionally roamed in this area. In exchange for the tea, these nomadic Arabs would provide us with eggs, which in the main were bad: this made the whole operation rather pointless! Having said that though, these exchanges did continue for a little while longer than expected . . .

Apart from tea making, the only use for this water was for our personal hygiene such as washing, including showers. We were allowed a 'ration' of one and a half gallons a day for this purpose, including use for drinking. Personal supplies did not go very far and it became necessary to share the shower water.

The water tasted so foul that we would not even use it to clean our teeth. Drinking it was out of the question, even though we had been assured that it had been purified.

In order to take a shower and conserve the water for others, it would be loaded into a canister of any sort. We would stand on a groundsheet out in the desert and pour this water over us. The water deposited on the groundsheet would be used more than once for other showers.

The level of hygiene, which applied at this time in the hot and dusty conditions of the Western Desert, (West of Cairo), meant that we as 'quasi' civilians, we were allowed to return to base once a month for a bath, and a day's return to the civilising influences of Cairo before returning to El Adem. This cycle continued for the full six months that we were there, until the advance was so far forward that other airfields and sea ports further to the west took the strain, and the operation at *El Adem* was no longer needed

Visits to the Scenes of Battle.

Some of the incidents, which occurred during my stay at El Adem, are well worth recounting.

The first of these was the exploration of the desert environment in which so many battles had taken place. On one of these days of exploration, we came across an untended ammunition dump left by the Italian Army in its hasty retreat to the west.

Being young and foolish we would seek out, and experiment with live grenades of all kinds. Some of these were 'thunder flashes', which made a lot of noise but emitted virtually no shrapnel.

We would hide behind any convenient solid metal object around the dump, pull out the pins which secured these grenades, and toss them as far as we could to await the explosion.

In retrospect I now realise how foolhardy we were, but at the time as young teenagers, the experience was exhilarating.

My friend with whom I shared this experience at the time was a young Canadian, also a late teen-ager like myself who had been transferred from the North Atlantic Transport Command to El Adem.

Throughout the period of our stay we had at our disposal a fifteen hundredweight, (15cwt) Ford truck, identified as a 'yellow peril' or 'YP' in the service jargon. This vehicle enabled us to explore the areas surrounding the airfield. This vehicle also served us well when the time came to return to Alexandria, and Cairo.

While on our exploration trips, we had to be careful to avoid the minefields. These had not yet been cleared or made safe. The minefields, which surrounded the airfield, were clearly identified for entry, but one would not dare venture into these areas without expert guidance. The boundaries were not delineated very clearly even though the entry path would be.

Once past the entrance into such a minefield, any return to the point of entry would be very hard to identify. This may be hard to appreciate, but to anyone who has been placed in that situation they will recognise that this statement is true.

I was actually able to visit the zone named the 'Devil's Cauldron', the scene of a battle which took place in this area before El Alamein. The result of this battle was the almost total destruction of the Allied tank forces taking part in it.

It was quite distressing to see the line of shattered British tanks, which could be viewed from the bottom of a sand valley, all knocked out as they appeared over the crest of the small hill, by the German 88s (the anti-tank guns used by the Germans).

Presumably these guns were strategically located in the valley below, awaiting the appearance of these tanks over the crest of the hill. In most cases the underside of the tank is its most vulnerable part.

The start of Flights to and from the UK

After about three months in *El Adem*, BOAC reopened the route to the UK. This route was operated during night hours only, and the departure and arrival at *El Adem*, was essential so that no part of the route to the North and West was flown in daylight, until later when conditions made this perfectly safe to do so.

The 'Liberator' type aircraft, used extensively by the US Air Forces in this war, carried out the non-stop operation from *El Adem* to the UK. The flights were piloted again by BOAC aircrew in BOAC rather than RAF uniform.

Captain O.P Jones, a well renowned BOAC pilot of the pre-war years, was one of the pilots who flew this route. I well remember his idiosyncrasy of always wearing spotless white gloves to fly his aircraft, even when operating under these wartime conditions.

The Liberators used *El Adem* both for fuel and the operational reasons described above.

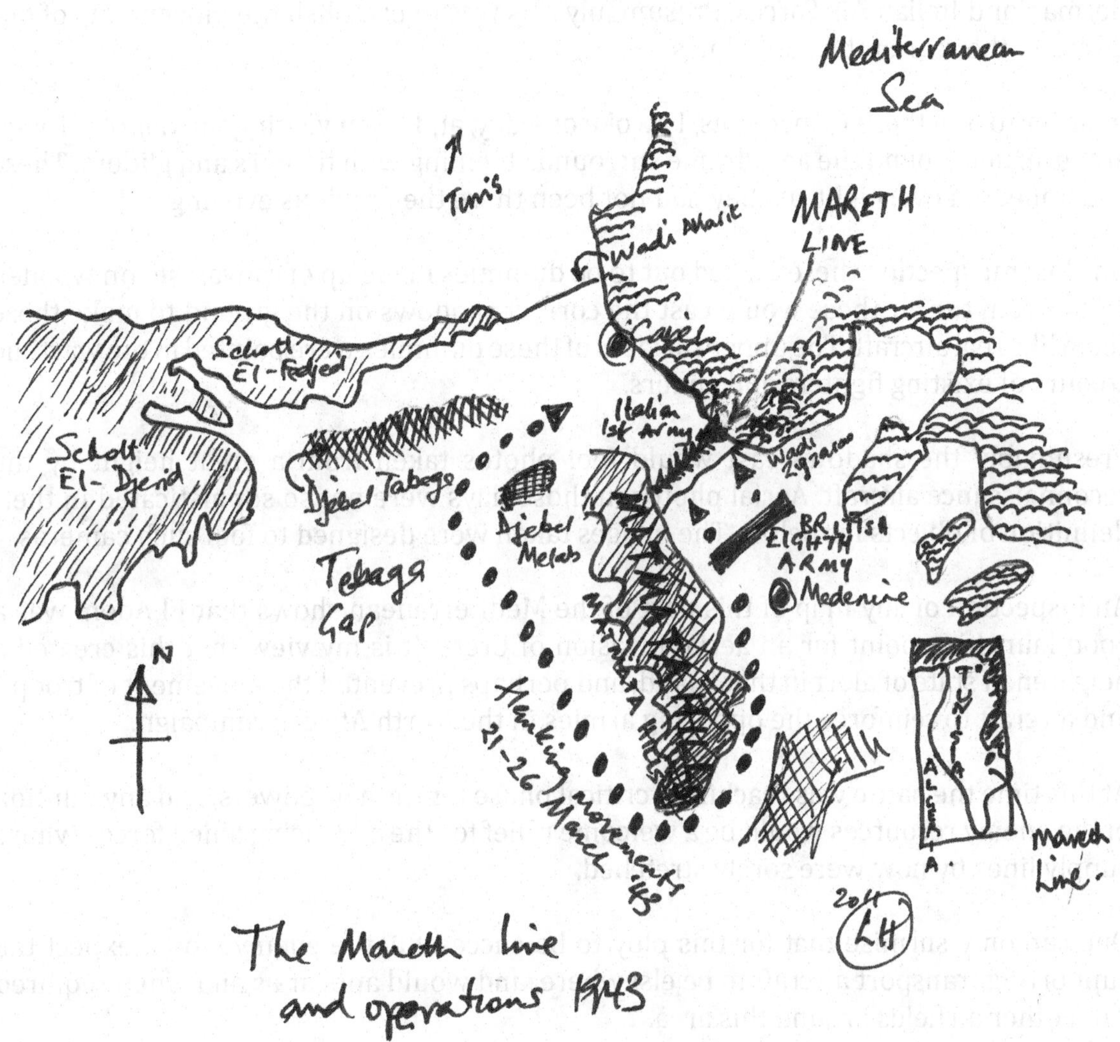

Mediterranean Sea
Tunis
Wadi Akarit
MARETH LINE
Schott El-Fedjed
Gabes
Schott El-Djerid
Italian 1st Army
Wadi Zigzaou
Djebel Tebaga
Djebel Melab
Tebaga Gap
BRITISH EIGHTH ARMY
Medenine
N
Flanking movements 21-26 March '43
TUNISIA
ALGERIA
Mareth Line
2011
LH
The Mareth Line and operations 1943

The Mareth Line 1943

Don Hill

Fooling the Enemy?

The next episode of note worth recounting preceded the next phase of the advance of the 8th Army.

El Adem, as stated earlier was the nearest aerodrome to the railhead from Egypt and because of this, was the subject of frequent incursions by reconnaissance flights by the German and Italian Air Forces. Presumably this was to establish the movements of our forces to the rear of the battle lines.

In order to fool these inspections, I awoke one day, and upon visiting the Control Tower at the airfield, found the aerodrome surrounds teeming with fighters and gliders. These had appeared overnight, as they had not been there the previous evening.

On closer inspection these turned out to be dummies made up of canvas, set on wooden stilts. From the air these would cast the correct shadows on the ground to make these seem like real aircraft. The upper surfaces of these dummies were painted in the wartime colours of existing fighters and gliders.

Presumably the shadows cast would fool photos taken from a great height by the reconnaissance aircraft. Aerial photos in those days were not so sophisticated in their definition of objects far below. The images taken were designed to fool such cameras.

An inspection of any map of this part of the Mediterranean shows that El Adem was a good launching point for an aerial invasion of Crete. It is my view that this created a heightened state of alert in that island, and perhaps prevented the movement of troops, and aircraft to reinforce the opposing armies in the North African campaign.

At this time the battle was reaching a critical phase for the axis powers, and any dilution of the enemy resources would be a welcome relief for the advancing allied forces whose supply lines by now were sorely stretched.

One can only surmise that for this ploy to be successful, the enemy would expect the supporting transport aircraft to be elsewhere, and would appear as and when required from other airfields around this area.

Once the next 8th Army advance re-started, these dummies disappeared as quickly as they had been introduced.

Our part in the Battle for the Mareth Line

The next incident of note was the part played by *El Adem* immediately prior to the battle for the 'Mareth' line.

The Mareth Line was a defensive line built by Rommel's forces, to prevent the 8th Army advancing into Tunisia.

By this time the North African landings to the west of Tunisia had taken place. The objectives of the British and American 1st Army, which had landed simultaneously in Morocco, and Algeria, was to advance to the East from Algeria and Morocco, to link up with the 8th Army, hopefully around Tunisia.

Once the 8th Army had breached the Mareth Line, the above objectives would be achievable. After a few setbacks, this objective was achieved in the time scale predicted.

The few setbacks, such as the battle for the Kasserine Pass, and the stiff resistance met by the 8th Army proceeding north along the Tunisian coast are instances during this campaign when little if any advance was made.

In fact the battle for the Kasserine pass, nearly caused the whole of the North African landings to falter. Had the German army been able to reach the sea to the east of Algiers, via the Kasserine Pass, the whole of the North African strategy and timetable would have been disrupted, and the subsequent invasion of Sicily affected.

Once the linkup between the 1st and 8th Armies had been achieved, it was only a matter of time before the axis forces were ejected from the whole of North Africa. This happened around April/May 1943.

The above is relevant to this story. It puts into perspective, the next part of this narrative. This involved my return to Cairo and subsequent transfer to Morocco.

The summer of 1943 was a time to consolidate the gains achieved after the North African campaign had concluded, and to prepare for the next phase: this being the invasion of Sicily.

I now return to the period immediately prior to the battle of the Mareth Line, and my part in this.

In order to prepare for the battle to breach the Mareth Line, extra troops had to be moved speedily to the front line from the distant rear areas.

We were told one day that a large number of troops, including Ghurkhas, had to be transported by air from El Adem to the forward airfields. These would be used to supplement the troops already in position for the battle about to take place. The additional forces would arrive by train from the holding areas in Egypt, and be carried by air to their destination.

It seems that the opposing forces did not expect reinforcements for the battle to eject Rommel's forces from so far back in Cyrenaica. They expected such reinforcements to use more advanced ports and airfields.

At any rate troops began arriving in considerable numbers, and were separated into groups of thirty or so, for immediate transport, once the transport aircraft to carry them arrived.

At the same time as these troops began arriving, a large number of Dakotas (DC 3) of the US Air Transport Command began arriving, from where I do not know. There were about two or three squadrons, numbering in all about 25 to 30 aircraft.

These aircraft and their mobile headquarters base, were set up on the opposite side of the airfield, some considerable distance from where the forces to be transported would be airlifted.

This US force was self-supporting, and would provide all the ground support needs for these aircraft throughout this operation.

As each aircraft was ready for departure, it taxied to the loading point near the airfield control tower. This area served as the assembly point for the troops who were to be transported.

Each group of soldiers was boarded and the aircraft took off for their appointed destination. This cycle was repeated many times, and the aircraft once unloaded of troops at its destination, would fly back to pick up the next load. This operation continued for a few days. Troops continued to arrive from the railhead, taken to the airfield and assembled ready for transport to the battlefront.

At the end of this operation, in which we were deeply involved, exhaustion was the order of the day. The operation had been non-stop. Troops had to be separated into aircraft loads. This meant apportioning these by battle formation, so that on arrival at destination, they would be delivered to their appropriate regiments

The above was done in an ever-changing environment, as each train arrival delivered a new body of troops, adding to those still awaiting transportation.

Along with the exhaustion, there was also a sense of satisfaction that the whole operation had been concluded without a hitch.

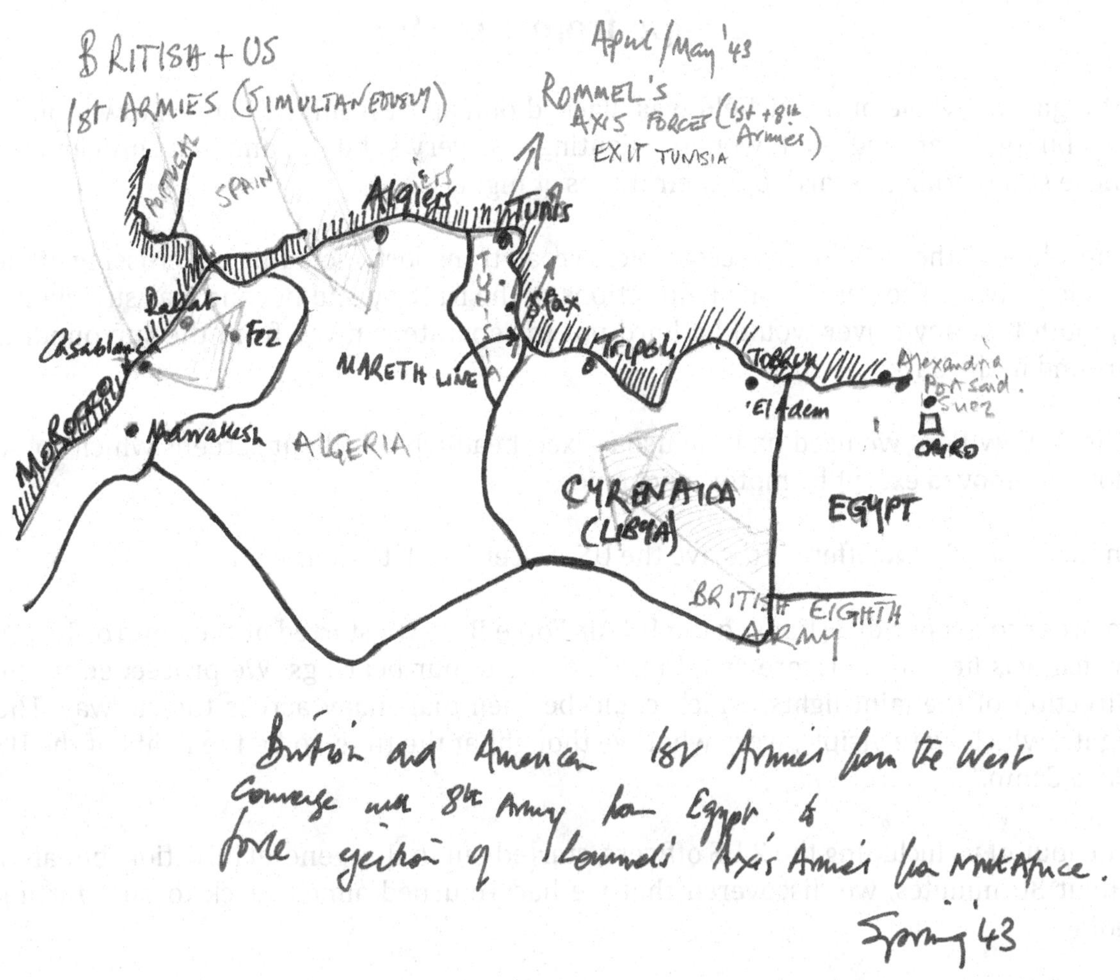

map showing routes of US and UK armies

In retrospect, it could be that this was one of the first major air transport operation of troops to the front line of the Second World War. If each aircraft had carried 30 fully armed soldiers, and 30 aircraft were involved each carrying out at least 6 or 7 flights over the 3 days, then in excess of 5000 troops had been moved some 300 to 400 hundred miles to forward bases in the space of 3 days.

When the operation was over, the US Officers located at the other end of the airfield were invited to the Officers Mess for drinks. We could not offer them dinner, as our cuisine was not up to the standard of the rations provided for their personnel. Even the tins of meat and vegetable hash available to the US forces were luxury items to us.

The purpose of the preceding narrative although of interest in itself, shows how, in the next part two of the BOAC staff, myself included, came to find ourselves in the middle of an active minefield. This occurred after we had delivered the US Officers back to their camp in the hours of darkness.

The saga goes as follows.

Don Hill

Escape from Disaster

At night the whole of the airfield was blacked out, apart from the control tower and a few buildings around the tower. Any lighting was very subdued and just sufficient for those still working to carry out their duties at night.

The whole of the airfield was accessible, to road transport, including the crossing of the single runway. The passage in all directions to the runway and beyond was sufficiently smooth that any driver would be hard put to separate runway from the surrounding ground in the dark.

The 'Yellow Peril we used had the usual fixed headlight blackout screens which could not be removed except by motor mechanics.

In this scenario, we offered to drive the US Officers back to their camp.

In order to get our directions to the US Air Force Base we started at the Control Tower, which was lit, and therefore could provide one of our bearings. We proceeded in the direction of the faint lights, which could be seen diagonally across the runway. The lights, which were visible, were what we thought at the time, to be the lights of the US Base Camp.

The four of us including the 2 US officers, started out in this general direction, but after about 30 minutes, we discovered that we had returned almost back to our starting point.

We found out for the first time, that in total darkness, there is a tendency for vehicles to move in circles even when the driver is convinced that they are driving in a straight line.

Having returned to our starting point, we re-aligned ourselves and set off again. After about 15 minutes we found the US Base and dropped off the 2 Officers. One of these indicated to us that he would keep a light on and pointed to the faint light about a mile away, which we all thought, was the control tower.

After about a further hour and a half's drive, we were no nearer finding our way back. The surface beneath began to get very rough and undulating, and it became obvious that we were lost. We therefore, very prudently as it turned out, decided that we should stop and rest until daylight.

Even though we were in the desert with daytime temperatures in the nineties, the nights were very cold. To keep warm we both wrapped ourselves around the warm engine, which in this type of vehicle was inside the driving cabin, located between the front two seats. We shivered through the next two hours until daylight enabled us to establish our location.

To our horror, we noticed that we had stopped inside one of the active minefields surrounding the airfield and of course nowhere near our intended destination.

On looking back we could see the wheel tracks we had made when entering this minefield. The engine was started, and very carefully we reversed the vehicle along the tracks we had made. At no time did we step off the vehicle.

We safely navigated our exit from this minefield, and in the early dawn light we reassessed where we were.

In the far distance we could see the very top of the Control Tower, estimated at about two or three miles away. We made a 'beeline' for this and arrived safely at the offices occupied by us below the control tower. We broke open the rations, kept there for emergency evacuation, and ate ravenously.

It was too early for the 'sumptuous' breakfasts provided by the Officers Mess Chefs, and the night's ordeal had left us very hungry.

The final episode in this saga was the abandoned take off in thick fog by a very senior army officer travelling back to the front in an RAF transport aircraft. Operational conditions were so bad that the pilot refused to take off, and was ordered to do so by this senior officer.

Flight rules state quite clearly that the pilot is always in charge, regardless of the status of the passengers. However on this occasion, the seniority of this officer, and the nature of his mission was made known to the pilot. The pilot against his better judgement, agreed to fly in the prevailing conditions. These were considerably below the safety margins for flight.

The aircraft aligned alongside the Control Tower, visibility was less than 50yards, and the aircraft duly took off. We could hear the sound of the engines as the aircraft disappeared into the fog. About 20 minutes later two bedraggled figures appeared out of the fog, which by now was less dense. The Senior Officer looked very sheepish, realising the consequences of his action.

It appears that the aircraft never left the ground. The pilot abandoned the take-off. The aircraft had come to rest beyond the runway threshold, and had been slightly damaged. Apart from the damage to the aircraft, fortunately no one suffered any injuries, although both were shaken by this experience.

Self-Catering in the Desert.

After about six months in residence at *El Adem* we were ordered to return to base. The three of us packed all our belongings, loaded sufficient fuel and food for our drive back to Alexandria and set off about mid-morning, intending to make one night stop on the way back, at either *Sollum* or *Bardia*. These were two towns on each side of the borders between Cyrenaica (modern day Libya), and Egypt.

While at *El Adem* we had learnt that we could heat up canned food by using an empty 4-gallon container of motor fuel, cut in half and filled with sand and small stones. Small holes would need to bored into the sides, below the sand level, to provide air circulation.

To this container would be added some of the motor fuel we carried. When this was lit, it would burn with an even fire. Pierced cans of food could be added to the fire. This meant that we could eat hot food on our journey back to Egypt.

We had acquired some tins of meat and vegetable hash from the US forces, and these, when heated were delicious, even when eaten straight out of the tin.

Further North African Experiences on our Return Journey

For the description, which follows, I have used the map on p351, of 'The Hinge of Fate', one of the volumes in Sir Winston Churchill's memoirs. The only maps of the area today do not show the towns through which we passed on the route from El Adem to Alexandria. If they do then their names have changed.

Many of the locations mentioned in the African saga which precedes these episodes, in particular *Takoradi,* and *El Obeid*, are also included in the intended journeys planned by Sir Winston Churchill in the Hinge of Fate. The roundabout routings were necessary at the time in order to reach Egypt in safety. These journeys took place before North Africa had been cleared of Rommel's 'Axis' forces.

I have recently re-read the 'Hinge of Fate', and reference to this has helped my memory to re-live the events described in this chapter. It is intended to help the reader to form a view of the North African scene as viewed through the eyes of someone who was out there during this period, albeit not in the front line but in a significant support capacity.

Again, the above is another digression from subsequent events, but provide further background to the environment and times in which these events took place.

The return journey took us to the east of *El Adem*, along a bumpy road, full of potholes created by the shelling which had taken place by both sides during the recent conflict. Little attempt had been made to repair these, as the battle was now so far forward that other ports and airfields were used to supply the advancing armies. These were much further west in Libya rather than Cyrenaica.

The return to Egypt started in 1943 after the month of May. By this time the final assault on the 'Axis' forces in the defence pocket around *Bizerta* in Tunisia had either been or was about to be successful, and the remaining enemy forces captured.

The route taken for our return to Egypt took us via *Sidi Rezegh* to the south east of *El Adem* to *Bardia*, a battered coastal town on the frontier between Cyrenaica and Egypt. Bardia was situated on the top of the escarpment. From there a tortuous road led down through a pass to the town of *Sollum*. Sollum was a frontier town on the Egyptian side of the border on the shores of the Mediterranean. It must have been at least 500 feet if not more below Bardia.

The road between Bardia and Sollum had been the scene of many battles during the North African campaign between 1940 and 1942. Both towns were occupied more than once by each side.

The road linking these two towns took us down a rocky incline, on a badly surfaced road again pockmarked with shell holes. The pass went by the name of *Halfayah*, but quickly became known as 'Hell Fire' pass by the allied troops who had fought to gain possession of Bardia from the 'axis' forces

We drove into Bardia, which was on the Cyrenaica side of the border from *Sidi Rezegh,* intending to settle down there for the night. Entry into Bardia was though a typical stone arch down a narrow street. On entering the main street we were met by a hail of rifle or machine gun fire.

It seems that the forces in residence had imbibed well, and were firing for the sheer fun of it. I can think of no other reason for this indiscriminate firing unless it was our unannounced and unexpected arrival. However, this seems unlikely as we did not appear to be the target, otherwise this barrage of fire would have been more effective.

We never found out the origin of these forces, but they were certainly on our side and not the remnants of any of the enemy forces. The battle had long since passed by and they would by now have been mopped up.

On the other hand they could have been a group of nomads who had wandered in to the town, after they had managed to get hold of arms and ammunition from the untended arms dumps, which abounded in that area.

This unprovoked fusillade suggested that we should beat a hasty retreat. This we did, and left Bardia by the way we had entered. This was the only road into and out of the town

We drove slowly taking the eastern fork, and after about two miles, we pulled off the road and set up camp.

As it was getting dark, we had no wish to traverse the pass in darkness. The road down through the pass to Sollum was both tortuous and dangerous. The state of the roads up to now indicated that the pass should be negotiated in daylight. There could also have been other hidden perils on that section of our journey in addition to the state of the road.

We had no maps to guide us, and even if we had these would have been out of date, because of the prevailing conditions.

When we arrived at our selected campsite, dusk was already with us, and we were unable to establish our exact surroundings, other than that we were still on the top of the escarpment and close to the cliff face. Our experience so far indicated that we should leave the road, in case some of the trigger-happy forces in Bardia should venture out on to the only road out of the town.

We unloaded our camp beds from the vehicle and set these up, as we had no desire to sleep on the ground, in case some scorpions and snakes decided to snuggle up to us under the blankets. Even snakes and insects need to keep warm somehow when the sun is below the horizon.

Serpents and other venomous insects abounded in the area, and we had no wish to have these as our companions for the night.

We lit up a fire using the method described earlier and threw three cans of food on this, suitably pierced to avoid any undue explosion. In direct heat un-punctured cans will expand and explode. This could have had serious consequences to our wellbeing.

As always when hungry, the heated food tasted delicious, as did the bottles of beer we had brought with us. After dinner we lay on our camp beds in the open air and each of us covered ourselves with three blankets. The desert nights were very cold, and we were advised to do this by those we had left behind at El Adem, most of whom were desert wise.

We slept in the open air.

The sky above was absolutely brilliant in the unpolluted night-time air. It was easier to gaze up and count the stars instead of sheep.

Sleep came very easily, even though we were unwashed and very dusty. Sand was everywhere, underfoot, in our clothing, and in our bedding.

We awoke at dawn, to discover that the two top blankets were soaking wet from the night dew. This was no doubt due to our proximity to the sea, and to the typical night-time condensation, which occurs in desert regions.

When I looked around at our surroundings, I saw one the most glorious sights it has ever been my privilege to see. The cliff face down to the bay far below, in the dawn light, was a reddish brown colour, interspersed with green foliage from the bushes growing out of the cliff face.

Far below was a bay of yellow sand leading to the rich blue Mediterranean waters. The waters running on to the sands created white and 'transparent yellow' ripples on the shore. There was a little vegetation around the sands to add colour and helped to enhance the overall view.

Part of the bay and cliffs were bathed by the early morning sunshine, while the eastern half remained a darker brown in the shade.

The sky to the east was a mixture of yellow, giving way to red and then blue. There was not a cloud in the sky, and the temperature surrounding us was pleasantly cool.

We made ourselves breakfast as before. The fuel for the fire was a mixture of sand laced with motor spirit, which we took from our fuel reserves. These reserves were stored in the 'Jerry Cans' we had brought with us, in case we could not find fuel 'en route' to complete on our journey.

We loaded up the vehicle, our faithful 'Yellow Peril',(YP), and set off down 'Hellfire Pass', until we reached *Sollum*. We did not stop there but followed the road to the east to Sidi *Barrani*.

The road itself was not close enough to the sea for us to stop and take a swim. We travelled on, still retaining the dirt and grime, accumulated over that day, and also adding to the previous unwashed period before leaving El Adem.

The road was still almost un-drivable, due to the irregular road surface. The 'YP' took all this in its stride and continued to perform well. The 'YP' had obviously been converted for desert use, and operated very reliably throughout its long journey.

Between *Sollum* and *Mersa-Matruh*, we passed a little known, and unregistered town by the name of *Buq Buq*. I am not sure whether this was between Sollum and *Sidi Barrani*, or after, but certainly before *Mersa Matruh*. No matter as this was of little consequence as we neither stopped there nor at Sollum during this part of the journey.

Our first stop after setting out that morning was at *Sidi Barrani*, a town made famous by a BBC radio show after the war.

We found that this town boasted a NAAFI store, which also provided hot meals. We halted and made up for the missing diet of the past two days by taking in a huge English breakfast with all the trimmings.

Having fuelled up both our starving vehicle, and ourselves, we set off to the east. The road surface was not any better, but at least we were driving closer to the sea, which could be seen, occasionally across the scrub-land to the north.

I later discovered that the whole area between the road and the sea was full of uncharted mines. These did not seem to trouble the local population, who by now had returned to these areas. Goats and sheep grazed peacefully over this land, together with their shepherds, who in the main were young teenagers, some no more than thirteen years old. They appeared totally unconcerned and unaware of the dangers of free movement in the mined areas. Perhaps their guardian angels watched over their 'well-being' (and their thirst).

We reached *Mersa Matruh* in the early afternoon, and drove right up to the beach. The water looked so inviting, that we stripped off completely and waded into the sea. It was full summer, and the sea was pleasantly warm. We lingered for about an hour, then dressed and restarted our journey to Alexandria.

This next part of the journey took us through *Fuka*, via *El Daba*, to *El Alamein*, and then on to *Alexandria*. The further east we drove, the more congested the road became. Nearly all of the road traffic consisted of Army supply trucks and staff cars. Very little non-military traffic could be seen.

We approached Alexandria, and after a tortuous drive through the streets of this town we arrived at a small square on the famous Alexandria esplanade. The blue Mediterranean lay to the north of this and looked really beautiful.

Alexandria, the principal holiday resort of Egypt at the time, had been relatively untouched by the war, even though the 'axis' forces had been within 70 miles, and for a short spell immediately before the Battle of El Alamein, even a little closer.

My boss, who shall be nameless, as are all the other characters in this narrative, advised us that he knew of a good hotel near the city square we had reached. I believe the name of the hotel was '*The Femina*'.

The hotel was of good quality for these times. We parked the 'YP' outside the hotel, uncorked ourselves from the vehicle and strode into the hotel lobby. Throughout the journey, the seating and driving arrangements had to be alternated, as there were only 2 seats in the front of the vehicle. The third passenger had to make do with whatever seating arrangements could be made in the back among the chattels, which we had loaded when we left *El Adem*.

We must have looked a sight with our dusty, grimy, and unshaven appearance. We hadn't shaved for over two days. Although the swim at Mersa Matruh refreshed us it only added to our dishevelled state. We did not shower with fresh water after the swim, which would be normal practice today. As a result the salt water we had gathered from the swim added to our grimy state. The salt accrued from this, integrated with the sand on our skin, and when dried became rather uncomfortable during this next part of the drive.

Even the clothes we wore, yellow desert shorts and shirt, were also in a deplorable state.

We fully expected to be ejected from the lobby, but instead we were made welcome and registered ourselves for an overnight stay before proceeding the following day to Cairo.

It was obvious that this hotel was well used to the appearance of persons appearing from the desert in such a disreputable state.

I recall the film *'Ice Cold in Alex'* and can feel for those persons in the film who arrived in Alexandria, and their first cold beer. They were in a similar state to us on their arrival.

After a good bath, a clean-up and a short walk along the promenade to stretch our legs, after the two days cramped in the vehicle, we returned to the hotel for dinner and a well-earned rest in the luxurious surroundings of our bedrooms.

The beds were so soft and comfortable after what I had been used to over the last 6 months, that there was a problem in trying to sleep. I had become unused to such comfortable surrounds: it would take time to adjust. Once again sheep had to be counted instead of stars.

The following day we took the well-used road to Cairo, a journey which took us about three uneventful, unremarkable hours . . .

Once in Cairo, we were put up by BOAC at the Heliopolis Hotel. This hotel was used to accommodate all BOAC personnel in transit, as well as the aircrew operating out of the then Cairo Airport,(at Heliopolis, on the outskirts of the City).

The airport was only a short ride by the 'Metro', which linked these two areas. This journey was far safer than a ride in a taxi between these two locations.

This is the final part of the North African saga, based on Egypt. The next part took me to the other side of Africa to Morocco. This is the subject of another part of this book. It also provides enough incidents of interest to be worth recounting.

The Sojourn in Morocco

On my return to Cairo, there was no new posting in the offing, so I was put out to grass and sent to join the BOAC complement at Heliopolis. Both BOAC and the RAF used Heliopolis airport. The days which followed passed in relative drudgery after the North African desert exploits.

Although I was still in the learning process about my job, I had not yet learned the patience of my elders and was searching for more adventure.

Around August of the year 1943, I was called back to Head Office, and advised that I was to be moved but not told where.

By this time the whole of North Africa had been recaptured, and my posting could have taken me to any RAF, or BOAC station in the Region controlled by the hierarchy in Cairo. The Cairo region ranged as far west as the Atlantic shores of Africa, encompassing Morocco, Algeria, Tunis, Libya, Cyrenaica, and to the east all the countries up to and including the present Gulf States, Iraq and Iran or Persia as it was then.

Officially I was still part of **216 Group** of the RAF, although I had relinquished this secondment after leaving El Adem.

I was told to move to the Continental Hotel in Cairo for the night, and early the next morning would be taken by bus to an unnamed airfield outside Cairo. The name given to this I discovered later to be **LG 224**. LG stands for **Landing Ground**.

LG224 was a very isolated and little known airfield in a remote part of the desert to the west of Cairo. Later I believe that a civil airport called Cairo West was developed in this area and became the main airport serving Cairo. I never found out whether LG224 and Cairo West were one and the same. At no time in 1943 could LG224 have been classified as a civil airport.

After about an hour's drive, the coach arrived at its destination, and we were led by a member of the RAF, to a waiting RAF DC3.

We boarded this aircraft and as I did so, noted that this was an operational aircraft. It was fitted with bucket seats along the length of each side of the cabin. Presumably it was fitted up for the drop of parachute troops in normal operational circumstances.

In the centre of the cabin, between the 2 rows of seats, were large crates presumably supplies bound for the same destination as us?

I still had no idea of my destination.

The aircraft took off, it was barely dawn, and all that could be seen below was desert. It was obvious that we were heading west, but that's all.

The seats were most uncomfortable. They were designed for troops with parachutes, and as we had none, the bare metal on our backsides caused me to squirm at regular intervals. There were about 8 other passengers all in RAF uniform, who were equally uncomfortable.

I rather hoped the journey would be short; otherwise it would become an endurance test. As it turned out this was not to be. The whole journey took a day and a half, during which time we halted for fuel at Tripoli in Libya.

About an hour after landing in Tripoli, we took off and headed west. At no time were we advised of our final destination. The other passengers also appeared to be unaware of their destination, or were not prepared to tell me. Perhaps the crew flying the aircraft thought we knew but never volunteered this information.

We flew for about another 3 to 4 hours. After our departure from Tripoli the sea was not visible, so it could bc assumed we were flying slightly to the south, but always in a westerly direction. We played cards, using the crates between us as a table. This significantly shortened our ordeal, as the aircraft was subjected to the normal turbulence associated with unpressurised air travel over the mixture of rocky and desert terrain below us.

Rocks and sand absorb and emit heat at different rates and as the heat rises, the mixing of these localised air masses in the lower atmosphere create this excess turbulence at these flight levels. I experienced similar conditions of turbulence when flying south to and from Malakal.

The route from Cairo to Malakal was partly over the river and partly over sandy and rocky terrain. This had the same effect as the rock and sand terrain over which we were currently flying.

Passengers travelling today have never experienced the 'joys' of flying for hours in continuous turbulence. Air turbulence these days is met for only short periods of a flight. In those early days, smooth flying conditions in Africa were the exception, and only encountered for the first hour or so after dawn or during night flights when the conditions on the ground equalised.

Night flying in Africa, apart from military operations, was unheard of at that time due to the lack of Navigation Aids. This was also due to the limited range of the aircraft. En route refuelling stops required takeoff and landing at airfields ill equipped for nighttime operations.

At the time in North Africa, secondary airfields were not equipped with runway lights, which could be switched on or off remotely by the control tower. In emergencies, it was necessary to lay down flares manually both on land or water to direct the pilots to their appointed landing zone

In BOAC this became the responsibility of the ground staff.

Just before dusk we started our descent, and after landing we disembarked for the night at a remote township in the heart of Algeria. We found out later that this was a town named *Biskra*.

Biskra is situated on the foothills of the Atlas Mountains some distance south of the town of Algiers in Algeria.

The night spent in Biskra, was just about the most uncomfortable I have ever experienced, including the Malakal and North African sagas to date.

The evening temperature was barely tolerable, in the high thirties or low forties. We were transported to a dilapidated Hotel in the centre of the town where we were to be accommodated for the night.

The bed linen in my bedroom was soiled and had also seen better days. Apart from being soiled, and dirty, these were covered in yellowish stains. Even though exhausted by the journey so far, I did not relish having to sleep on the bed provided.

My fellow passengers and I decided to explore the town, but after walking down the only main street and sweating profusely from the heat, we returned to the Hotel. Dinner was awful. The last course was cold rice pudding which no one touched.

After a very fitful sleep on top of the bed linen, I awoke and went down for breakfast, before returning to the airport to continue my journey to an unknown destination.

The breakfast consisted of the uneaten cold rice pudding from the previous night. After a couple of mouthfuls my colleagues and I abandoned this sumptuous repast, and decided to go hungry. The morning coffee was undrinkable, even though I am normally very partial to French coffee.

After take-off, it became apparent that we were bound either to the north, to the Algerian coastline, or west to the Atlantic coastline. The route to the west involved at some point, the crossing of the Atlas mountain range. My knowledge of geography indicated to me that this aircraft and the height of the mountain range were incompatible.

The DC3 was an unpressurised aircraft, and the Atlas mountain at its highest points were above the level at which unpressurised aircraft could fly safely with passengers on board.

We were not provided with oxygen for the journey, although no doubt the pilots' were, in case of emergency. I therefore, assumed that if we were to fly to the west we could only cross the Atlas Mountains in good weather, through some of the passes which were present in that range.

The aircraft climbed steadily, but as it did so, the land beneath remained close to us, so it was apparent that we were approaching the mountain range. By the position of the sun clearly we were travelling in a westerly direction. Our destination should therefore be somewhere in Morocco.

Immediately after crossing the Atlas Mountain range, we started our descent. We landed at an RAF airfield near *Fez*. This airfield went by the name of *Ras el Ma* and was equipped with only one runway.

The RAF had only recently occupied this airfield. It was needed to support the delivery from the UK of short-range aircraft needed to reinforce the Air Forces in North Africa. These were to be used for the invasion of Sicily, and Italy.

The invasion of Sicily was about to take place from Tunis and perhaps Libya. The manning of this airfield by BOAC staff also allowed a new air route to be opened by BOAC between the UK and Egypt.

Initially the movement of such military aircraft was merely a trickle, but later the numbers grew at an alarming rate. This necessitated a hurried move by the whole unit from Fez, located around the fringes of the Atlas Mountains, to a safer venue at an airfield close to the town of Rabat close to the Atlantic shoreline of Morocco.

I now found out that my role in this operation was similar to that performed at El Adem, but with the added function of returning the delivery crews back to the UK.

The aircraft transporting these pilots back to the UK would have to fly out to sea by night, to avoid the enemy aircraft which patrolled the French Atlantic coastline.

The aircraft, which were destined to return these pilots to the UK, would arrive with military supplies, also destined for the front line. These DC3 aircraft, were adapted for longer range flying, and were fitted with extra fuel tanks located at the front of the passenger cabin. Access to the flight deck was by a narrow passage no more than 2 feet wide between these tanks.

The RAF organisation at the airfield at Ras el Ma was an ADRU (Air Despatch and Reception Unit), and also a Staging Post as already described for El Adem. A Group Captain supported by many RAF officers ran the station. My brief was to report to the BOAC Manager not the RAF Commander. However, a few members of the RAF establishment were made available to us to support the loading and unloading of aircraft.

An RAF staging post provided not only an ADRU function, but also minor engineering facilities for aircraft in transit. Major maintenance and assembly functions were carried out at the maintenance unit located near the seaport of Casablanca.

Casablanca was also a major US Army and Air Force base, whose Medical facilities were used jointly by US and British forces. The base at the airport had an RAF Doctor but no hospital facilities.

Although still not in the RAF, I was accommodated in the Officer's quarters. Sleeping accommodation consisted of a series of wooden chalet type houses, each accommodating four officers. Each of the two bedrooms was shared by two of these. I shared my accommodation with an elderly gentleman, aged in his late forties or early fifties. At my age I found it difficult to distinguish with more accuracy, the ages of older people.

I shall not name names, as I subsequently was embarrassed to find out that the gentleman I shared the bedroom had homosexual tendencies: not towards me but a young sailor he had met during a visit to the town of Fez. He confessed this one evening when I noted that he was weeping in his bed, and enquired the reason for this.

It appeared that in civilian life he was a happily married family man and his action appalled him. At my age, barely 20 now, I became a father confessor to this much older man.

The walk between the sleeping accommodation and the Officers' Mess abounded with funnels driven into the ground and used as urinals by all the station personnel. This was fine as long as there were no female personnel on the base.

Later however this hygienic solution to everyday problems, had to be revised, as more and more females began to transit this station 'en route' to *Algiers* and beyond. Initially this necessitated their passage from aircraft to the transit lounge by a circuitous route, which bypassed these indelicate eyesores. Eventually these were removed and proper toilets and communal showers introduced. Living conditions became more civilised.

Fez and its Inhabitants

The city of Fez in 1943 was a beautiful Arab city, which comprised both a new and old town. The indigenous French settlers occupied the newer part. The old part of the city was very similar to any other town of Moorish origin,

The main Hotel in the town of Fez was located between the outskirts of the new town and the start of the old town. The hotel was named the 'Palais Jamais'. Presumably this was, in translation, the 'Never, Never Palace', (or even the 'Neverlands') but interpreted strictly as the 'Never Palace' by staff locally.

The Hotel was built long before the new town was developed, and was constructed to fit into the atmosphere of the locality in which it had been built.

In front of the Hotel was the city square, and market, which formed part of the old town.

From the square, the Hotel presented an imposing appearance. It comprised a long faced, two storeys high building, built in the style of a Moorish palace. The entrance to the lobby was through a central archway, also constructed in the same style.

The main structure of this hotel housed the lobby, dining and reception rooms, and a limited number of bedrooms. A walk through beyond the lobby, led to the most beautiful part of this Hotel, a terraced garden about 100 yards in depth, with a width equivalent to the entry façade. A central, partially paved and cobbled path led to the more remote parts of these grounds.

During the walk through these gardens, the rippling sounds of a stream could be heard but not seen, as the dense foliage hid this. Around the path, which led to the hotel rooms in these grounds, an occasional fountain could be seen, spraying out water and cooling the atmosphere.

The garden was well laid out with flowers of extravagant colours, mainly various shades of red and yellows. *Bougainvilleas* grew up around the chalets and trellises. Coupled with this were bushes and trees of all descriptions native to the Moroccan environment. The chalet type accommodation was partly hidden from view by the foliage from the trees, and surrounding bushes

The most wonderful scents emanated from these both at night and during the hot days, especially in the damp environment created by the running water and fountains.

Most of the hotel rooms were in this garden. Those in the main building were more opulent, but less alluring. The guests in the main would request accommodation in the garden chalets.

The accommodation in this garden was made up of half wood, half cement chalet type construction. The style of each chalet conformed to the traditional Moorish architecture. The colour of each differed, adding to the range of colours in this garden.

Each chalet would have only one bedroom with en-suite facilities, and would be totally separate from any other chalets in these grounds.

To reach the communal areas and restaurant from these chalets, guests would be required to walk through the garden. A walk through this garden in the evening would be an enchanting experience, as the paths to the main building were lit with subdued lighting emanating from the trees.

The aircrew that arrived at *Ras el Ma* to deliver their aircraft would rest overnight at the 'Palais Jamais' before returning to the UK the following day.

The aircrew ferried these aircraft from the UK to Fez, while other pilots, who were based in North Africa would take these aircraft to the front line battle zone. All this was in preparation for the landings in Sicily.

Because we had the responsibility for receiving, accommodating, and organising the return of these RAF personnel back to their UK base, we were able on occasions to sample the delights of this accommodation.

The comments made in this narrative are first hand experiences, subject to any lapses in memory, and correctly describe the facilities and beauty of this hotel as I remember this.

The contrast between the accommodation at the airport and the hotel is indescribable. I shall not attempt to make this comparison. Any reader who has read both accounts will be able to judge these differences for themselves.

Fez and Espionage?

One day during my stay at *Ras el Ma*, I and another officer were invited by a colleague to go with him to the old town to celebrate the end of the Islamic feast of Ramadan. A gentleman he had met whilst on a special assignment had given him this invitation.

On the appointed day we went to town in search of the place to which we had been invited. This journey took us through the main square in front of the 'Palais Jamais', to a narrow road to the left of the hotel, which led into the heart of the old town.

We arrived at what appeared to be a solidly built house, alongside which were some houses less solid in construction, and rather dilapidated in appearance. These were situated deep in this part of the old town. The streets very narrow with the upper floors of some these houses overhanging the street, making it seem even narrower.

The door of the house was made of wood with rather ornate carvings, and studded with metal embossing. The general external appearance belied what was inside. Apart from this house the rest of the houses in this narrow street appeared to be both ramshackle in appearance and in need of urgent repair

We knocked on the door. A liveried servant opened the door to us, and took us to meet our host.

We entered into the most beautiful courtyard, open to the sky, with a gallery on the upper floor, covering all four sides of the courtyard. The pillars supporting the upper gallery were all covered in marble both cream and pink. The walls on all sides were made up of blue and white mosaic tiles. On the side of each wall under the gallery were Moorish arches. These were also covered with the same type of tile, but with golden overtones. I recall the arches also had a hint of red. Potted plants covered in multi-coloured blooms grew up over and around the arches. The foliage from these, added extra beauty to these surrounds.

In the centre of the courtyard, was an elaborate fountain. Water was spraying out from its centre and trickled down the sides into a large marble saucer, with a further marble saucer below that.

At one side of the courtyard, under the archway, was a single low-tiered bandstand, on which three musicians, seated on a raised dais, were playing what to me sounded like Arabic music.

On one of the other sides, was a large very low table, oval in shape surrounded by a number of cushions. This was where we were to dine.

The other two sides comprised the entrance archway, and presumably the other provided the stairs by which the upper floor could be accessed. Naturally this is supposition, as we were not allowed to visit this part of the property.

The centre of the courtyard was open to the sky, and as it was night, the blackness above broken only by the myriad of stars, added to the beauty of this environment.

Our host turned out to be a well-spoken person of Moorish origin. He spoke perfect English with no trace of a foreign accent. He made us very welcome.

Whilst in conversation, among the pleasantries of the introduction he mentioned that his wife was a Mancunian by birth, but tradition demanded that we would not be meeting her.

Although present in the house, cultural circumstances dictated that she would not be joining us at dinner. At that time Islamic custom was that women of the household could not form part of any social gathering when all the guests were male.

Whether the same rule applies if some of the guests are female I cannot state.

The meal itself, all of which was exquisitely cooked consisted what must have been about fifteen courses, I never counted these exactly as after the first three courses we had already over eaten, and had to rest back on the cushions as is the custom between courses. Part of the etiquette demanded that we should belch to show our satisfaction at the repast so far.

No menu was supplied, so we were unaware of the number of additional courses yet to come. My friend indicated that it was not a good idea to refuse to partake of any course otherwise our Host would be offended. We struggled through to the end.

No cutlery was supplied at any time, and we were required to eat with one hand only, I believe this to be the left, as the other is considered to be culturally unclean in that society . . .

At the end of the meal our host produced a selection of Malt Whiskeys for our use, which as a strict Moslem he would not partake.

Our enquiry about their provenance resulted in the explanation that these were bought in from, or had been given to him in Gibraltar, during one of his frequent visits to that fortress.

We said nothing at the time, but after leaving our host to return to base, we could not readily understand how such luxuries could be in the possession our host, and how he could obtain ready access to the fortress of Gibraltar, which at this time was closed to all servicemen, unless special permission had been granted before going there.

The quality of the spirits also implied that this gentleman was not all that he appeared, and that he must have a position of great trust with the British Government.

The fact that he had a Mancunian wife, spoke perfect English and French, and could travel unfettered in the war zones, indicated that he must have connections with the covert services of both Britain and America. I have omitted so far to indicate that he was afforded the same level of freedom by the US services.

An explanation that comes readily to mind is that he had been placed in position during the fall of France, to act as a sounding board and provide information to the allies prior to the North African landings.

His location in the heart of the old town would make it difficult for him to be apprehended by either the Germans, or the Vichy French who controlled this territory before the allied landings in 1943.

My transfer to Casablanca for Treatment.

After I had been in Fez for about one month I became unwell, and the RAF doctor indicated, that I would have to go Casablanca for treatment. The only hospital in the area was a US Army Hospital, just outside Casablanca, and near to the airport serving this town.

I was not bedridden so could be flown down to the airfield just outside Casablanca in an Avro *Anson*. This aircraft was part of the Casablanca establishment for just such an eventuality.

The airport at *Casablanca* without doubt would have been the same shown in the final scene of the film 'Casablanca' which starred Ingrid Bergman, and Humphrey Bogart. In the film very little of the airport appeared as it was blanketed in fog when Ingrid Bergman departed with her film husband. Presumably the fog was used so that any airport could have been used to simulate a departure from that place.

What I remember of *Casablanca* airport at the time was the presence of power lines close to the approach to the runway. On landing these overhead power lines appeared to be dangerously close to the runway threshold. This was not apparent in the film.

The only realistic part of this film version was the *Languedoc* aircraft used for the departure. This aircraft was the main aeroplane used by Air France at the time. It would have been used by the airline to transport passengers from this airport

However again I digress.

images of Avro Anson and Languedoc

On my flight to *Casablanca*, I was seated behind the only pilot on board as he navigated the foothills of the Atlas Mountains on his descent from *Fez*, via *Meknes*, to the airport at *Casablanca* which was at sea-level. The journey was quite an experience as the pilot, as well as flying and navigating the aircraft, had to activate manually all the controls, flaps and undercarriage.

For the next three days after landing at *Casablanca*, I lost my Officer status, as the US did not recognise my uniform, and to them I became the equivalent of an enlisted man.

I was not well enough to argue the point and was taken to the US transit camp, where I had to overnight, and assigned a bed in the enlisted men's dormitory. All the beds were 'double-deckers'. Fortunately I found an unused one at the lower level. Not being very hungry I did not go to the canteen for a meal.

The following morning I was transported to the hospital with others from the transit camp. On arriving I was accepted and assigned a bed in the enlisted men's dormitory, undressed and got into bed to await my summons for treatment.

Although, my complaint was minor in nature and not life threatening, it was very painful and certainly not of a sexual nature. Apart from this nothing more is to be said.

The operation took about fifteen minutes, after which I was taken back to the ward. By the same afternoon I was well enough to take some food and attend the common room available to the enlisted men.

The conditions offered to enlisted men in the US forces, were far superior to those offered to Officers in the British armed services in Fez.

Perhaps this explains the differences in the fighting potential of both forces, as the British were perhaps hardier, and more likely to endure the hardships, which a battle environment requires.

My companions in the ward were all US personnel, and came from all parts of the US. Some were barely literate, and came from the more remote parts of the USA. This applied to the patient in the next bed to mine who hailed from Tennessee.

This man was a PFC (Private First Class) and very homesick. I was a good listener as he described in great detail the home environment he so missed.

As I was to be discharged the following day, I did not raise the issue of my officer status, neither with my companions nor the hospital staff, particularly the nurses who were all of officer status.

That evening I attended a USO concert for the troops. The main guest of this show was Al Jolson, who by then appeared to be in his late fifties. He sang all the old songs, which had made him famous. These went down well with the audience, who appeared to suffer from nostalgia about their homeland. Music is the best way to trigger memories from the past.

The songs which Al Jolson sang evoked for them memories of their homeland, and especially those parts of the USA from whence they came to fight in North Africa.

Many of them had not travelled beyond the borders of the USA before, and some not even outside their home state.

I was less affected by nostalgia, as neither the singer nor the songs evoked any such memories for me.

My return journey to *Fez* was by the same route. We landed in *Fez* in the early afternoon, after which life continued with nothing worth reporting during the rest of my stay there.

Before I leave this period of my life, it is worth noting, that with today's knowledge of the perils of tobacco, it seems that the US forces tried to kill their patients in hospital with kindness.

Each morning while patients were in the hospital, they were given not offered, a packet of two hundred *'Camel'* cigarettes. Presumably patients were required to smoke these in a day as each day another packet of '200' appeared automatically.

I shudder to think how many packets a patient would have accrued, if he had been hospitalised for 3 to 4 weeks. No wonder a black market in cigarettes flourished.

Our own cigarette rations while in the desert consisted of *'Woodbines'*, which no one outside the British forces would touch with a bargepole. I cut my smoking teeth on these while at *El Adem*. Prior to this I was a non-smoker.

Shortly after my return to *Fez*, the whole station was moved to another airfield close the Atlantic coastline of Morocco, and near to the Capital city of *Rabat*. This new airport was located about five miles outside *Rabat* at a place called *Sale*. The airport thus became known as *Rabat/Sale*.

The move from Fez to Rabat in Morocco

The journey from *Fez* to *Rabat*, was undertaken by road, and passed through *Meknes*, which was at this time one of the larger cities in Morocco, much more so than Fez.

The town of *Meknes* was situated on the lower slopes of the Atlas Mountains. It is located in the triangle formed between *Fez, Rabat and Casablanca*.

Sale was close enough to *Rabat*, and could be reached after a late night in town in about forty minutes at a brisk walk. This walk was undertaken frequently, as the last transport to base, had frequently left by the time we reached the pick-up point outside the 'commandeered' *Hotel Balima*

The *Hotel Balima*, the main Hotel in the centre of the new town of Rabat, had already replaced the *'Palais Jamais'* in Fez, as the Hotel allocated to house the transit RAF and BOAC aircrew 'overnighting' in this town.

Once we had been safely installed in this new location, BOAC was to re-link the route from the UK to Egypt and all points west and south from there.

This new air link was to be operated by a new aircraft in the BOAC fleet, the Avro York. The link initially did not include the flight from the UK but was restricted to the North African sector only with the aircraft based in Cairo. The Avro York was a derivative of the Lancaster bomber, and although this aircraft continued in service with BOAC after the war, it was not commercially viable.

The aircraft was a high winged monoplane. Passenger vision was not impaired; as all the windows were below the wings. From a passenger viewpoint it was a great aircraft to fly in, even though it was unpressurised, with a height restriction of 10000 feet with passengers on board.

The *Avro York* had an ugly shape, having a fat, almost square fuselage, linked to the wing and engine sections of the operational bomber

Unlike the US transport aircraft of the time, the DC4, which was constructed, with a tricycle undercarriage, the Avro York still had an operational tail wheel, and no nose wheel.

The tail wheel would be firmly grounded while the aircraft was stationary, and throughout the loading process. It would only lift off the ground during take-off, and then only after a suitable speed had been reached. This aircraft was easier to load, as the main body of the aircraft could be reached without special ground equipment. On the other hand the DC 4 required special ground equipment to reach the loading compartments at a height of around six feet.

Persons working in today's civil air transport scene, take for granted that suitable loading facilities are always available to make their loading task easier. They never give a thought to the cost of development and introduction of such specialised items of equipment.

As aircraft get bigger so even today's equipment may have to be redeveloped, and introduced at considerable cost to the provider of such items.

The operational restriction, which applied to the 'passenger carrying' AVRO York, made the aircraft unsuitable for a direct flight over the Atlas Mountains. The direct route from Rabat to Egypt would take the aircraft near isolated peaks in the Atlas mountain range, with heights around 9 to 10000 feet. Thus the route it had to follow was to the north of the mountains along the coastal regions of Algeria.

In bad weather and heavy cloud the peaks in the Atlas Mountains, although few in number, could have represented a danger to this operation.

Although desirable, there were no such restrictions imposed on the flight of military aircraft. Military pilots always carried oxygen for such occasions, and the altitude that could be flown was limited only by the height limitations of the aircraft.

If there had been height limitations for military aircraft, the Burma to China route would never have been operated with DC 3 supply aircraft, and the whole of the Burma campaign, could have taken a different turn.

The task of the 'ADRU' in Rabat now included the handling of civil aircraft operations as well as the main reason for its existence. This was to provide the facilities for the RAF to deliver operational aircraft to the front line, and provide ground assistance to RAF Transport aircraft. It also had the responsibility to reposition the aircrew back to their home base once they had delivered their aircraft. This operation, which started in a small way in Fez, grew considerably at Rabat.

The Arrival of BOAC Female Ground Staff

To aid in the expansion of the Civil Air operation in Rabat Cairo Headquarters in their wisdom had decided to post at Rabat three female members of the Cairo establishment. This was to support, the Station Manager, and myself in the ground handling operations.

The Cairo staff apparently did not recognise how the presence of these three individuals, would affect the performance of the RAF personnel stationed in Rabat, all of whom were exclusively male.

The RAF Officers in particular were affected, as these women shared their daytime activities in the Officers Mess, although at night they were accommodated off base in the town hotel reserved for the transit aircrew. Each evening they had to be returned to town by one of us acting as 'chauffeur'.

The presence of these women created unnecessary friction among the station personnel, necessitating, in one case the transfer of one of the officers, because of his involvement with one of them. These women frequently changed the direction of their affection, with various members of the station establishment. In some cases this attention was even directed at some of the BOAC pilots when they 'overnighted' in the same hotel.

It is not necessary to elaborate more on this situation, other than to state that at no time was I involved in any of these wrangles. This would have been difficult as all the male members of the BOAC staff were located in the male only quarters at the airfield.

In any case in the eyes of these ladies, we were not of true officer status as they carried the same badges of rank as ourselves. We were therefore small fry and unimportant in their long-term strategy in searching for permanent post war relationships.

The above may appear to be a cynical view of the situation, but that is the way I saw it.

This attitude did not detract from the fact that I was friendly with all three, since it was not only necessary to do so in order to carry out our joint responsibilities on the station, but also because as individuals they were very pleasant purely on a platonic basis.

My Association with the US 'CIC Corps'.

In two of the rooms in my accommodation block, were two American gentlemen with whom I had become friendly. They identified themselves as US CIC agents, and would frequently be missing for days at a time, for what purpose I never discovered, nor would they divulge.

CIC stands for Counter Intelligence Corps, and the reason why these gentlemen should have been on an RAF station rather than the US Naval establishment nearby at *Port Lyautey* was never revealed.

Were we under suspicion? Was their function so secret that not even US forces were to be made aware of their presence in Morocco? They never wore uniform, and both were very well read and literate. Far more so than those members of the US forces I had come across so far, both in Cyrenaica and Morocco. I placed their level of intelligence on a par with senior members of any University Faculty.

To one of these we introduced the game of Rugby Union(RU) football, and he took to this with great gusto, as he likened the rules to the football played in the US, even though in the US game, the ball can be thrown forward which is 'taboo' in the RU rules.

Another member of the station establishment was *Michael Aldridge*, a Flight Lieutenant, who later became famous on television. My own post war memory of him was watching him on the BBC Sunday evening comedy programme, 'Last of the Summer Wine' where he played a 'dotty' professor. Sadly Mike Aldridge is now dead.

I also became very friendly with the young French Liaison Officer who lived on the base. Through his connections in Rabat, he introduced me to the French Society families in town. The great majority of these were from the ranks of the French armed services, and comprised in the main of Generals and other high ranking Officers and their wives and daughters. I was able to converse haltingly in French, and it was easy to be accepted by them.

The mothers of the younger elements of this society watched over their daughters with great assiduity, to ensure that none strayed from the family hearth. Therefore all friendships were of a strictly platonic nature unless one intended to become seriously involved. In such cases this had to be made known in advance through their parents.

Throughout my stay in Rabat, my relationship with these remained purely platonic. I was not in a position to commit myself in the ongoing circumstances. Some of the fathers were pushy in this respect, and tried to get me to commit myself.

Any serious long-term relationships would be destined to fail, as it could not be guaranteed to continue after a posting away from Rabat. Inter station holiday travel in BOAC during the war years was not possible, and frowned upon by the powers that be in Cairo.

For nine of the 15 months I was in Rabat, life was very pleasant and civilised. One could almost forget that there was an ongoing war, far to the north east of Rabat. However each duty day brought this home to me.

Rabat and the RAF Football Team

The RAF station establishment consisted of around five hundred to six hundred service personnel. Among these were a number of men who in peacetime had been professional footballers, some played for UK 'First' and 'Second' Division sides with others in the 'Scottish League'.

Playing together on a daily basis made this a formidable team, who throughout my stay in Rabat never lost a game. Apart from the inter service games, they were frequently challenged by teams from outside the British forces. On two occasions challenges came from the combined services of the French Armed forces.

The forces, which threw down this challenge were drawn from all three of the French armed services representing the whole of North Africa, They came from Morocco, Algeria, and Tunis. In both home and away matches the team from the RAF Staging post in Rabat beat them handsomely.

At the time the French team representing Rabat were languishing at the foot of their league, and the population of Rabat adopted the RAF team to their hearts. They arranged matches with all the other senior teams in both Morocco, and Algiers, none of which were able to beat this array of part time footballers from our base.

After the defeat of the Combined Services team, the Football authority in Rabat allowed this team to play all its home games at the Rabat stadium. Each home game attracted a capacity crowd. All the personnel on the base were allowed free access to these games.

Eventually three members of this team were asked to play for the local Rabat side. As soon as they did so, the performance of the local team improved dramatically, and they began to win their matches. Eventually that season the team won the championship of Morocco, beating the professional teams from Casablanca, Agadir, Marrakech, and Meknes on their way to the title.

Due to the fact that the RAF team members were serving personnel, these players could not be paid as professionals. Arrangements were made so that instead of payment, part of the gate receipts, were to be given towards the formation of a Malcolm Club in town.

Malcolm clubs had sprung up at many overseas locations in North Africa and the Middle East, no doubt sponsored by some benefactor unknown to the writer but clearly known to many as 'Malcolm'. These were places situated in the centre of towns at which off duty servicemen could relax.

Apart from locally produced entertainment in the form of dances, these locations would also be the venue for entertainment provided by visiting ENSA parties and local theatre and music groups.

This particular Malcolm Club in Rabat was successful and financially secure from the revenues earned by the football team, and especially these three 'quasi' professionals. It was therefore, no surprise to me that the team remained intact, and were never subjected to the threat of a transfer. No doubt the local Station Commander and his administration sergeants saw to this.

As the months advanced, and the operational commitments reduced, so many of the RAF personnel were transferred away. When the establishment had been reduced from around five hundred to just one hundred, these elite footballers remained even though in some cases, this meant moving them to other duties.

The Operation at Rabat

DC3 aircraft in civilian livery carried out the main operation of returning the delivery aircrew. The pilots also wore the BOAC uniform. This allowed the aircraft on the way out to Rabat from the UK, to land in Lisbon ostensibly as civilian aircraft, although the load carried out from the UK consisted of cargo destined for the war zone, which by now was the threatened invasion of Sicily, and southern Italy.

Eventually converted Liberators, which could carry around thirty six passengers plus aircrew at a time, replaced the DC3 operation to and from the UK. The non-seating layout of these aircraft required 16 of these passengers to be seated on the mail sacks stacked over the bomb bay. The other 20 would spread out on 'biscuits' in the rear part of the fuselage. A 'biscuit' is a square straw filled mattress.

The choice locations for the returning aircrew would be the 20 positions at the rear. As soon as any of the aircraft was positioned for loading, there would be a rush for this prime site regardless of the consequences of this movement. The unauthorised embarkation of these persons would cause the aircraft to sit on its tail wheel, even though this aircraft had a tricycle undercarriage!

The RAF personnel of non-officer status did not resist this unauthorised embarkation by the pilots, who were mostly of officer status. This action would cause the nose to swing up and the whole aircraft 'to sit up and rest on its tail'.

The position of the aircraft after this made the loading of the hold in the nose-loading bay very difficult. It would now be about fifteen feet off the ground and unreachable by any loading device available on the station.

Even when this forward compartment was finally loaded, the presence of these bodies at the rear would continue to exert sufficient downward force to leave the safety tail wheel, still in touch with the ground. To place the aircraft in its static loading position, the engines would have to be started, and revved up with full braking, with chocks in place. Only then would the aircraft right itself

Before the Liberators took over the Rabat to UK route, there would be occasions when at least 15 DC3 aircraft would be waiting to undertake the journey back to the UK. Each of these would be fully loaded for their return journey with returning crewmembers, and forces mail.

The range of the DC3 was so marginal for this operation, that the weather conditions over the Atlantic, and the landing conditions in the south west UK had to be exactly right, for the operation to be undertaken. Awaiting these conditions would cause this backlog of departures to build up.

Any departure 'window' would be very small, no more than 1 hour. After this departures would have to be delayed a further day.

When the conditions were right, and all 15 pilots of the DC3s, (not those on board as passengers) agreed, the departures would start. The whole operation had to be completed in about 30minutes, to allow the same weather conditions to be met by all these aircraft. There would be many false alarms before the right conditions prevailed.

If one pilot out of those waiting to go was not happy the whole operation for that night would be aborted. 'All for one, and one for all', was the philosophy employed.

On a busy night these transport aircraft would take off at two minute intervals.

Forced Landing on the shores of Portugal.

On one of these nights, one of the aircraft, due to engine trouble was forced to land on one of the beaches in Portugal. At the time Portugal was a benevolent neutral, as distinct from Spain, which was a belligerent neutral.

The aircraft landed safely, and no one was hurt. However, in order to maintain their neutrality, the local Portuguese inhabitants were quick to realise that all the passengers were in RAF uniform so they approached the aircraft with civil clothing. This allowed the passengers to change into these before deplaning, without prejudicing the neutrality of Portugal.

The passengers were dispersed back to the UK by other means, and eventually the aircraft was also flown out and returned to service. I believe the pilot, who was involved in this incident, was transferred to the 'Ball Bearing' run, carried out by Mosquito aircraft to and from Sweden. On one of these 'ball bearing runs', enemy aircraft eventually shot down his aircraft and he was killed in action.

The flight to Sweden had to be made during the night hours, as the route took the aircraft very close if not actually over enemy territory.

The Transit through Rabat of King George VI.

I am aware that one should not write about the movements of Royalty, I believe this story will cause no offence to anyone reading this.

When civil aircraft started operations through Rabat from the UK, word came to the BOAC Catering establishment that a special VIP was expected and that this person had requested a chicken meal for the onward journey to Cairo.

The request caused a great deal of confusion, as the Airline Catering resources were not up to providing this sort of catering on the York aircraft.

After a great deal of 'to and fro' activity, everything was ready for this aircraft. It transpired that the VIP on board was King George VI who was visiting the troops further east in North Africa.

When the aircraft arrived a request came from the aircraft to ask if Sir Hugh Stonehewer-Bird was present, and if so could he please board the aircraft to talk to His Majesty. The King did not disembark.

Sir Hugh Stonehewer-Bird was in North Africa, as part of the non-military establishment in Algiers, but was not in Rabat to greet the King.

Apparently after the departure of the aircraft the truth transpired, both the Royal entourage and the station personnel had misinterpreted the request for 'Chicken'.

His Majesty was apparently referring to Sir Hugh Stonehewer-Bird when he requested 'Chicken.' It seems that when both were young they knew each other well, and that 'Chicken' was the nickname used by His Majesty to refer to this gentleman.

photo of Pilot Officer 71919–Don Hill

Return to Cairo and Reposting to Sicily.

The next part of this saga took me back to Cairo, as I was to be reposted back to the war zone, this time in southern Europe.

My return to Cairo was in the *Avro York*, seated in the tail of this aircraft. The rearmost cabin, was fitted out as a Galley, and had one seat. Because cabin crew were required to be active for the journey, the seat had been designed to be used only for landing and takeoff. It was certainly not the most comfortable. This particular flight carried no cabin crew thus this compartment was available for my sole use.

The flight from *Rabat* to *Tripoli,* skirting the Atlas Mountains, was very turbulent, and the rear part of this aircraft apart from the up and down movement, also swayed from side to side. The feelings felt were similar to those experienced by 'bad' sailors traversing the Bay of Biscay by sea in rough weather.

I was not the best of travellers at the time and not very comfortable. In later years with much more air travel under my belt, and the advent of pressurised aircraft, I became a seasoned traveller and actually came to enjoy my air journeys.

We landed in Tripoli, and remained on the ground for about thirty minutes. The state of the airport building, at what was still called *'Castel Benito'* named after the infamous *Benito* of recent Italian history, was a disgrace.

Despite the potential turbulence to be experienced on the next part of the journey, I could not wait for the aircraft to be ready to depart. The state of the toilets in the terminal building rendered these unusable by any normal civilised person.

We took off as predicted. The remainder of the journey apart from the turbulence was uneventful. We landed in Cairo just before dark.

The next day I reported back to Head Office, and told that I was to proceed to Augusta in Sicily. This was a return to flying boat operations. This pleased me greatly; I still had no great love for the landplane operations.

Before I was to proceed to Augusta,(a harbour on the East coast of Sicily), I was to become an RAF officer, as civilian personnel were still not allowed into this part of the war zone.

I reported as requested to RAF Headquarters in Cairo, and was granted a Civil Commission as a Pilot Officer, (Number 71919); given £45 Egyptian pounds and sent to *'Gieves',* the serviceman's tailor in Cairo to be fitted out. A letter of authority with full rank details, was provided for *'Gieves',* with the authority to tailor for my outfit, and including any discount due for its provision. The RAF stores to which I was directed issued the remainder of my kit, which was the battle dress, and RAF Officers' hat and badge and forage cap, worn by all at that time.

About 4 days later, it was necessary to prepare for my departure to Augusta. This journey required me to fly from *Rod el Farag* to *Augusta* in a Catalina flying boat.

Augusta is situated on the east coast of Sicily, midway between Catania and Syracuse It had been an Italian Naval and Airship base both before and during hostilities; the bay was a large natural harbour more than adequate for flying boat operations.

The distance between Cairo and Augusta was around 1200 miles, but the journey took forever, as the cruising speed of the Catalina, seemed to be about 100 miles an hour. It has been known for the Catalina to make no forward progress when the head winds were greater than the maximum forward speed.

I boarded the flying boat, through the side bubble which was opened from the inside, and was shown my seat which was in the mid-section of the aircraft.

The Catalina was an RAF aircraft, with the appropriate roundels and camouflage colour. It was not fitted out for passenger travel. Seating arrangements were the same as that provided for my journey on the DC3 from Cairo to Fez.

At the rear of the passenger cabin, in the raised section of the tail, was the throne, open to view for all to observe. No privacy was offered.

We left the Nile at Cairo by early dawn, and arrived at Augusta some 9 to 10 hours later.

My stay in Sicily, my marriage there and our return to the UK, and eventual de-mobilisation constitutes the next chapter of this story.

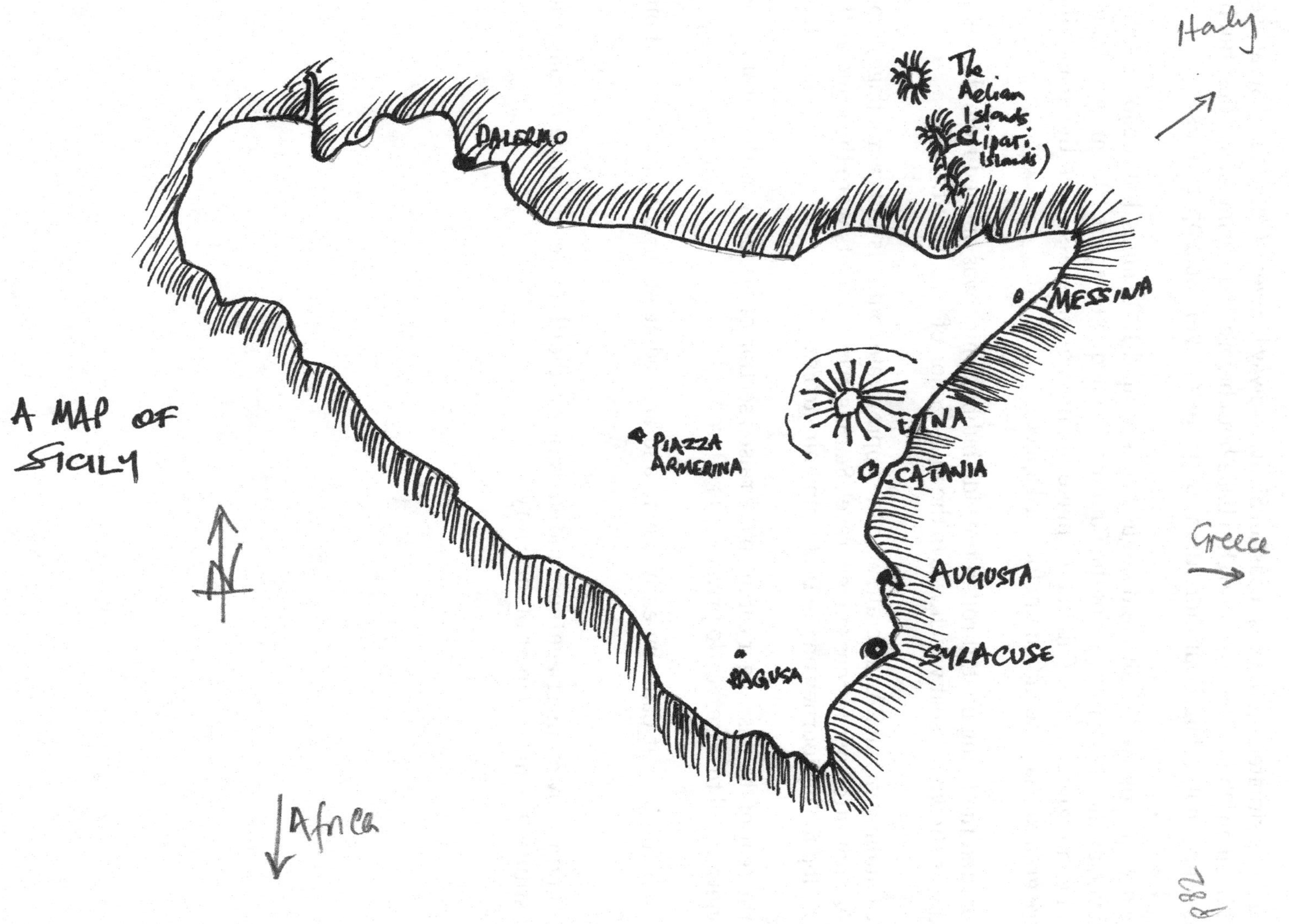
Italy
The Aelian Islands (Lipari Islands)
PALERMO
MESSINA
ETNA
CATANIA
PIAZZA ARMERINA
AUGUSTA
SYRACUSE
RAGUSA
Greece
A MAP OF SICILY
N
Africa

Chapter 3 Sicily and beyond

(...to Rome, via Dakar in the Senegal)

This part of the book starts when I arrived in Sicily for the first time. If my memory serves me right this period was shortly after Naples in the south of Italy was in Allied hands, but the battle to the north for Rome, had been halted by the failure to capture the Benedictine Monastery at Monte Cassino. The landings at Anzio had not yet taken place, but those at Salerno had.

By the time I left Sicily for the first time in October 1946, the war in Italy and the rest of Europe had been over for about a year. The Far East conflict had finished in August of 1945. RAF operations in Sicily were almost negligible, and the main emphasis of the Sicily base was converting to Civil Air operations. The Italian Air Force had taken over all weather forecasting, after a period of tandem operation with the RAF.

This sets the overall scenario after my spell in North Africa and Morocco.

The Environment

On landing at Augusta in Sicily, the Catalina flying boat in which I had travelled to my new posting taxied to the mooring buoy located near the *Capitaneria*, (the Harbour Master's domain?) in the harbour.

The harbour at Augusta was a large natural inlet on the East Coast of Sicily, between Catania to the north, and Syracuse to the south. Before the invasion it was an Italian Naval base and harboured many warships of the Italian Navy.

In later years after this story ends, the US Mediterranean fleet used Augusta to harbour some of their ships, additional to those berthed at Naples. Naples is still the current headquarters of the US Navy in the Mediterranean.

The harbour at Augusta in 1944 was unsuitable for merchant ships, as it had no loading and unloading facilities. Today the harbour has a large oil refinery on its western shore, refining the oil obtained from Libya. Presumably the port facilities have been adapted to load and unload tankers plying between these two countries.

When I arrived in Augusta, the Royal Navy had practically abandoned the base; a small detachment of the Senior Service remained, under the control of two Naval Officers, one a Lieutenant Commander, and the other a Naval Lieutenant who was almost the spitting image of Bruce Forsyth, complete with jutting chin.

During the occupation by the Royal Navy all the buildings constructed on the base to house the Italian Navy, had been renamed after famous Royal Navy,(RN) admirals of the past. Among these were Nelson, Collingwood, Rodney, Frobisher and Drake. There were others but their names escape me.

The Collingwood building was the largest of these and housed the RAF NCOs and other ranks. It also provided full catering facilities for those persons housed in this complex.

The other buildings housed the RAF officers, the administrative offices, and the Officers' Mess. The two Naval Officers were accommodated in the Officers' quarters until their departure.

The *Capitaneria* was the administrative centre. It was situated on the north side of the bay, as were all the other naval buildings on the base, and was open to the harbour with a landing jetty close by.

The BOAC staff occupied offices on the ground floor of the Harbour Master's building. The rest of these premises were given over to the RAF contingent. This also included the Naval detachment already installed in that building.

More about the Environment and Location

The town of Augusta, and the ex-naval base, was on the northern side of the harbour. To the south across the harbour was the road to Syracuse. Syracuse itself could not be seen from Augusta or anywhere else in the harbour area, although as the crow flies the entry to the town is no more than 5 to 6 miles away. However, for the journey by road it was a good 30 minutes' drive.

The town of Syracuse had its own separate harbour immediately to the south of the bay of Augusta. The harbour there was barely usable at the time, as it had suffered badly from the recent invasion. Small vessels still plied to and from Malta.

Many of the buildings, which were now occupied by us in the naval base, had also suffered considerably and were pockmarked by small arms fire, and from the bombardment by the allied navies and air forces, prior to and during the invasion of this island. No attempt had been made to repair this damage during the period that these were occupied by us.

At the furthest inland end of the harbour was a large airship hangar which was now disused. It provided an excellent landmark for those aircraft, which would land here. The hangar was sufficiently high to allow an airship to be accommodated within, and must have been the equivalent of at least a 10 storeys building.

A small breakwater was present. This protected access to the harbour from the open sea, thus making the inland water relatively smooth for the flying boat operations. This breakwater was located on the northern shore, and was only accessible from the naval base.

On the north side of the bay was the town of Augusta, a smallish town of around ten thousand inhabitants. It comprised one main street, which led to the Naval base and in which the RAF was located. There were two other streets, which ran parallel to the main street. Access to the naval base was through a manned security gate, leading from the main thoroughfare.

On Sunday afternoons and evenings, this main street would be filled with strolling couples. They walked both on the pavements and on the road making it impassable to vehicles. It seems that this is a normal custom in small towns both in Sicily and Southern Italy. This habit presumably was developed to allow young men and women to parade under the watchful eyes of their parents, with a view to meeting up with a person of the opposite sex. Everyone wore their Sunday best, just like the Easter Parades on 5th Avenue in New York during the 20s and 30s.

When I got to know Catania better, I noted that this practice but on a smaller scale was also the norm there as well. Catania is the largest town on the east coast of Sicily, and lay to the north of Augusta.

In the puritanical environment of the southern Latin nations, the Sunday parades were a must, otherwise a whole generations of spinsters and bachelors would have evolved.

At the opposite end of the town was an old castle, which we were reliably informed was used by Mussolini to house political prisoners. It not only had a forbidding appearance, being of medieval origin but access to it was not easy either.

The railway station was at the opposite end of the town from the base. There were no through trains from Augusta. All trains stopped and had to backtrack to the main line from Catania to Syracuse. The location was sufficiently far from the base that road transport was needed to get to there.

Any journey by rail from the railway station would pass by a series of salt producing paddy fields. The salt fields were visible, immediately after leaving the station on the single-track railway from Augusta. These saltpans were located between the track and the open sea.

All the salt pans were just below sea level allowing water to be introduced directly from the 'unpolluted' sea, and not from the water in the harbour.

Once covered with water, the access to these saltpans was shut to allow the seawater to evaporate. The salt deposits which remained were scraped up into salt mounds, and bagged for subsequent export to the remainder of the country, under the watchful eyes of the equivalent to our excise customs officers.

In Italy these are the '*Guardia di Finanze*', (Financial Police).

Salt is indeed big business.

Even to this day in Italy, salt and tobacco can only be purchased in government-controlled shops. All such shops can only be set up with government approval and must be licensed. Salt from these saltpans had to be sold direct to the government. No private deals were allowed. This is not to state however that the MAFIA had no say in this, as this was a monopoly to be exploited.

From the security gate looking towards the base, were a number of buildings, the largest of which accommodated the air force personnel. This was located near a small inlet from the main harbour.

Immediately beyond the gates and to the right, were a number of ground floor only buildings, (not Bungalows) which housed mainly the security staff that controlled access to and from the base. At some point during my return posting, my family and I were accommodated temporarily in one of these.

My return posting was after the war, and is the subject for a later episode in this book.

Further down this road leading from the gates to the *Capitaneria*, were four superior two storey buildings assigned as Officers' quarters. These were on the left hand side of the road. On the other side from these buildings was the Officers mess, entrance to which led to a private garden and a small pier at the water's edge. Launch mooring facilities were available on this pier.

Near to the officers mess was a tennis enclave, with only one hard court.

The garden itself was typically Mediterranean in style. It was constructed on a slope down to the water's edge. To reach the water's edge there were a series of flat stone steps. On each side of the path were flowers and bushes, which in the summer created a heady scented atmosphere. A few garden seats were present in the garden where one could sit and take in the beauty of the garden. Trees placed strategically around the garden provided the necessary protection from heat of a summer's day in Sicily.

The air force unit, and some BOAC staff, who were already present when I arrived, had moved from the island of *Djerba* off the North African coast of Libya. All the boats and material present at that base had been moved lock, stock and barrel to *Augusta.*

My immediate boss was a BOAC gentleman who had been given the rank of Squadron Leader. We both occupied the same office in the *Capitaneria*.

In our office was an inbuilt wall safe, to which the two of us had keys. This will become significant later in this narrative.

The Pay Run

The shortage of officers on the base made it necessary for the station commander to appoint all of them to specific duties, additional to those for which they had been assigned.

My arrival coincided with my appointment as Motor Transport Officer, Deputy Adjutant, and occasional Duty Officer. This was additional to my duties as Air Transport Officer.

I was ill-prepared for these extra responsibilities, not having been trained in the workings of the ways of the services, and especially those of an adjutant, one of whose duties was to hand out summary justice to those RAF personnel who had trespassed against the law.

The collection of money to pay both the military personnel and those employed locally, was a task to be performed in turn by the officers. This entailed a journey to Catania once a month, to collect the money from the Bank of Sicily, the only functional bank available in Catania at the time.

The currency in use at this time was the allied currency used in place of the 'Lira' throughout the occupied part of Italy. The local population had little love for this currency, but even less for the 'Lira', which by this time had become seriously devalued. When offered the allied currency they had to accept it, which they did with bad grace.

Pay was issued in 'Lire' (plural), as the Bank of Sicily in Catania continued to deal in this currency despite the presence of this alternative Allied currency.

The drive to Catania, would take about one hour, but when the Station Commander made the journey, he would be upset if it took more than forty minutes. He must have been a racing driver among his hobbies in civilian life. There will be more about him later.

The drive itself would take us past the railway station, down a dusty road, to the junction of the main road from Catania to Syracuse. After about 10 minutes on this road, past a small village named Villa Smundo, the road would wind up and down some fairly tortuous bends linking Catania with Syracuse, passing on the way the smallish towns of Lentini, and Carlentini, the plains of Lentini, past some walled off orange and lemon groves, to a tree lined avenue which led to the entrance to Catania from the south.

Today the Airport for Catania is located at Fontana Rosa on the Lentini plains, but in those days, it was occupied by the RAF and not called Fontana Rosa.

On the journey back from Catania, with money on board, we were advised never to stop even though we were frequently confronted by groups of armed civilians. We would accelerate through such unauthorised checkpoints. On one occasion, on return to base we discovered bullet holes at the rear of the vehicle, although we heard nothing at the time.

On the pay runs, two armed service personnel would act as guards throughout the trip.

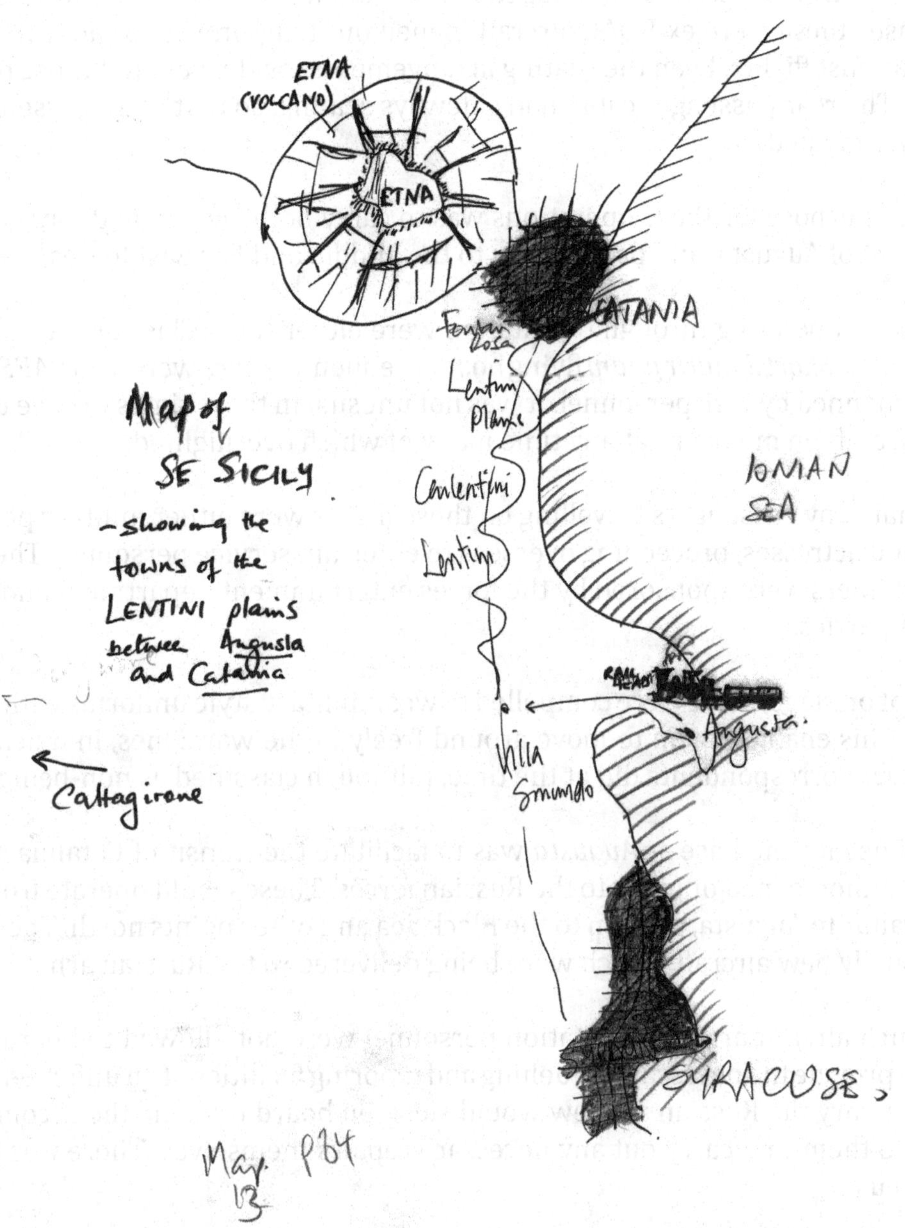

map of SE SICILY showing intervening towns Lentini

Flight operations via Augusta

Only crews in RAF uniform were allowed to operate into Augusta. The great majority of these were BOAC pilots, but some were serving RAF officers and would wear the badges of rank they had while in the RAF. The others, like myself, were granted civil commissions for the duration.

The aircraft would also be camouflaged in RAF colours complete with RAF roundels. In some cases these were ex BOAC aircraft loaned out temporarily to the RAF for the UK to the Far East flights. Even the seating arrangements inside were not those of a civilian aircraft. The rear passenger cabin had sideways seating, so that extra passengers could be accommodated.

The main purpose for these operations was to carry both civilian and forces mail to all points east of Augusta, and particularly to the Middle and Far East forces.

The aircraft operating through this station were either the C Class or the later version known as the *Short Sandringham* flying boats. Frequently, there were also *RAF Sunderland* aircraft manned by RAF personnel. It was not unusual in these times to have up to six or seven aircraft on moorings at any time many of which overnighted.

In the main any passengers travelling on these flights were either military personnel or actors and actresses, proceeding overseas to entertain service personnel. These groups of entertainers were sponsored by the forces entertainment department and identified as ENSA parties.

When not on stage, these were compelled to wear military style uniforms with no badges of rank. This enabled them to move around freely in the war zones, in much the same way as war correspondents did at the time, (although classified as non-belligerents.)

Another use for the base at *Augusta* was to facilitate the transit of Catalina flying boat aircraft, either loaned or given to the Russian forces. These would operate from the USA via Gibraltar to Augusta, then on to the Black Sea and other points north. The *'Catalinas'* were usually new aircraft, which were being delivered to the Russian armed services.

When such aircraft arrived, all station personnel were not allowed to board, but were asked to provide the necessary refuelling and mooring facilities. If an unforced night stop was necessary the Russian aircrew would sleep on board refusing the accommodation offered to them, and carry out any necessary repairs themselves. There was little trust between us.

Later we established that this lack of trust was not due to animosity on their part, but the considerable number of luxury items purchased by the crew in the USA. These were very precious to them and were being taken back to Russia, either for their personal use, or on orders from the higher authorities in Russia.

In early 1944, the south of France was still occupied and thus not available to allow the aircraft operating into Augusta to over fly. The aircraft routing from the UK was via Gibraltar, to Augusta, then on to Cairo and points east.

Following the invasion and reoccupation of Southern France by the US forces, flights from Augusta to the UK could now be routed through the Toulouse gap landing at *Biscarosse,* a lake close to Bordeaux and the Atlantic Ocean, in an area south of the Cognac region better known by the brandy of the same name.

The Weathermen at Augusta.

The station of Augusta possessed a major Meteorological Office manned by RAF personnel. This office provided both the RAF and BOAC,(and as well the Russian flights),with their weather forecasts. It was manned twenty four hours a day, seven days a week.

The weather forecasts and maps produced by this office provided data for all military and civil aircraft operating in the central and southern Mediterranean.

Many of the officers, mainly Flight Lieutenants and Squadron Leaders became household names, as BBC weather forecasters in post war Britain. Most of these were Welsh by birth and carried the name Davies.

If anyone wishes to examine the BBC archives for the weather forecasters in the immediate post war years, it will be found that the name Davies appears more than once.

These officers made good bridge companions, and we would frequently play with them this game in the officer's mess.

When weather conditions were marginal, the bridge sessions would continue all day. 'QGO' messages would be sent out to all stations notifying them that the station was closed to all operations. On some days the 'QGO' message may have been used a little recklessly. **Q** codes were three letter codes of specific **Q**uestions with specific answer codes for airport visibility, landing access and local high altitude ground obstacles etc.

'QGO' in the RAF terminology indicated to all other stations, that *Augusta* could not accept flights due to inclement weather conditions. QGO would declare the landing area to be below the permissible landing criteria, based on cloud and visibility limits.

These shortened codes to describe various weather situations in the RAF, were all used before long range Radio Telephony became the norm. Station to station communication was carried out in Morse code and it was for this reason that so many Radio Officers were used both in the RAF and BOAC, during this period. Subsequently after the war, ICAO took up this three letter Q code worldwide for communications when approaching an airport for landing permission.

Once the new technologies became available, radio officers became redundant and these techniques unnecessary. Pilots were able to communicate directly with ground stations using High and Medium frequency voice communication.

The Robbery

My first major incident experienced at Augusta occurred shortly after my arrival.

At this time BOAC employed a young gentleman as an office clerk. His first name was '*Lino*'. I forget his second name.

On a particularly hot day we were sweltering in the non-air-conditioned office, when this gentleman suggested that if the window security railings were removed the windows could be fully opened. We could therefore benefit from the cool breeze coming from the harbour. After a short discussion, my manager agreed to this proposal.

Strangely enough after a couple of hours, two men arrived and duly removed the iron bars from the two windows, facing the open harbour.

The next day one of the Met Officers and myself were going to a Rest Hotel, high up on the eastern slopes of Mount Etna at an altitude over 5000 feet, for two days' rest.

In pre-war days this hotel had been a luxury resort for winter skiers, and was constructed along the Swiss Chalet concept. All windows had an inner and outer casement, each opened independently. Double-glazing was unheard of in those days.

The Allied forces had commandeered this hotel as an R and R (Rest and Recreation) centre, for all ranks. A two days' rest session at this hotel provided a welcome relief from the oppressive heat of Catania and Augusta during the summer months. In summer the daytime temperatures could be well over 40 degrees, whenever the wind blew in from the Sahara desert. In Egypt this desert wind is named a *Khamseen* (15 day wind). In Sicily it is known as the *Scirocco*. Elsewhere, near Marseille, it is the *Mistral.*

I left the office late on the previous evening, having ensured that the safe was securely locked. I did not have any need to open the safe during this period, locked the outer door to the office and returned to my room on the base.

After dinner in the mess, and having arranged for the early transport to the station, bade my colleague goodnight, and returned to my room for a late bath, and sleep.

At 6.30a.m. the next morning, I took my overnight bag to the waiting vehicle, and departed for the station to take the early train to Catania.

On arrival at Catania about an hour later, we took a '*Carozza*' (a horse drawn carriage), to the 'R and R', (Rest and Recreation) centre in the town.

The transport to the hotel on Mt Etna would not leave until late morning. We sat around the centre talking to those running the establishment.

About an hour after we had arrived at the centre, there was an urgent telephone call for me to return immediately to Augusta. I was also advised, without fail to remain with my colleague until the Military Police would arrive to take me back to Augusta for interview.

When the police arrived, I was notified for the first time, that the safe in our office had been broken into (not forced), and all its contents had disappeared.

I was taken back to Augusta together with my colleague, for interrogation since I was the last person to leave the office the previous evening. Although I had not opened the safe, I had checked that it was locked.

I was advised later, that the break-in was through the window, whose bars had been removed the afternoon previous to the robbery, and that the thieves had approached the building at night by boat from the harbour.

Whether the boat had come from the town of *Augusta*, or from further afield was never established, but it was obvious that the robbery had been well planned in advance. Whether it was MAFIA inspired or carried out by local miscreants was never revealed.

My colleague confirmed that at no time until picked up had I been alone, and that my overnight bag had been in sight at all times to the both of us. After a search of my room, including the lifting of the odd floor tile, I was allowed to return to the officers' mess for a meal.

Fortunately I was able to prove my innocence in this affair. I did have a cast iron alibi, as my colleague who was a senior member of the RAF staff at Augusta vouched for me. He confirmed that at no time was I or my bag out of his sight during my absence from base.

Any absence from my colleague throughout the eight hours, could have implicated me or at the very least allowed suspicion to remain.

The money and contents of the safe were never found, but shortly after, the office clerk '*Lino*' failed to turn up for work, and all trace of his whereabouts were lost.

The amount of missing money was not large, and was no great loss to the station's finances. I cannot imagine that anyone who had taken the money could have lived the rest of his life on the proceeds.

Needless to state, the rest period planned by us at the hotel on Mount Etna never materialised. This was to occur much later during my stay in Augusta.

The American Deal

After I had been in Augusta about six months, I was appointed Mess Secretary. This task required me to control the stock and expenditure incurred by the Officers' Mess for drinks supplied to the bar. Receipts from bar sales had also to be accounted for. The rule was that the profit margins had to be a maximum of 10% of turn over. The cost of drinks had to be 10% or less than the cost of the supply.

Special ledgers were provided to record daily consumption, revenue, and stock levels. These ledgers were inspected on a regular basis by the RAF Audit section. A stock check was included as part of the inspection.

When the Navy left, the station inherited a large supply of Plymouth Gin and Scotch whisky. This became a part of our bar stock and sold at the bar. The Navy had abandoned these supplies when they left. They did however take away all the stocks of Rum.

The supplies were discovered in the cellar, and quickly became absorbed into the bar stocks of the Officers' Mess. No supporting paperwork existed so these could not be absorbed officially through the books.

The supplies left were far in excess of that which could be used by the members of the mess. As Mess secretary, I had to find a way to maximise our return on these surplus stocks. The members of the Officers' mess were in the main beer drinkers. The origin of such beer did not matter as long as it tasted of beer.

The US forces were at the time located in Palermo on the other side of Sicily. I contacted my equivalent in Palermo, as a result of which, a barter agreement was reached by which they offered to exchange, twelve cases of Rheingold American beer (forty-eight cans per case) for each case of whiskey, which we could supply them. They also agreed to pick up these supplies and bring us the beer. This exchange involved one Case (twelve bottles) of whiskey for approximately five hundred and seventy cans of beer. About half a dozen cases of whiskey was part of this exchange. The amount of beer delivered was enough to last the mess until our departure from the island,(just under three thousand five hundred cans of beer were delivered, swapped for the whisky that nobody English chose to drink).

As Mess Secretary it was necessary to charge the officers for each can of this beer at the same price as for the normal supplies, I was not allowed to supply the bartered beer free.

At the next audit inspection, the accounts were submitted and found to be in order, except that our bar profits were far in excess of those expected. The audit officers indicated that they need only account for the sales plus 10% profit, plus remaining stock, which by now consisted mainly of Beer, and Gin, with very little Whiskey. The extra Whiskey and Gin did not appear on their books. These had to be discounted as they were a legacy from the Royal Navy and never ordered through the normal RAF supply channels.

The auditors suggested that we dispose of the excess profits, by purchasing suitable equipment for the mess. This we duly did, by buying and installing a very advanced Radiogram, together with a number of '78' records, bought in the town.

After this any surplus would have to be disposed of by using this to organise a Ball at which many of the local residents were to be invited. This was a PR exercise and given full approval by the RAF hierarchy

When we had done as ordered, the books were regularised. The auditors were very complimentary about the financial stability of the officers' mess accounts.

It only goes to show that by judicious financing, it is always possible to improve on profit margins. It only needs the right circumstances.

The above sequence of events enabled us to be more readily accepted into the Augusta 'high society', who at this time were still resentful and suspicious of our intentions towards them.

In the years from 1941 to 1945, I had rapidly become very worldly wise. I had learnt to fight my battles, both within myself and against others, and thus matured far more than my 22 years belied. Even though, as I thought at the time, I had matured, I was ill equipped for any extra responsibility which could be placed on my shoulders. This will become self-evident, in the next element of this narrative.

My Fall from Grace

I thought at this time that I had matured sufficiently to take on additional responsibilities. It was only later in 1945 that I was proved wrong.

Towards the end of 1945 and early 1946, my Station Manager left me in charge of the BOAC operation at Augusta. He was an RAF Wing Commander who had replaced my erstwhile boss, the Squadron Leader who by then had been transferred back to the UK.

The Wing Commander's rank was real not fictitious, (like those held by my ex-boss and myself). These were 'CC', (Civilian Commissions) granted to us so that we could operate in the war zone.

By this time the RAF presence at *Augusta* had diminished greatly, and the BOAC establishment included some two hundred local personnel needed to maintain the workshops, the boats, and the maintenance of the properties on the base.

When it became time for my Station Manager, the real Wing Commander to be 'de-mobbed' from active service,(so that he could rejoin BOAC as a civilian,) he could not wait for a replacement to arrive before returning home. He suggested, and London agreed, that he should hand over the responsibility for running the base to me, until a new manager could be sent out.

By this period of the war, with free access to the UK, the station at *Augusta,* was no longer responsible to the Cairo head office, but came under the direct control of the UK.

In retrospect, my promotion albeit temporary, was a bad one both for BOAC, and myself. I still had a lot to learn about managing myself, and those for whom I had a responsibility. I placed my own personal ambitions ahead of my responsibilities to the station and its personnel. Perhaps my lack of full maturity showed itself, as I allowed my ego to control my actions.

I spent less time on the base than I should have, and more in Catania where I could court my wife to be. I had met my wife to be at a dance held by the station, which she attended with her mother and younger sister.

In the long run, my lack of management style and responsibility may have held me back in later years. However, on the upside, my wife and I have been together now for fifty six years* since 1946 when we married. We now have 5 children, and 12 grandchildren to keep me young in heart to this day. In addition I have 5 very caring and loving in-laws, the husbands and wives of my children.

It took me a long time to recover the lost ground, once the new Station Manager arrived and once again had to play second fiddle. I suppose there must have been an element of resentment on my part, although I did not recognise at the time that it was my failure to consolidate my position, which caused this sequence of events to happen.

Looking back objectively this sequence of events was a further step in my development as a person. It allowed me for the first time to recover from the shock of my demotion in status, and to weigh personal ambition, against my love for a person other than myself. As it happened I chose the right course, and in due time I was able to recover the lost ground in my career.

**at the time of writing in 2002*

The Acquisition of a Car

The increase in my social activity whilst in charge of the BOAC element of the Augusta base coincided with the opportunity offered to me by the closure of the Naval base at Messina on the north east coast of Sicily.

The local Naval Commander wished to return to the UK by air, rather than await the naval transportation that was planned to take him and the remainder of the naval personnel back to the UK.

As principal transport officer, I received a phone call from him to enquire about the possibility of an air passage back to the UK for himself only.

It so happened that there was an RAF Sunderland, which had been held up at Augusta on its flight back to the UK. The engine repairs had just been completed and it was ready to depart the following morning. I asked the pilot if he was prepared to take a senior naval person on his flight the next day. He agreed to this.

I phoned back to Messina, and indicated that a flight had been arranged, provided he could arrive the same day or very early the following morning.

About four hours later, a staff car complete with pennant appeared at the entry gates to the base. I hurried to meet him and introduced him to the pilot who was to carry him back to the UK. He thanked me profusely and handed me the keys to his staff car and indicated that I could use the car for my own use, as there was no point in returning it back to Messina to be abandoned.

The availability of this car was also responsible for my downfall, as it made me independent of RAF transport or train to get me to and from Catania.

When the new station manager arrived, he commandeered the car, as the BOAC Station Manager at the time had no personal transport. He must have assumed that the car went with the job, whereas in truth he should have relied on the RAF to supply him with vehicles on request. The action of taking over my personal transport was a further cause for resentment on my part, as I regarded this vehicle as mine, and not the prerogative of the station manager. It had been passed over to me for a favour granted to its previous user and was not a station asset for BOAC.

More about the RAF Station Commander, and Some Competitions.

When I first arrived in Augusta, the RAF Station Commander was a Squadron Leader. Aside from his responsibilities as station commander, he was also the heir to a considerable fortune based on a well-known chocolate factory in the UK. The chocolate made at this factory is still, I believe on sale to this day. I do not partake of chocolate so cannot vouch for this without useless research.

As a result of his wealth he was not very frugal with his money, as we found out when during our frequent games of Poker he lost more often than he won. Perhaps he was a philanthropist who could not wait to give away his money.

While station commander he had three hobbies, these were: **the conversion of an Italian Naval speedboat, which was engine-less, into a modern speedboat** with a five hundred Horsepower engine-the engine had been acquired from the RAF base at Catania, where he was a frequent visitor where he bought an abandoned aircraft engine, badly in need of repair and refit-); **maintaining his interest in flying** as he was a qualified RAF pilot this he did by borrowing an operational RAF fighter aircraft from the Catania base, and flying this over Augusta harbour to show us all his aptitude for this form of transport, and finally **arranging competitions for the station personnel**...

Concerning the first of these hobbies, he had the help of the RAF Marine Sergeant (who also had post war engineering ambitions), to help convert this derelict craft into a first rate speedboat. This task involved not only a partial redesign of the hull, for the projected speed, but also to contain and fit the new engine to the existing shell.

The new engine was far heavier and larger than the previous engine, which should have been in-situ; the conversion task took them about four months to complete, as it was only a hobby and not part of their general administrative duties.

When the boat was complete he arranged to race this from one end of the harbour to the other. The intention was to pit this boat in a race, against the power of the standard air sea rescue type launches which were present on the base. These launches were used to carry out the Air Traffic control duties required for the operation of flying boats. Such duties have already been described in earlier chapters and need no further elaboration.

In any event, this was to be a handicap race, at which station staff were allowed to place bets.

The course was a straight run of around four miles, within the harbour. The Control Launch was to be given about a half mile advantage. The odds were in favour of the Control Launch, as there was no evidence to suggest that the redesigned Speedboat would last the distance without either the hull breaking up, or the engine or propeller design failing at maximum speed.

As it transpired those betting against the speedboat's success lost their money. The speedboat overtook the launch well before the finishing post. Having succeeded in this venture, the station commander lost interest. The Marine Sergeant continued to fine-tune this craft. Presumably this experience was to serve him well in the post war marine sport environment.

The flying hobby of this Squadron Leader needs no further description, (except to say he was probably showing off how well he could handle the aircraft's controls to all and sundry).

The last event, which I recall during this period, was a handicap race to get to the port of Syracuse by 12 o'clock on the day of departure. The method of reaching there either by land or sea had to be notified in advance so that each method could be given a handicap departure time, with the intention that all should arrive about the same time.

The actual race turned to be a minor disaster, with a touch of deviousness on the part of the winner.

The station doctor decided to go by Star Class yacht, which had been inherited from the Italian Navy, and used by the RAF personnel. Another officer had borrowed a Mule from a local farmer. This he intended to take the shortest route by crossing over untilled fields and roads. The BOAC marine officer, an ex-Naval man, was to use a four oar whaler which would hug the coast round the promontory leading into the harbours at Syracuse. Another was to row across the bay to the Syracuse road, and then cycle to the venue using a bicycle carried on the rowboat.

The last two including the station commander were to proceed to Syracuse, one by a flat-bottomed non-seagoing boat, and the other the station commander, by his staff car.

The station commander hoped to be in Syracuse before all the others, so that he could present the prize.

As it turned out only the station commander and the officer using the flat bottomed boat, reached their venue, and even then the station Commander came second.

You may well ask why the others never reached their intended destination.

This is why!

The **'Star' class yacht** set out in good time, but *no one had told the yachtsman how to turn the yacht* in the prevailing conditions: he had to be collected by the Air Sea Rescue Services while well on his way to Crete . . .

The **Mule rider** made good time until the mule reached the entrance to Syracuse: *it then refused to move any further* and eventually it had to be transported back to Augusta from whence it originated . . .

(The mule rider had been involved in an all-night poker session with the station commander, self and two others, and actually had to be reminded that it was time to set out early enough for the competition).

Both he and the station commander participated in the race with very little sleep if any. The **staff car driver** knew that he could afford to take a nap, as he could cover the journey well within the prescribed time, the other (the mule rider) was handicapped to start at 6 a.m.!

The **'oarsman-cyclist bi-athlete'** never made it to the other side of the harbour as he ran out of puff, and decided to return to the starting point instead!

The **'Whaler'** (with the BOAC marine officer and a passenger), had to abandon the journey before even leaving the harbour because the BOAC gentleman had succumbed to a recurring bout of malaria and the remaining crew member could not handle the craft on his own, especially as it involved a row out into the open sea!

A watchful eye was kept on the progress of all and so no lasting damage was done to any of the participants, apart from the element of shame for their failures.

The **winner** played a crafty game as he had reconnoitered the intended route, and discovered that prior to reaching the promontory separating both harbours, there was a small man-made rivulet, which linked the two harbours together, meaning he literally took a short cut legally to the finish line . . . The outlet in the Syracuse harbour was very close to the meeting venue, arranged strangely enough by the gentleman himself and agreed by all the other participants. ***The flat-bottomed craft he used not only had a 9-inch draught but was also powered, so very little effort was needed to reach the required destination*** . . .

Humility prevents me from identifying who the flat bottomed winner was in that competition . . .

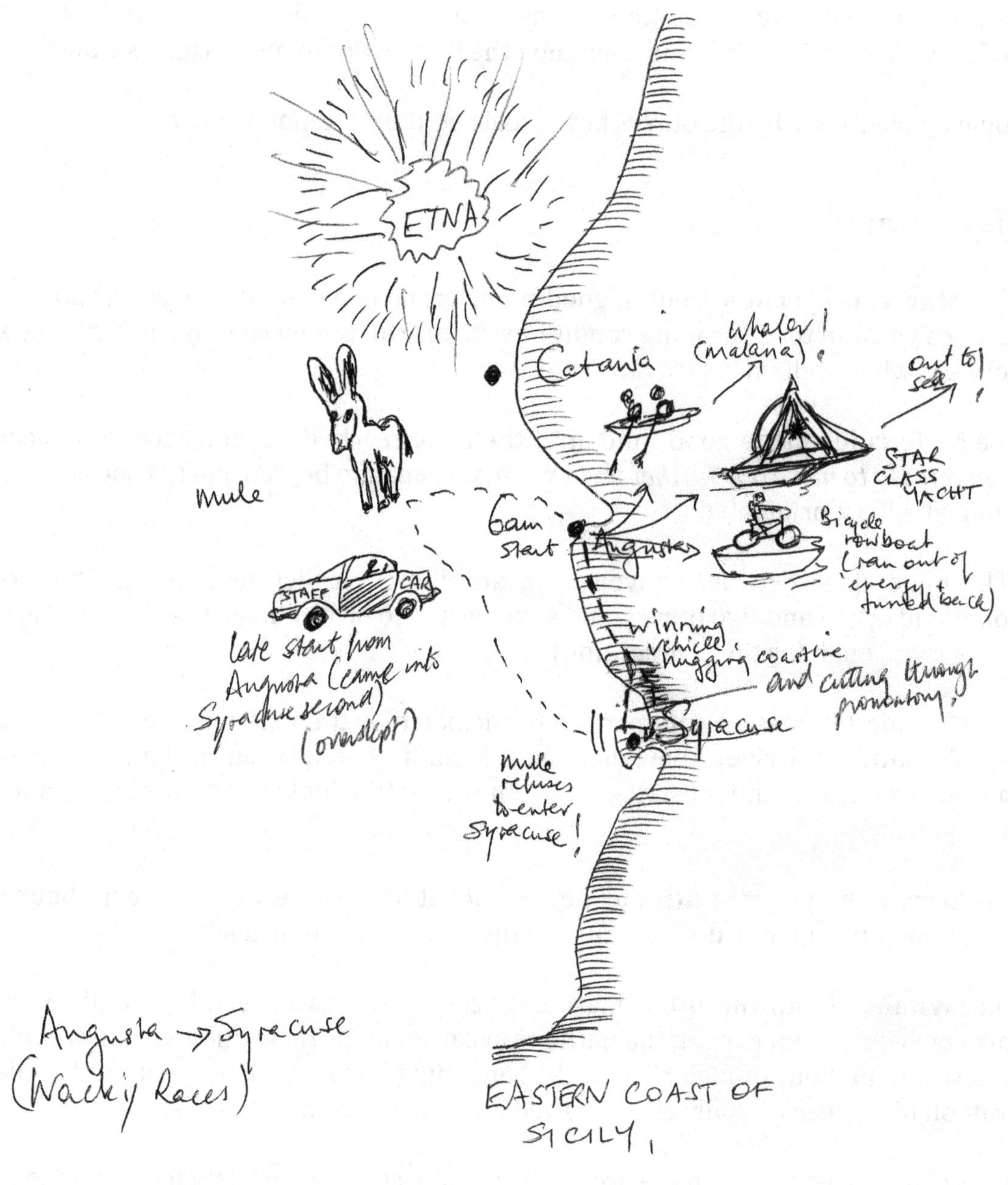

cartoon Map of the Augusta-Syracuse 'wacky' races

My Marriage and return to the UK.

During the middle part of 1946, it appeared that my disaffection with my situation had come to be recognised by the incumbent manager. Presumably this had something to do with my transfer back to the UK for further posting.

I had known my wife to be, for about six months when my transfer became known to me. This was in July of that year, and because of this I proposed to her and was accepted. We became engaged on the 16th July 1946, a date I remember well.

At this time, I had made known to her of my impending departure, but not what awaited us on our return to the UK. This I was unable to do for the reasons stated below.

I had last set foot on UK soil in the mid-thirties (aged twelve or so) when I left those shores with my family. I therefore had no idea what life would be like there as an adult.

At that time it was normal practice for overseas staff to obtain permission from home base before marrying. This I failed to do, but when I did so somewhat later, I received their blessing, so all turned out right in the end.

Financially, I was ill equipped for marriage, having been rather profligate with my salary. With very little money and no property, my future looked rather bleak. However in the immediate post war years, I was not the only person to be in this position.

We married in August of that year, and as it turned out this was the best decision I had made so far in my life. In the year 2002, we are still together and comfortably off, with five married children, and many, many grandchildren and great-grandchildren, some of who are now also adults.

All of my children are also married. We must have done something right in this world, where so many marriages fail after a few years. This is mainly due to a lack of tolerance on both sides, and the inability of some to keep to their marriage vows.

We are both firm believers in the solemnity of the marriage vows, which should be observed, regardless of any temporary difficulties. Constancy, Tolerance, and Perseverance are the watchwords for a long lasting marriage. This is made much easier when faithfulness is included as part of one's beliefs.

Everyone has faults, and in any marriage, if it is to succeed, both parties must support these, and talk through any periods of instability, which may occur.

I have digressed from my story, to state some home truths, which have been learnt over the past fifty years or so. I believe it is important to pass these on to both my immediate family, and other readers brave enough to have read this story so far.

The Honeymoon, and Trials

To continue the story,after the wedding, we proceeded to Rome for our honeymoon. At that time the only way to get to Rome was by steam train. We left Catania in the late afternoon, and crossed over via *Messina* to the mainland.

By the time we reached the mainland it was dark so we decided to halt on the way. This meant backtracking to Reggio Calabria, the nearest large town on the south coast of the mainland. This was an impromptu stop and we had not pre booked our accommodation. We could not, or were not allowed to register at any of the main hotels in this town. It took a while before we found a most unsuitable accommodation but were allowed to register.

The first night of our honeymoon was spent in very uncomfortable circumstances, but it still remains a pleasant memory.

I believe to this day that the reason we were not accommodated at the better hotels in this town, was due to the residual resentment of the local inhabitants, and not because these hotels were full. This could be because I as an RAF Serving Officer had married an Italian girl. Inter marriage at this time was frowned upon, and it took a lot of courage on the part of my wife, to endure the taunts of many of the local population who thought ill of her, even though there was no element of truth in their supposition.

We were to come across similar feelings of resentment even in Rome, after we had registered into the *Albergo Reale*. This was a first class hotel in the centre of Rome, commandeered by the Allies to accommodate visiting Officers to Rome.

The resentment encountered was not at the hotel itself, but during our sightseeing visits to the town.

The return journey was uneventful but tiring. Travel was by steam train, and wherever one was, even in the first class compartments, the engine smoke pervaded the compartment. The fumes would be worse if the windows were opened to allow any cooling breeze to enter. The compartment we occupied was at the front of the train. I shudder to think what passengers in the rear compartments had to endure. Much of the smoke passed over our heads.

Large parts of the journey were covered on a single track, and there were frequent stops to allow trains to pass in the opposite direction. Every few hours the train was diverted to a sidetrack to await the passing of these.

On our return to Augusta after the Honeymoon, we were re-accommodated into quarters, which were more suitable for our new marital state to await our transfer back to the UK. This transfer took place in October 1946.

One of the last episodes worth recounting during this part of the 'first *Augusta* saga' was our encounter with the US Navy.

This is how it happened. The harbour was large enough to allow the US navy to use it for their large ships, which at this time were based on Naples in southern Italy. Today the harbour at Augusta is more widely used by the US Navy.

On this particular day, my wife and I were sitting in the garden after lunch. This was the garden referred to earlier. There were two garden seats opposite where we were sitting.

Two gentleman obviously of US origin came and sat down in those seats. They had just used our tennis courts and were dressed in white shirt and shorts. One was about 30 and the other in his early fifties. We got into conversation with them and shortly after, the station engineer and his wife joined us. We chatted for a while, and as a result they offered us return hospitality for the use of the tennis court. This was to be on the US vessel in the harbour.

They indicated that they would send a launch to pick us up the following night and we were to dine on board.

The next day at around 7 pm we went to the jetty, at the bottom of the garden, and awaited the launch. It turned out to be the Admiral's launch. It was only when we reached the ship, the USS *Kearsage*, a large Aircraft Carrier, that we realised that the two gentlemen in the garden had been the Admiral and his aide.

The Admiral greeted us on our arrival on board, and after dinner, a special film show was put on, at which we were accommodated alongside the Admiral and his aide in the front row, on the top deck of the carrier. We were also sent home in similar style.

It just goes to show that it is not possible to judge people by their appearance on first acquaintance.

Return to the UK and an Unknown Future

We left *Augusta,* and after landing in near Bordeaux, to refuel, we landed in Poole harbour, the UK base for the flying boats.

On reporting back to the head office in London I was granted leave, prior to my posting to the Flying Boat base at Lilliput, near Bournemouth.

From London, we proceeded to *Aldwick* near *Bognor Regis* where my mother was staying. This allowed me to introduce my wife to my family.

After a short stay we travelled direct *to Bournemouth*, via Southampton and found accommodation in *Parkstone*, near Poole Harbour where I was to start work.

I found to my surprise that the 'second-in-command' of the flying boat base at the Harbour Yacht Club was my erstwhile manager, the Squadron Leader I had first met on my arrival at Augusta.

There is little to report about my sojourn in the UK, until my return to *Augusta* for the second time in early 1948.

During this UK stay, apart from getting to know the weather conditions, which were quite different from those I had become accustomed to whilst overseas. There is little of interest to write about.

The main landplane engineering base was at 'Hurn Airport', where all the maintenance for departures from Heathrow was carried out. This meant that all aircraft arriving at Heathrow had to fly to that base for servicing prior to their next departure from London.

No major maintenance work was possible at the time at London Airport. There were no hangars, only a conglomeration of huts, to which passengers would report for departure.

After about six months at Poole supporting the flight departures, I was transferred and placed in charge of the ground operations at Hurn. This meant a change of accommodation, as the Parkstone place was too far from Hurn for this to be viable.

By this time, our eldest child had been born, and trying to find suitable accommodation for a young couple with a small child was very difficult. No one wanted to know, and after two or three short stays in accommodation near to Hurn, I was forced to request a transfer back overseas.

Fortunately one of the persons at home base, to whom I reported, was one of those with whom I had shared a flat in Cairo. He was very sympathetic to our plight and initiated a transfer back to Augusta.

One reason for the existence of the small establishment at *Hurn* was due to the frequency of operations to and from London Airport. On each flight there were passengers, either proceeding to or returning from holiday. Each of those departing had to be processed prior to embarkation.

The other and main reason for the establishment of the Hurn base was the frequency of diversions from London, due to the prevalence of smog conditions. This prevented the landing of aircraft of all airlines operating into and out of London at the time.

Before the Clean Air Act, 1956, London, had not yet been declared a smokeless zone, and the winter coal fires from all the houses, created the ideal environment for the 'pea—soupers' of those days.

'Pea-soupers', are normally caused by the prevalence of coal particles in the atmosphere. The presence of these particles creates the ideal condition to turn a misty night into the dirty grey fog of a 'pea-souper'.

In 1948, some forms of assisted landings were available, but these were not as sophisticated as those available today. Auto Landings driven by computers on aircraft were only a dream at this time.

Landing limits for safe operation, were far more restricted than today, as a consequence as soon as the limits were breached, up to 30 or so aircraft of all nationalities would descend on Hurn. All the passengers had to be deplaned, and transported to London by rail. The same applied to the Mail and Cargo on board, when these aircraft were unable to reposition back to London.

The airport at Hurn was not suitable for International arrivals and departures, as there were no Customs and Immigration facilities available. These had to be brought in from Poole Harbour and until these arrived, no passengers could be deplaned.

When the conditions persisted for any length of time, the aircraft would remain at Hurn and prepared for departure. Passengers and their baggage and any other load, had to be transported by rail from London to Bournemouth West, where they had to be collected, processed and placed on board their aircraft.

It has been known during my stay, for all the staff at Hurn, to be on duty non-stop for over thirty six hours, until relieved by staff coming from London to take over duties. These enforced hours began to play havoc with my home life, as my wife was with a small child in unfamiliar circumstances, and living under great hardship.

At the time my pay was a mere £7 or so a week. Much of this went on accommodation and food. There was very little for extra luxuries, essential to modern day living. So it was against this background that my request for return to an overseas posting was made.

In 1948, I was barely 25 years old but had experienced conditions not felt by even those twice my age. This toughened my wife and myself for the life experiences yet to be met by my next few overseas postings, and the arrival of our two other children.

This is another story yet to be told. This deals specifically with those stations to which I have yet to be transferred, each of which have episodes worth recounting.

BOURNEMOUTH, POOLE, THE HARBOUR, + ENVIRONS.

HURN

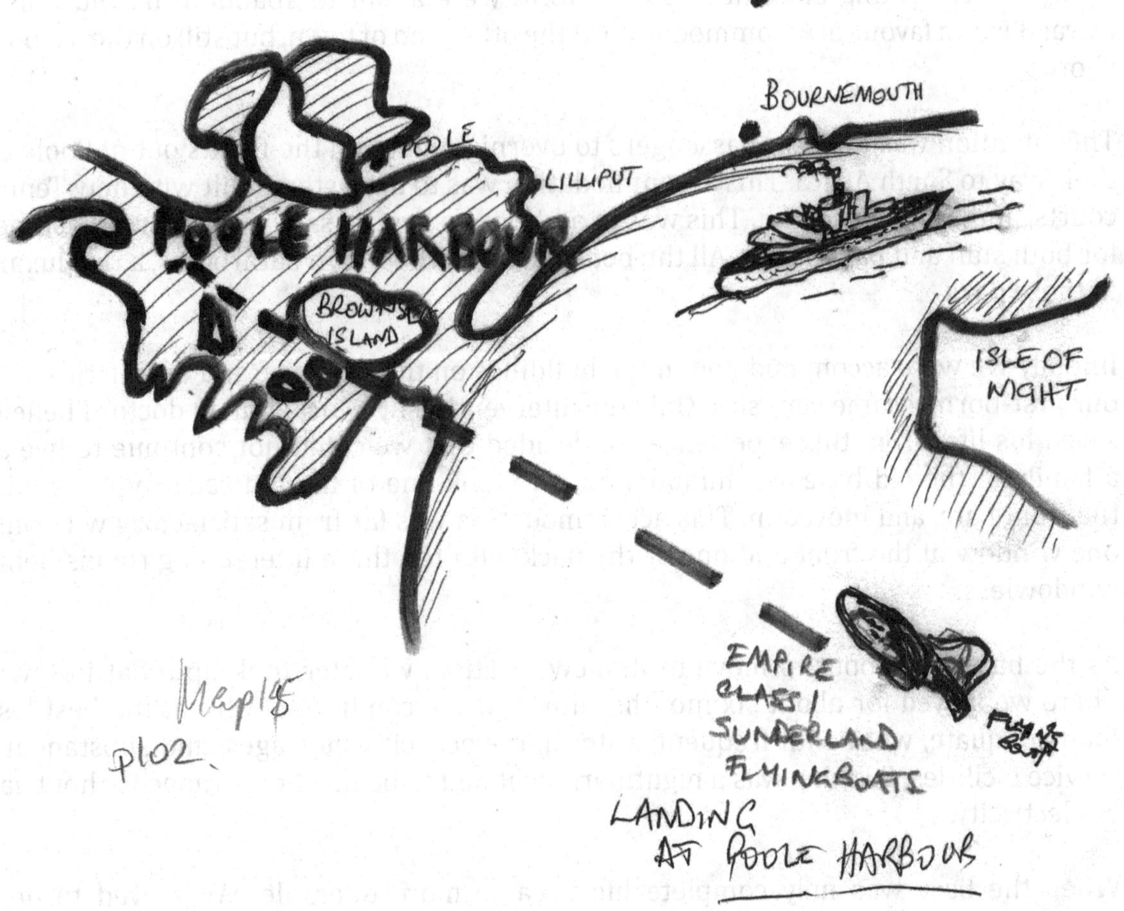

map of Poole harbour and G AEUE flying boat

Return to Augusta.

To return to Augusta, the journey back required us to be at the departure point in Poole harbour early in the morning from where we were staying in *Christchurch.*

Passengers travelling on the flying boats from London, were taken by road the previous night, and accommodated in *Brockenhurst*, a townlet about midway between Southampton and Poole. We were transported there the night before departure, to link up with those passengers coming from London.

The following morning we departed from Poole for Augusta, via *Marignane* near *Marseilles,* landing later the same day at Augusta.

On arrival we were met and spent the night in temporary accommodation until something more permanent could be arranged.

Someone more senior had replaced the previous manager. This was because great changes were taking place at Augusta. BOAC were about to abandon the Old Italian Naval Base, in favour of accommodation at the other end of town, but still on the harbour shore.

The intention was to allow passengers to overnight here on the flights out of Poole on their way to South Africa. This accommodation was to be custom built with new Tennis courts, and a snooker room. This was in addition to first class dining and rest facilities for both staff and passengers. All the bedrooms had their own bathrooms, a real luxury in those days.

Initially we were accommodated in the buildings on the old base, and during this stay, our first-born became very sick. Only the intervention by a local Italian doctor I believe saved his life. From this experience we decided that we could not continue to live as a family in the old base accommodation, and took one of the old security houses by the front gate, and moved in. This accommodation was far from satisfactory with only one window at the front and one at the back with the three intervening rooms being windowless.

As the base was about to move to its new location, we later took up a flat in town. There we stayed for about six months, although the conditions were at the best less than adequate, what with frequent water and electricity shortages, and substandard service facilities. Cooking was a nightmare, as it had to be done on a range without gas or electricity.

When the base was fully complete life became more tolerable. We moved to new premises on the base, with all 'mod cons'.

The new base facilities included a jetty from where passengers could disembark directly on to dry land, thus avoiding transportation by launch from the aircraft. Aircraft would continue to taxi as before to the mooring buoy, but once moored it would be winched back until it rested between the two platforms. This allowed the passengers and baggage to be discharged directly on to dry land. Baggage could be hauled by trolley direct from the aircraft to the base hotel.

All the flights to and from the UK would overnight in Augusta, and this set up made the handling and distribution of overnight bags much easier. A full first class hotel service was offered to these passengers at the base hotel run by BOAC catering staff. This included a cinema at which films sent out from the UK became a regular feature.

Although the flying boats, were operating well and different versions of the original C Class had been developed, which carried more passengers than the earlier types, the running costs of maintaining the facilities at each route station, made their operation economically unsound.

The C Class had been replaced by the *Sandringham* for a short while. Then along came the *Solent*, which carried a far greater number of passengers, and included a better observation platform at the rear.

For a little while the *Golden Hind* class was used. These two aircraft were even larger than the *Solent*, but the death knell had already been struck, and the days of flying boats in BOAC were numbered. After about eighteen months in all, I was transferred back to the UK, and put on indefinite leave until a further posting became available.

It is worth mentioning in passing, that one of the clerks employed by us, by the name of '*Cala*', in later years became a personality on Italian television, as did his son after him.

The story now continues with my progress on the walk through life after Augusta.

Transfer to Dakar in Senegal (1949)

It was about this time that the British South American Airways were running into financial difficulties, having lost a few aircraft as well as operating the wrong type for the routes they were flying. The BSAA operation was to and from the UK to South America and the Caribbean. Essentially the route between the UK and South America via the Caribbean must have been viable initially or BSAA routes would not have been granted their routes.

BOAC took over the route from BSAA and replaced the BSAA Tudor aircraft with Argonauts, a Canadair derivation of the DC4 fitted with Rolls Royce Merlin Engines.

When the takeover occurred a whole new route structure became available, and I was hastily summoned back from leave and transferred to Dakar in Senegal.

When I was sent on indefinite leave, my wife, child and I returned to Catania to stay with her parents. More permanent accommodation in the UK was still difficult to find on the salary I was earning at the time.

Initially the posting was not a family one. No suitable family accommodation was available in Dakar and the whole station organisation was under review after the takeover of this route. I therefore left my wife in Italy and proceeded to Dakar on my own. My wife was now pregnant with our second child, whom I never saw until she arrived to join me in Dakar.

When I arrived, Lancaster aircraft were still operating the South American route. These only carried around six passengers due to the narrowness of the fuselage.

The manager to whom I reported, had arranged accommodation for his staff *in a third rate hotel in the town.* Two people had to share each room. Bath and toilet facilities, were along an outside covered passageway at first floor level, and around the corner on another side of the building. No meal facilities were available in this hotel, and it was necessary to go about two hundred yards down the road for the nearest eating establishment. This was particularly irksome following a long spell of fifteen hours of duty, a large part of which was at night. These long days followed each other in sequences, with another spell following immediately the same night.

(Needless to say, aircrew that overnighted, were accommodated in top grade hotels, with full meal facilities).

The only point in favour of this arrangement was that the manager shared the same hotel accommodation as his staff, but his room had a bath over which he and his wife cooked some of their meals on a Primus stove.

The conditions met, were like a return to the primeval environment related at the start of my career. The environment at Dakar was much more civilised, but the incumbent manager still made little use of this to improve his staff living conditions.

Perhaps the reason for this frugal attitude was that he was intent on spending as little as possible in order to cut the operational costs of this new station on the BOAC network. Initially Dakar was mainly a fuelling stop on the South American route, and as such very little revenue accrued from it.

The town of Dakar, and its airport at *Yoff* some five or six miles away, was the most westerly point in Africa, and the nearest to the South American continent's most easterly airport of *Recife.* This made Dakar the ideal launch point for the transatlantic crossing.

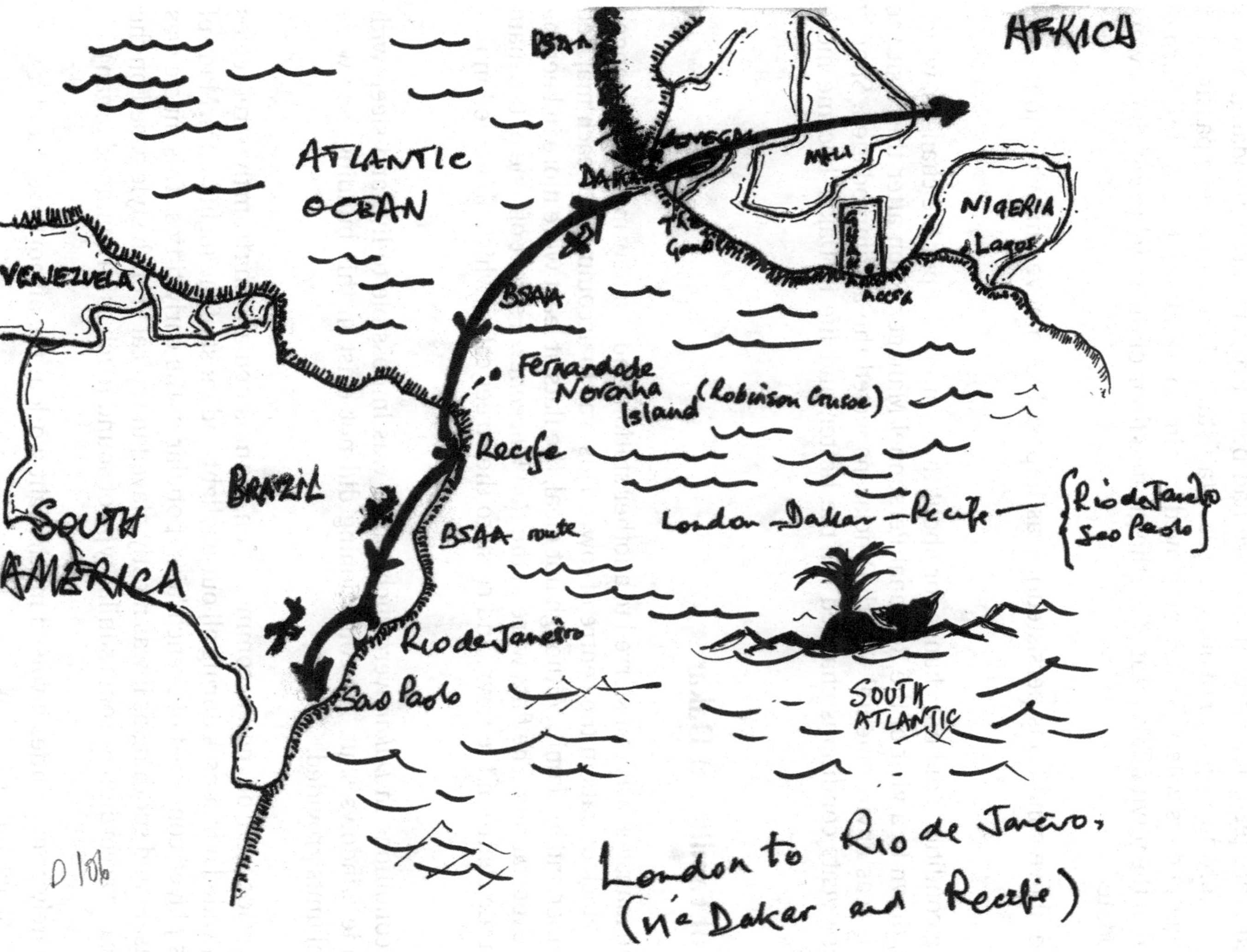

map of Yoff Airport of Dakar in Senegal to Recife, Brazil

Dakar itself at the time was a very cosmopolitan town with a good deep water harbour, and a very large French population, many of whom were military personnel located both in the town, and in nearby barracks.

The main streets abounded with street cafes, from which popular French music of the day blared out loudly, invading the surrounding houses and our hotel in particular.

Most of the local French residents would populate these pavement cafes, and life could have been more pleasant for us if only we had been properly accommodated and in conditions more appropriate to our overseas staff status. It so happens in passing that the Manager and his wife, who was employed by him on behalf of BOAC, spent much of their time in the town office located on the ground floor of the hotel in which we were accommodated.

While the above conditions persisted it was impossible to have our wives join us in Dakar.

Our living conditions did not change for about three months. I put the changes, which followed, down to a visit of the Regional Personnel Manager. Soon after this visit the BOAC Overseas Environmental Health Official inspected the accommodation. Shortly after these visits conditions changed for the better, and life in Dakar became more tolerable.

Arrival of Families at Dakar

Firstly the manager was transferred to another station, and the new manager arranged to lease a block of flats in the centre of town. This was to accommodate each married staff member and his family. Although not ideal, the flats at least were more in keeping with our expectations. The flats were in the *Rue Vincennes*, a street off one of the main streets in the centre of the town, and close to the street cafes, which abounded in this area.

Climatic conditions in *Dakar* were such that it was impossible to live and sleep with the outside windows shut. Air conditioning did not exist in this building, nor were individual units provided.

While in residence in our new accommodation, the music emanating from the street cafes nearby, invaded our senses during all our daylight and most of the night hours. Many of the tunes played consisted of French 'airs', popular in the early fifties. This music was very pleasant and soothing as it was mostly played in typical French style based on the harmonica or accordion or some similar type of sound (such as a Hammond organ).

Unfortunately as our duties involved much night work at the airport, we found it very difficult to sleep during the day.

During this stay in *Dakar*, both the manager and my immediate boss changed more than once and gradually the 'Avro Lancaster' was phased out and replaced by the *Argonauts* in a full first class configuration of around forty seats.

The South American through traffic was very seasonal, and steps were taken to turn Dakar into a feeder station for West African Airways flights operating from Lagos via Accra, through Robertsfield Airport,(Monravia) in Liberia, through Freetown, Sierra Leone and penultimately via Bathurst,(now Banjula) in The Gambia. These flights would deposit passengers bound for the UK, mostly Colonial Office expatriates travelling back to Home Shores, and return with those passengers arriving on the inbound flights from the UK heading out of Dakar.

BOAC_C-4_Argonaut_Heathrow_1954.

DH Comet 1 BOAC Heathrow 1953.

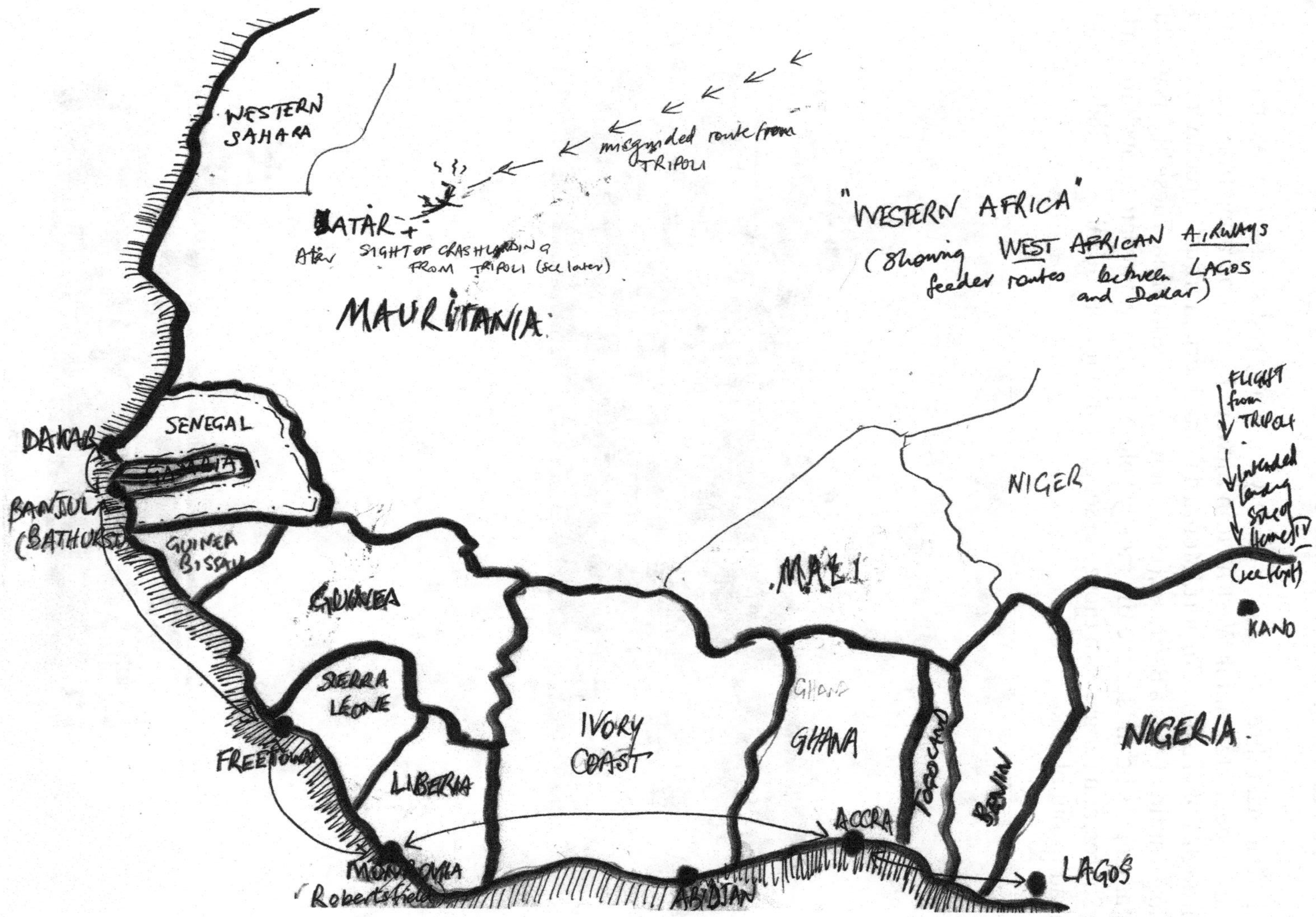

map of West Africa Airways feeder routes

All the BOAC transatlantic flights arrived from both directions during the night hours, so all passengers had to be accommodated temporarily in the Air France Rest House facilities near the airport to await their connecting flight

At certain times of the year, the night hours on the airport tarmac teemed with the flight of Cantharide* blister beetles. These were very top-heavy insects that lumbered around in the night atmosphere, and would give a very uncomfortable sting if touched. By being careful it was possible to dodge these when proceeding to and from the aircraft.

The fact that these beetles are the source of Spanish Fly produced out of their crushed body parts made these trips even more hazardous, as the uniform of the day consisted of short wide bottomed shorts, into which these insects could fly with careless abandon, but with disastrous effects to the person wearing this uniform due to the potential pharmacologic effect on the local blood circulation.

I never suffered this indignity, but one of my colleagues did, and became very distressed as a result.

**Cantharis vesicatoria* when crushed is the source of so called 'Spanish Fly' aphrodisiac.

The West African Airways flights would arrive in the late afternoon, and depart early the next morning. The Bristol Wayfarer, a very ugly looking aircraft specifically designed for the transport of cars across the English Channel operated these flights.

At least two of us were on duty during the night hours, to cope with the reception, and accommodation of those passengers trans-shipping to and from the BOAC flights. Coupled with this were the in-flight control of the inbound long distance flights, and liaison with both the inbound and outbound crews to allow these to be interchanged. at Dakar. Passengers also had to be taken to and collected from the Rest House.

The rest house was not a true hotel. No staff were available, to wake these passengers in time for their impending departure. This lot fell upon the BOAC personnel whose task was to identify the rooms occupied and arrange to wake these in the middle of the night.

When a shift was over following the departure of the Wayfarer bound for Bathurst and further points south in West Africa, we were exhausted and ready for bed. This was not always easy in the existing living conditions described earlier. One never quite recovered from the previous shift before it started all over again the same evening.

During the rainy season, the journey time by air to Bathurst in the Gambia was a mere twenty minutes, even by the plodding Bristol Wayfarer, not the fastest of aircraft in those days. The same journey by road could take up to two days, due to the conditions of the road between these two locations.

To get to Bathurst by road, it was necessary to travel many miles inland from Dakar, before reaching a point on the Gambia River where vehicles could cross. There was no direct road access by bridge near the coast due to the width of the Gambia river mouth.

The air route became a popular way for local traders to supply their stores in the Gambia. As I recall the airfare was about £5, and the profit margins on the goods carried was more than enough to cover this fare.

Had they been allowed, this flight would have been filled with such passengers, to the detriment of passengers wishing to travel to more profitable destinations further down the route.

In addition, there was this constant battle with the local traders who wished to maximise their profit margins by trying to carry far in excess of their baggage allowance in the form of goods. This became a regular feature of all such departures, when these refused to pay any excess charges. They would argue until just prior to departure in the hope that we would relent to ensure that the flights left on time. After we removed some passengers because of these altercations, the traders became wiser and peace and harmony was re-established.

The traders would normally fly out to Bathurst on the morning flight, and return the same day, on the afternoon flight from the south. The time between these two flights was such that they could carry out their trading and dispose of the goods brought in.

During this stay in Dakar, three episodes come readily to mind, which are worth recounting,

'Robinson Crusoe' and a Forced Landing

The first of these was the forced landing of an Argonaut on its way to Recife from Dakar. Before reaching landfall in South America, engine trouble forced the aircraft to make an emergency landing. This landing was on the island of *Fernando de Noronha*, situated some one hundred miles from the South American mainland. This island purported to be the self-same island, which was written about by **Daniel Defoe** in the 'Robinson Crusoe' saga.

The Brazilian Air Force eventually took all the passengers and crew off the island, and the aircraft itself was later flown to Recife then back home to the UK, to be reabsorbed into the Argonaut fleet. The aircraft registration as I recall it was GALHU.

Although not directly involved in the subsequent events to extricate the passengers, and recover the aircraft, we all maintained a great interest in its outcome. The crew was all well known to us.

In between flights, many crew members awaiting their next flight would spend the afternoon at the beach resort near the airport. Special daily transport was arranged, to take the off duty staff and their families, and crewmembers to the beach at *'Ngor'* near the airport at *'Yoff'*. The crewmembers travelled back and forth from the UK on a regular basis, and with these frequent beach trips many became friends of the resident BOAC families. This is why we all became concerned when we heard of this incident, and relieved when the outcome was known.

Crash Landing at Dakar

The second incident of note was the crash landing at night at Dakar itself by an incoming Argonaut. This necessitated lengthy repairs, but eventually this aircraft also returned to service.

The airport at Dakar was constructed on a raised part of the land with the sea on three sides, on one of which were two hills, named appropriately as *'Les Mamelles'*. The approach in either direction was to a single runway with a lip of around three feet at one end. Landing aircraft approached from the sea, and had to clear the runway threshold before touch down.

On this occasion, the aircraft at landing speed touched the lip on the runway threshold with its nose wheel before touchdown. The result of this was that the nose wheel buckled and was pushed back towards the front cargo hold. Part of the nose wheel remained in touch with the runway, so the aircraft slithered to an emergency stop without further damage.

Passengers were all safely disembarked; none were hurt, and the aircraft taken back to the tarmac. A later inspection of the damage revealed that by pure chance the load in the forward hold had borne the full force of the nose wheel collapse, and consisted mainly of high density 'rubberised' goods that had absorbed the shock from the collapse of the damaged nose wheel and prevented much more serious damage with possible loss of life.

Apart from the initial shock caused by this incident, everything returned to normal very quickly, and a full inventory of the damaged cargo on board reported back to the BOAC insurance service back home. Fortunately the passenger bags were in the rear hold, and remained undamaged.

Desert Crash Landing, North of Dakar.

The last and most serious of the incidents during my fifteen months stay in Dakar was quite unconnected with the normal operations through that station.

At around ten o'clock in the morning of 26th May 1952 while on duty at the airport, the Air Traffic Control tower advised us that a BOAC aircraft G ALDN a Handley Page

Hermes IV,(nicknamed 'Horus') was in distress and about to force land in the southern Sahara Desert since it was lost and fast running out of fuel. It requested directions as it had lost its bearings during the night on a flight between Tripoli in Libya and Kano in Northern Nigeria. A quick set of bearings taken by the authorities, at both Bathurst, (in the Gambia) and Dakar, plus another station in the region, placed the aircraft to the south east of *Atar,* a French Foreign Legion outpost in Mauritania about four hundred miles to the north east of Dakar.

Having established the aircraft's location the next thing was to direct this aircraft to *Atar*, the nearest available airport. The landing strip at *Atar* was unsuitable for this type of aircraft but it at least had all the medical, and rescue facilities ready to hand.

The response from the aircraft was that it would try to make for *Atar*. As it happened it could not, and had to force land in the desert. The pilot reported the landing, and advised that only light injuries had been sustained by some of the passengers, but in the main all was fine.

It was now necessary to locate the exact location of the aircraft and mount a rescue mission to recover the passengers and crew. Once the aircraft was located 115 km SSE of Atar, an air rescue mission was launched from Atar. The first priority was to locate a medical officer. This was done and he was parachuted down but on landing he sustained injuries from which he subsequently died at the site of the accident.

During this emergency it was deemed essential for one of the Dakar staff to go to Atar to supervise the evacuation, and recovery of the passengers and crew. Initially I was destined for this role, but eventually a more senior member of the staff undertook this obligation, leaving us to communicate with London, and organise any recovery aircraft which would be needed to operate, between the crash site and Atar, and between Atar and Dakar. Only a very light aircraft such as the Avro Anson could land at both the crash site and at Atar, which was not equipped for this type of incident.

The eight crew and ten passengers were asked to try to clear a landing site in a suitable spot for a very light aircraft to land. This operation resulted in the death of the First Officer, 'Ted Haslam' from the heat and the exertions needed to construct this landing site, and perhaps also as a result of injuries from the crash landing.

The Foreign Legion base at Atar, arranged for a food and water drop, to sustain those passengers stranded at the scene of the accident. At the same time a convoy set off from *Atar*, including another doctor, but they indicated that it could take up to three days for them to reach the scene of the accident, due to the nature of the terrain and the distance involved.

Meanwhile at Dakar, the US consulate was asked if the US could provide assistance, and as a result they arranged for a helicopter to be sent. This would be carried to Dakar in a US Transport aircraft from Libya, but this helicopter would have to be assembled after arrival at Dakar before it could become operational.

Our London base offered a DC4 'Sky Master' aircraft, and this quickly replaced the helicopter offer as a more suitable alternative. This was to land at the crash site and gather a few passengers at a time, for transportation back to Atar and then onto Dakar. This decision was the correct one, and after about three days all the passengers were back at Dakar. The land convoy had not reached the crash site before all seventeen remaining passengers and crew had been evacuated.

The cause of the accident was later found to be due to a navigational error. The route from Tripoli to Kano was about 6 degrees west of due south. The aircraft setting for the journey actually carried the aircraft some 60 degrees west of due south. There were no navigational aids on this route, and it was normal practice, for the navigator to base his position by Dead Reckoning, a method of navigation frequently carried out during the war when the same 'in flight' conditions applied over enemy territory.

'Dead Reckoning' navigation is where time and ground speed and possible drift are taken into account to establish one's position relative to the ground on a route navigation chart. Corrections would only be made once true bearings could be established from one or more radio stations. In Africa such stations were conspicuous by their absence. The crew could have used astral navigation to pinpoint their position, but did not consider this to be necessary at the time.

Apparently it was a passenger who alerted them to the problem. When dawn broke he could not see the sunrise to the east from the port side window where he was sitting and so alerted the crew to the fact the aircraft was not travelling 'southwards'.

The remnants of this aircraft was sold to a UK salvage company, who had hoped to recover its outlay by the salvage of the more sophisticated parts of the aircraft, especially those in the Flight Deck.

Representatives of this company arrived in Dakar some time later, and having visited the crash site with much difficulty, they discovered to their horror, that all had been in vain. The nomadic Arabs, had gutted the aircraft, and had taken everything from the aircraft including instruments, galley equipment, and aircraft seats and décor. The remains of the fuselage are at RAF *Duxford*.

picture of BOAC Handley Page Hermes IV

Relocation of Staff, and Crews.

Meanwhile on the personal front, BOAC had constructed two new buildings adjacent to each other, to accommodate all the station personnel in one location, Up to now these were spread around the town. This accommodation would also be used to accommodate the crews who would overnight, thus saving the Hotel costs. Single members of staff and the crews would be housed in one building, and the families in an adjacent block.

The families could use the rest rooms and dining facilities available in the main building, although each flat was fully equipped

The only problem about this new venture was the location of the site. This was on the edge of the French residential quarters, but the northern aspect looked across the start of the African quarters. Immediately below the main building was a walled compound, obviously occupied by a family group and near relatives. The compound comprised a series of huts, but all cooking facilities were communal and in the open air.

The women of this compound would spend a large part of the day, preparing the food for cooking. The staple diet comprised food which was indigenous to Senegal, and most plentiful. This consisted mainly of peanuts, and manioc roots. I presume all the beating in large stone pots with a type of baseball bat, was a way of pulverising these two elements, into a pulp prior to cooking.

This diet was supplemented by dried fish, which was hung out to dry in the compound. This type of food was both plentiful and cheap in the local market.

Each mealtime the whole family would gather together, chat and make loud sounds to the accompaniment of a rhythmic drumbeat. Night-time was the same. The African chants and drumbeats continued late into the night.

We had plenty of time to study this element of the Senegalese culture, as it all took place directly under our window whilst we were accommodated temporarily, in the main building awaiting the completion of our flat.

Apart from this, life was quite tolerable now, despite the tropical heat and occasional violent rainstorms. We were relatively close to many of the main food and clothing stores. The main market was only a short distance away, and there were many pleasant walks either towards the sea, or the main harbour. Outings to the beach near the airport, continued. The families would spend most afternoons at the beach while the husbands were at work.

On my next vacation to the UK we had arranged to spend this time in Italy with my wife's family. We still had no home in the UK where we could spend our holidays so Rome was the cheapest alternative, as well as the best option.

My wife's family had moved from Sicily to Rome whilst we were in Dakar, and it was a good opportunity to see them again and learn more about Rome.

While away, I was to attend in the UK, an advanced Flight Operations course. The course would last ten weeks. It was designed to equip attendees for the changing scene about to follow in the aviation industry. All overseas staff members were required to be operationally qualified to allow the Airline to dispense with the Operations Officers, who were unqualified for any other overseas ground duties. BOAC had inherited these from both BSAA and the RAF in the immediate post war era and was now rationalizing its operations structure.

Those staff that were retained, (for overseas appointments after reappraisal), had to be fully competent in the commercial and operational aspects of the airline, in order to significantly reduce the overseas' staff complement.

The level of operational training would be designed to bring such staff up to the level of the US equivalent of Flight Dispatchers. The title of flight dispatcher in the UK today is quite unlike that given to US government-licensed personnel who hold this title.

In the UK today the responsibilities of a flight dispatcher have been eroded to the point where those staff only co-ordinate the pre-departure preparation of an aircraft whilst on the ground. No operational duties are now included in this role, unlike those that applied when the title was first introduced.

The ten week Advanced Operations course comprised lectures and tests, on Air Navigation Law, Meteorology, Flight Planning in all forms, and an understanding of the mathematics which support flight planning across uncharted routes using spherical

Trigonometry. No computers or calculators could be used on this course.

Fortunately I passed this examination with good marks. I have a certificate to this day to prove this.

While I was on this course, my wife and children remained in Italy and only re-joined me immediately prior to our return to Dakar.

While in Rome, my wife (who has 'good connections' in Government through her now, late Uncle), managed to ask for me to be transferred to Rome. I was unaware of this at the time, but soon found this out on our return to Dakar.

My wife's uncle had founded the **anti-Mussolini party**, *'Il Partito Popolare'* in Italy. *Alcide de Gasperi*, then the Prime Minister of Italy was a protégé of her uncle.

Apparently the Italian Ambassador in the UK expressed a wish to BOAC that it would be in the interests of the airline if I could be transferred to Rome. BOAC granted this request and I was soon on my way out of Dakar.

The flight back to the UK in the Argonaut was very pleasant. The part of the journey at night, took us along the African coast north via *Port Etienne*, in French Mauritania, past *Villa Cisneros*, in the Spanish Sahara, passing the Canary Islands to the west. By this time dawn was breaking from the East, and the high peaks of the Canary Islands bathed in the early morning sunlight was a vision of beauty. The peaks themselves protruded from above the layered cloud far below. The whole panorama was a mixture of pale blue and pink. The mountains themselves were a light shade of purple.

The flight, at a height of around eighteen thousand feet, was incredibly smooth but very noisy, as we were sat in the four facing seats at the front and close to two of the four Merlin engines. At night the exhausts from these glowed red and the engines crackled and spluttered intermittently, presumably when the flight engineer changed to different fuel tanks.

When I reported back to the UK I was told in no uncertain terms that my posting was not the wish of my General Manager, but this had been ordered and *that I should never again use these means to get a favourable posting.*

Later in my career, this gentleman and I were to be reconciled when eventually I was posted back for Head Office duties.

Fortunately my recent course success stood me in good stead, as the duties in Rome were purely operational. With no involvement in the commercial aspects of the airline, BEA was responsible for all ground service duties at *Ciampino*, (the international airport serving Rome at the time).

All the aircraft passing through Rome and handled by BEA would be parked at *Ciampino East*, on the opposite side of the airport from where I was to work. The two areas were separated by the only runway.

The town of *Ciampino* was only a short walking distance away from the terminal buildings at *Ciampino East*. Many of the local staff employed by BEA would live there.

The BOAC Operations office was located at Ciampino West, where all the operational services were situated. All Italian and US aircraft would operate from these terminal buildings at Ciampino West.

Our place of work was therefore isolated from the rest of the BOAC operation in Rome. We were however required to attend the East Side to carry to them the weather forecasts and flight plans to brief the crews in transit. Those who were joining their flight in Rome would call in to the office on the west side before going over to the east side

The *Via Appia Nuova* was the main road link from the city of Rome to the airport. At this timc this road was also the main road link to Naples and the south. The main motorway to the south was in the process of being built together with the Rome outer ring road to by-pass the city from the north, some parts of which had been completed.

The time spent in Rome was between the years 1952 all the way through to early 1958; this was a total period of five very happy years, envied and rightly so, by all those I met subsequently.

Our principal duties were to carry out **'in flight control'** on all BOAC aircraft flying into and out of Rome. These duties included the Control of all aircraft in flight to ensure that they reported their progress at 30-minute intervals. We were also required to respond to any requests for in-flight weather conditions. We would also watch the weather conditions and initiate reports to the aircraft if these changed significantly.

The office was fully equipped for this purpose, and all messages relayed to and from the aircraft were received directly at our workstation in the office.

Another of our duties was the crew allocation to each flight when these were not in direct transit. We were also required to complete flight plans for each aircraft operating out of Rome. The routing and prevailing weather conditions would determine the route to be flown, and the minimum safe amount of fuel to be taken on board for the journey. On any one tour of duty there would be anything up to twenty aircraft in flight, as nearly all flights to the south and east of the UK would operate through Rome.

On any one night up to one hundred and twenty crewmembers might have stayed more than one night (or more)to await their next flight out. Some of the crew changes involved were very complex, in view of the different flight time limitations imposed by the National Governments of the airlines, which we had to control. In addition to which each day we had to cope with at least a ten per cent sickness rate, mainly from the crews returning from the Far East. This frequently necessitated last minute crew roster changes. In the case of Cabin crews this was not too difficult, as these were less subjected to the restrictions, which applied to the operating crews.

One could not assign an operating crewmember to a route for which he had not the necessary route qualification. For example if the aircraft from Rome was due to return via German air space, and had to land en route, then one could not assign a crew member who had only been cleared for the direct route over France to the UK. This was even more restricted when the crews, in question, were not UK based, such as those from Australia. It occasionally became necessary to request the positioning of extra crew from the UK to meet some of these restrictions.

In addition to these duties, we were required to calculate and produce Flight Plans, for all the different aircraft types operating through that station. At the time all the aircraft operating through Rome, were propeller driven. Propeller driven jets, and pure jets appeared later during my stay. For these we had to be trained separately at a later date.

Each of the aircraft types in current use and their route patterns demanded different techniques in order to calculate the times and fuel requirements for each journey. Due to the continuing turmoil in the Middle East around this period, frequent re-routings became necessary, some of which became very marginal due to the operating range, and route to be followed by some of these aircraft.

All the flight planning techniques employed were taught to us during the operations course I had taken, but I never realised at the time how soon this knowledge was to be used in earnest.

For those who are interested, all flight plans had to be calculated and completed by hand, there were no computers to assist, as there are today. Each aircraft in use operated to one of the following rules;

Flight Planning at **Constant Speed Cruise**:*(for the Hermes type* aircraft)

Flight planning at **Constant Power Cruise:***(for the Argonauts)*

Flight Planning in **Long Range Cruise**: *(for the Lockheed Constellation).*

All of these techniques we used on a regular basis in Rome.

For those interested, the following definitions are given;

Constant Speed Cruise occurs when engine power at the start of cruise is set and as the weight of the aircraft is reduced by the fuel consumption the airspeed increases. Power has to be reduced at regular intervals to maintain the planned air speed, implying a reduced fuel consumption as the power required decreases.

Constant Power Cruise occurs when the engine power is fixed at the start of the journey and remains unchanged until landing, with the result that as the fuel consumption reduces the aircraft's weight so then the air speed progressively increases because of the constant fuel burn.

Long Range Cruise

This type of flight planning is the most complex of the above alternatives, and used for those aircraft, for which long distances have to be flown between landings.

This type of fuel and cruise planning requires the airspeed to be set at stalling speed plus 5 %. minimum. In this variety, on the above flight planning themes, the optimum height and speed have to be re-calculated every one or two hours and height and power adjustments made accordingly to maintain this optimum situation. This type of planning was particularly useful on those routes, which operated to the East of Rome, on non-stop flights to Bahrain in the Arabian Gulf (Persia), via the direct route over Syria, or in war conditions via Northern Turkey to by-pass the war zones.

All flight plans had to be prepared according to the weather conditions based on the forecast route and destination weather conditions. In some cases this involved rerouting aircraft around the bad weather areas. Aircraft in those days never flew above 20 000 feet and bad weather over the Alps frequently required re-routing for passenger comfort, and also on occasions, for safety reasons.

Later new flight planning techniques had to be learnt to cope with the newer jet type aircraft. This necessitated, further courses in the UK, which I undertook and passed successfully, but this is the subject of another story later.

I hope by now that the reader will come to understand the complexities of this new task, which added to the experience gained during my overseas service so far.

Gradually as a result of this additional training and use of it, I matured from a young adult, to one who became much more responsible and worldly-wise, well able to cope with what the future held in store for me.

A few episodes occurred during this stay in Rome, which are worth recounting, two of these are personal, and the rest operational. The personal notes are for the benefit of my family, who wish me to record the family history.

The first of these was the birth of my third child in 1957, a son at the *Ospedale Salvator Mundi* in Rome.

Tour of Italy to Re-register my Car

The second was the purchase of our first car since we married. This car was a **Morris Oxford**, complete with UK registration plates (**MGC 326**).

Cars with Foreign Registration plates could only remain in Italy for a period not more than six months. The car was purchased from the Morris Dealer in Rome, who also supplied the necessary Carnet providing us with a car for six months only, unless a new Carnet could be issued from outside Italy.

Arrangements had been made with the Automobile Club of Nice, to allow all foreign registered cars in Italy to be reissued with a new Carnet. This meant a very welcome journey to Nice every six months for this purpose. The first two occasions that we made that journey it was a very pleasant experience as it enabled us to drive through North Italy, twice a year from Rome.

The shift pattern which operated for us in Rome covered a four day cycle, of twelve hours each, (two at night, and two day shifts each starting and finishing at 9 o'clock). This pattern allowed us four days off in between turns of duty. This was enough time to take the car to Nice and return, before the next turn of duty was due.

After two such trips we decided to 'nationalise' the car and made the necessary representations to the authorities. We had to pay the import taxes due so that we could be given a Rome number plate. The original number plates were kept, and served us well when we had to return the car to the UK, The car behaved impeccably on the journey back to the UK, and we were able to repatriate this car with very little trouble. This we did by changing the number plates before we loaded the car on the Channel ferry as we still had in our possession the original UK registration document.

The Comet 1 Disaster to GALYP

Enough about these personal episodes, the next had more tragic consequences. I refer to the Comet 1 disaster to GALYP, the registration of the aircraft. This eventually led to the grounding of all aircraft of this type until the Modified Comet 3 and 4 appeared.

I happened to be on duty, on the 10th January 1954, and had both briefed and seen the crew prior to departure. I was subsequently required to make a deposition at the British Embassy in Rome as to the state of mind of the crew immediately prior to their departure. I was able to assure the interrogators that there was nothing untoward in their behaviour, and they all appeared perfectly well.

We were in the habit of flight watching each aircraft out of Rome, until control was transferred to the next control area, which in this case would have been Milan Air Traffic Control.

The last communication received, from the aircraft after departure was something to the effect of:

'Climbing through 20,000 feet at *Orbetello*, switching to Milan Control'.

These may not be the exact words but the meaning of the message was clear.

Two things happened immediately after this.

Firstly the air traffic control centre at Milan reported no contact with the aircraft, but the flight through the Milan area was so short, (in view of the speed of this aircraft), that we could not take any action except to notify the UK.

After this other events happened very quickly and the UK stated that they had been unable to contact the aircraft. It was about this time that the Italian police advised us that a fisherman off the island of *Monte Cristo,* (near the island of *Elba*), had reported an aircraft falling into the sea. From this point the rest of the Comet 1 saga has been fully documented by others, and it is not necessary to repeat this nor dwell on this tragedy.

Flight Control for Comet Aircraft in Rome.

One of our main duties when the Comet operations started through Rome was to provide ground assistance direct to the aircraft prior to their arrival in Rome. Fuel on the Cairo-Rome sector was quite critical, and any doubts about the landing conditions had to be reported to the pilot in flight, before he would descend below 20000 feet.

Coming from Cairo, the time at which a landing decision had to be made, was when the aircraft would be approaching the isle of *Ponza,* and *Naples* to the south of Rome. Any decision to divert to *Elmas* (the airport for Cagliari) in southern Sardinia had to be made before then; otherwise the aircraft would continue its approach to a landing in Rome, regardless of the ongoing weather conditions.

The operation from Cairo would bring the aircraft into the approach to Rome at about 3 to 4 AM. Anyone who knows the weather conditions at Ciampino will readily appreciate that this is about the worst time of the night for fog to engulf the single runway from the end nearest to the river Tiber

The single runway at Ciampino was constructed on a slope, with the approach from one end bringing the aircraft in over the Alban Hills, with *Monte Cavo* as its highest peak on to the runway, landing towards the river Tiber. The other approach would cross the river and land towards the *Alban Hills.* The latter approach was the one used most frequently.

On some days around midnight until dawn, fog would form over the river, and would drift gradually towards the runway, spreading from the lower end of the airfield to the higher part towards the Alban hills.

When this situation threatened we had to take the car and proceed to the high part of the runway to count the number of runway lights, which could be seen from that end of the runway threshold. The term used for this was **RVR,** *(Runway Visual Range*). If ten or more lights could be observed, the approach from the Alban Hills would be recommended: otherwise the landing would have to be aborted.

Sometimes the journey between the Control Tower, (where we were located), and even the drive to the runway threshold would be fog bound, and the runway could not be seen, because visibility would now be about fifty yards or less. Then the fog would clear suddenly and the visibility became crystal clear, with the lights of the villages and towns on the slopes of the Alban hills, twinkling in the darkness.

As stated earlier, the Control Tower was located on the west side of the runway, about midway from the two runway thresholds.

Normally when the fog drifted in from the river, it would only cover about half of the length of the runway but would include the Control Tower.

Thus what appeared to be a blanket cover of fog from the observation post on the control tower, the fog would only affect part of the airfield. Only a runway inspection from the higher end of the runway would determine this situation. In most cases any approach to land from the direction of the Alban hills, would be well within the landing limits, whereas from the other direction, the landing conditions would prohibit this.

Our responsibility was to make our way to the Control Tower after the runway inspection to advise the captain of the situation, together with any recommendations.

Many is the time the aircraft landed safely but had great difficulty in taxi-ing to the Terminal Building as it ran into the fog bank after having landed safely.

Misty conditions at Ciampino were the exception rather than the rule. The visibility would either be good, or extremely foggy. Whether these conditions are applicable today I cannot state. All my visits to Rome in recent years have been via the new airport at *Fiumicino.*

The ILS detective Story

The last incident worth narrating is that of the peculiar behaviour of the *Instrument Landing System* (**ILS**) at Ciampino. This system was the only landing aid available to pilots operating into Rome. The **ILS** facility was available for both approaches to the airfield at Ciampino.

The story, which follows, applies to only one of these two landing aids.

Pilots would arrive in clear conditions, and whilst correctly aligned for the approach to the runway they would test the **ILS**. Each pilot wanted to establish a level of confidence in this facility, in case it had to be used in earnest during inclement weather conditions.

The **ILS** always functioned perfectly for all approaches from the Alban Hills, but was only intermittently successful, when the facility was tested whilst approaching the airport from the city of Rome and the river

During these tests the facility on this approach would be perfect for a while but suddenly for no apparent reason the directional indicator would indicate a sharp swing to the left, even though the pilot could see that he was still correctly aligned.

This intermittent performance meant that the facility could not be used safely until the cause for this deflection could be found.

To establish a cause, we maintained a log of each occasion the pilot would indicate that he was testing the **ILS** facility, and the outcome of this test.

It was pure chance that we came to compare our log with the train schedules into and out of *Ciampino* railway station.

The railway station at *Ciampino* town ran parallel to the runway, but little more than one to two hundred yards to the left of the approach from the direction of the river.

The regular train service would start in Rome and proceed to *Ciampino,* and after a brief stop would continue to the towns and villages on the Alban Hills. The track at the time was electrified with overhead lines.

A comparison of these schedules with the log revealed that nearly all the reported **ILS** failures coincided with the movement of trains on the part of the track arriving or departing from the railway station. Once this was established, and after further tests it became apparent that the cause of the **ILS** deflection was likely to be due to power surges on the overhead lines, whenever a train was in the vicinity of Ciampino.

Once this had been brought to the attention of the Italian Air Force authorities, they came to some agreement with the rail authorities, and the intermittent failures ceased. The Italian Air Force who at that time were responsible for running the operational aspects of this airport also helped to address this problem with the rail authorities.

The responsibilities and tension of my duties greatly added to my character development, and served me well later in my career.

Chapter 4 Moving On . . . Hatton Cross

(Algiers, Accra and 'back-to-Blighty')

My departure from Rome and transfer to Algiers

The day came after five years in Italy to leave Rome. In those days it was the rule that no one on overseas service with the airline should remain at the same station longer than this period of time.

My wife, whose family all now resided in Rome, was saddened at this news but also because her father was not very well at the time. It was therefore decided that no matter where I was to be posted, she would remain for the time being in Rome with our three children.

As it turned out my next posting was to *Algiers,* which at the time was not a very safe place to be for my family. This was in early 1958, when the French forces were in conflict with the FLN of Algeria. The FLN were a group of so-called 'terrorists' (so called by the French on the one hand, yet 'freedom fighters' by the Algerians). These were mainly native Algerians, and normally not of French extraction.

The fight between these two factions around the town of Algiers occurred mainly during the night. The FLN would descend from the hills to the south and infiltrate the towns and villages on the plains between the foothills of the Atlas Mountains and the Mediterranean. Occasionally 'Terrorist' activity took place during the day, with small groups entering the town and tossing hand grenades into the roadside cafes in the main streets of the town. These would be filled with customers of all types, both French and Algerian.

Many of the French population were actually residents of Algeria. The French population who hailed from Metropolitan France, would call these citizens *'Les Pieds Noir'* or when translated into English 'The Black Feet'.

I had to travel to *Algiers* from *Rome* via *Paris.* The journey from *Paris to Algiers* was in a **Breguet** type aircraft. This was a monster of a plane for its time and accommodated around two hundred passengers on two decks. It was designed and built by France solely for the mass transportation of its overseas population from various parts of Africa, to and from the French mainland. It not only had a relatively short range, but also was not pressurised. Not a graceful aircraft it was nevertheless very effective for its purpose.

Though long and uncomfortable the journey itself was unremarkable. This aircraft is not the speediest in the Air France fleet.

London had placed me in charge of this station, and had reporting to me sometimes two ground engineers, and one catering officer on temporary assignment, plus one other person to assist in the ground handling duties.

This was a temporary posting of about six months duration, while the airfield in Tripoli, (***Wheelus Field***) a US air force base, was to be transformed from a military to a civilian airport and the runway extended to make it suitable for the larger type of aircraft, which would be flying between the UK and West Africa.

'Wheelus Field' had taken over the functions of the erstwhile Castel Benito airport, which up to now had served the town of Tripoli in Libya.

Algiers was to be only a technical stop. It would be used when the weather conditions at either destination were marginal and high loads prevented the uplift of sufficient fuel to operate from Kano in Northern Nigeria, to the UK direct. Barcelona in Spain could also be used as an alternative halt.

The main handling agency for these operations was to be Air France. They would be responsible for providing the bulk of the engineering and passenger facilities for these operations. Air France would also provide us with the necessary funds during our stay, and arrange any accommodation we needed. Accommodation was hard to obtain, due to the large number of French forces and their dependents sent to Algiers to control or combat the opposing forces.

For the first few weeks we had to move frequently from hotel to hotel, some of which were well outside the town itself. During this period we had to live out of suitcases, and take our meals wherever we could. The daily meal allowance had been set absurdly low, and much lower than that we would have to provide to any crew who may have had to overnight. After suitable protestations, we were put on a par with the crew meal rates, and were able to use the better eating establishments.

All the operations, for which we had to standby, were in the very early hours of the morning. A curfew existed in the area outside the town of Algiers itself. After dark we could not move from the town to the airport without a special escort.

The airport *Maison Blanche* (**The White House**) was about a 25-minute fast car ride from the town in the direction of the foothills to the Atlas Mountains. At night this area was a danger zone, with the FLN frequently infiltrating down to the main highway to await the passing of military convoys, which they would attack.

All movements down this highway at night were strictly controlled. The driver of any vehicle allowed to operate this route, had to carry a blue flashing light placed on the roof of the car. Each journey would require us to report in at each check point en route. There were many such checkpoints between the town and the airport.

Failure to report would cause the army to come out in force to search for us.

The above procedure would be carried out nightly, however the curfew rules would only apply to our return journey on the way back from the airport. Air France provided us with the necessary transport together with a driver for the trip in both directions.

Once at the airport, we would await the first notification of the departure of our aircraft from Kano. Once airborne the pilot would indicate his destination as early as possible to allow us time to return to Algiers.

Frequently the destination of Barcelona/UK could not be confirmed until about two hours after departure, and the weather and fuel situation had been recalculated in flight. Only when the pilot confirmed that he would be overflying were we able to stand down and return home.

Any early return would always involve us in the checkpoint routines outlined earlier as this would involve the return to our hotel within the curfew limits. Air France made the special arrangements with the authorities to allow us an unhindered return to our hotels.

When the aircraft had to land for refuelling, then the whole night would be spent at the airport, and the curfew by then would have been lifted and return to our Hotel would be normal.

For the first few weeks we were intermittently accommodated at the Hotel Albert in the centre of Algiers, close to the war memorial, and the Government offices. After this period had elapsed, our long-term accommodation at this hotel was confirmed and we all stayed there until the station was closed. My room was on the fourth floor overlooking the road which led to the square and war memorial. This is of some significance later on during our stay.

As I was in charge of operations: my greatest fear was that one-day we would have to cope with an enforced stopover, as there would be no accommodation for the passengers.

This did happen once for an emergency repair and caused considerable upset, as the only accommodation available was only sufficient for the operating crew. If they had not rested, the whole operation (after the repair) could not continue. This was due to the flight time restrictions imposed on flight crews by National Governments, to ensure the safety of all civil air operations worldwide by providing sufficient rest.

The time was early summer, and fortunately the weather was fine. Having explained the situation to the passengers, they were most co-operative. Arrangements were made to feed them at the main hotel, after which they were taken to the main beach to await the completion of the repair, and their return to the airport. The whole stay was over ten hours, during which time we were all totally occupied with the wellbeing of these passengers.

Apart from the minimum arrangements, Air France did not assist us greatly, providing only the financial resources and transport necessary to meet the needs of this emergency. At no time did they provide any ground staff resources especially since station was not equipped to handle such emergencies by foreign operators.

Don Hill

The Start of the 5th Republic of France

During our stay at the Hotel Albert, it was usual for the square around the war memorial, and just below the hotel, to resound to the blare of military music, for one or other of the military occasions frequently celebrated by the military forces of France.

This was a regular feature to which we became accustomed. However on one particular day while in the hotel, we heard unusual noises outside, and on going out onto the balcony we could see a restless crowd gathering around the square.

While the music was playing a noted and very popular French general appeared in a motorcade from the opposite end to where the hotel was located. His arrival caused a great deal of enthusiasm from the crowd who surged forward, and surrounded this motorcade.

We were too far away to hear what was being said. The end result was that the crowd, which by now had grown considerably, rushed up the steps behind the war memorial, and started to occupy the nearby government offices.

The military forces around for the celebration, instead of stopping this riotous activity participated in the overthrow of the current regime in Algiers. The next stage of this takeover was what appeared to be whole French population of Algiers showing their happiness, by driving into this area sounding their horns just as they did when they recently won the World Cup at football

I have on film, a short excerpt of this occasion in 1958.

My first task was to get to the British Consulate, to notify London to stop all flights until advised that the situation had normalised. The journey on foot to the Consulate was hazardous, but there was no way we could reach the airport to use the Air France facilities. The British Consulate's private communications links had to be used to notify home base about the situation.

Some parts of the Army continued to remain faithful to their oath of allegiance to the old regime. These had to be forcibly evicted from the Post Office, radio station, and other important parts of the town. The port facilities were also taken over by the new forces.

After the initial euphoria the situation remained tense for about three days. Reports came in that forces loyal to the old regime were moving in from outlying districts, to restore order. This could have caused a serious confrontation leading to what would become civil war.

The uprising in Algiers quickly switched to the mainland in France, and General De Gaulle became the rallying point for what had started as a local insurrection in Algeria.

map_of_french_wine_regions.gif (600×680)

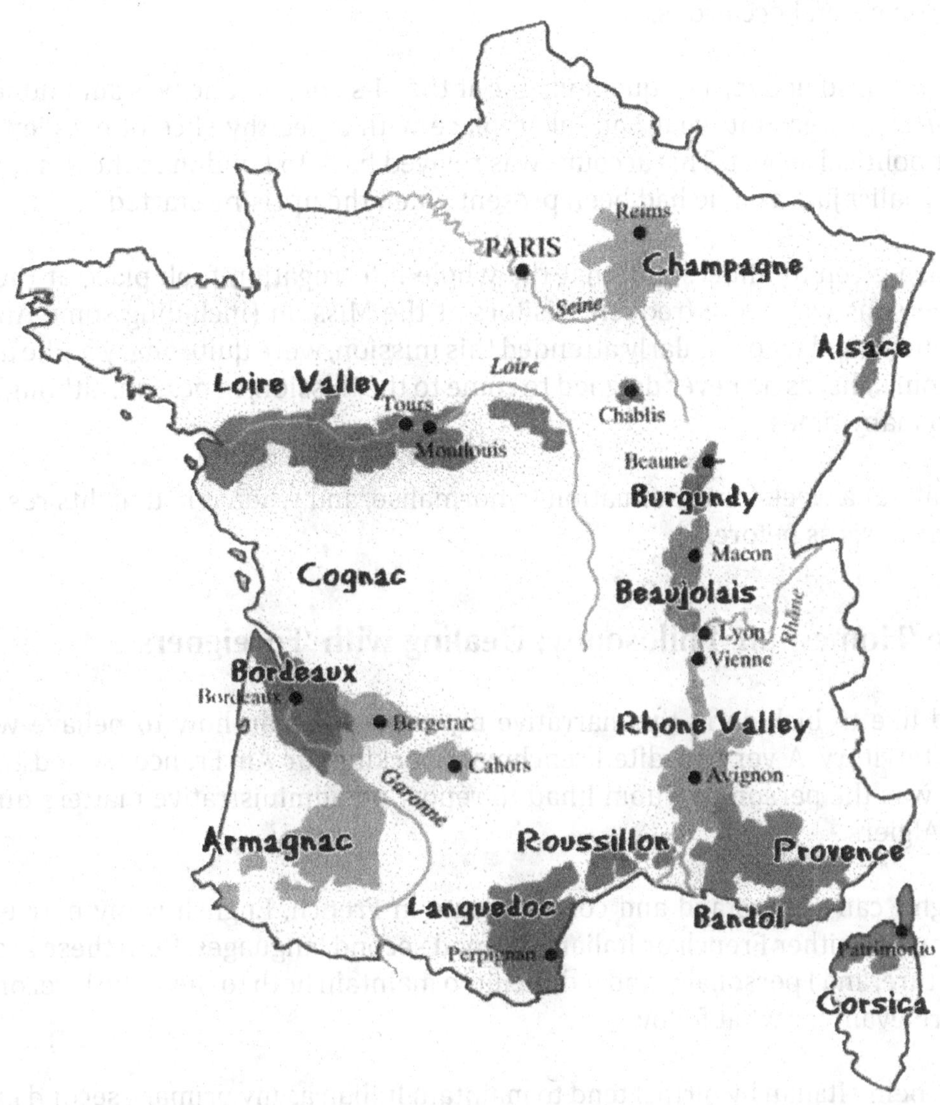

The local insurrection now became the way forward and the birth of the new Republic.

'***The old order changeth yielding place to new***...' and from that time on the 5th Republic was born and lives on to this day.

It so happens that a few days later General De Gaulle, and his faithful generals visited the war memorial where the uprising had started. From my prime position on the balcony of the hotel, I could see him in his motorcade directly below me. Security was very lax, and no attempt made to prevent us from standing on this hotel balcony.

It is interesting to note that during this uprising certain journalists from the UK appeared and reported back on the uprising. To do so they had obtained their information from the British residents in Algiers at the time and would not condescend to meet them at the '*Seaman's Mission*', located close to the Port of Algiers. This mission was the regular meeting place for all the British residents including the British Consul who attended in person, on several occasions.

I gather from someone, a frequent visitor at the Mission, that he was summoned to the *Hotel Aletti*, to recount what had taken place with a healthy slice of his views on the current political aspect. This account was relayed back to London in the first person by this journalist just as if he had been present when the uprising started.

I was also given to understand that the whole interrogation took place at the bar. All those persons who were frequent visitors at the Mission (including some Anglophile Frenchmen), and who regularly attended this mission, were quite angry at the aloofness of this journalist as he never deigned to come to the mission, in person, although invited to do so many times.

It took about a week for the situation to normalise, and when it had flights resumed on the same basis as before.

A little 'Homespun' Philosophy: Dealing with 'Foreigners'

I would like to include in this narrative my experience on how to behave whilst on French territory. A very erudite Frenchman working for Air France passed this on to me. He was the person to whom I had to report on administrative matters during my stay in Algiers.

Although I can understand and communicate in French, English is my native tongue. With practice either French or Italian are good second languages. Both these are similar in structure, and I personally find it difficult to maintain both to the same level of fluency. This is relevant for what follows.

My wife being Italian by birth, I tend to maintain Italian as my primary second language, so that when I speak or listen to Italian, I think in that language and do not need to translate mentally into English. For me to convert from Italian to French takes about three months, until then Italian continues to dominate as the second language.

After about three months in Algiers, I struggled to make myself clear to this French gentleman. Up to now all my dealings with him had been in halting French, undergoing translation mentally from English.

On this particular day, I was unable to explain myself clearly in French, because the subject was complex and technical in nature. This gentleman stopped me and spoke back in impeccable English. When I remonstrated with him on this point, his reply gave me food for thought. This I want to share with any reader of this book particularly those who go abroad on business, and expect the world to communicate with them in English.

(I exclude tourists from any criticism that follows as they are only in that country for a short stay).

When I asked why I was allowed to struggle with my French for so long, his reply was:

'When I am in your country I always use your language to communicate with the local population. It is only right therefore, that when you are in my country you should communicate in my Language.'

Of course he was right, and I had to apologise and thank him for helping me out. I continued to converse with him in French, and as time passed, my French improved to the temporary detriment of my Italian. French took over as my first foreign language for the remainder of my stay in Algiers.

I believe this (psychological) difficulty arises only when both languages have a similar grammatical structure, and that those who speak both French and German do not have the same problem. As I do not speak German this can only be a theory to be tested appropriately.

I pass this on to those in the commercial world who expect to do business abroad.

I had a similar experience, but in a slightly different form, earlier in my career when I was in Augusta. ***Prince Feisal*** of Saudi Arabia and his entourage were in transit on one of the Flying Boats bound for the UK. This would have been around the year 1944-1945.

As a mere underling, I was not allowed to speak to the Prince directly, but only through an interpreter. On this particular day I asked the interpreter to advise the Prince about something, (the exact nature of which I forget), and when this was translated to the Prince he took his interpreter to task in the most perfect English. He told him exactly what I had said, and not the version passed to him by his aide.

The above is a salutary lesson, that whatever is said in one's mother tongue to a 'foreigner', should never be offensive to the listener, as there is every possibility that your remarks are being understood and may cause offence.

This lesson also applies in reverse, and can be used to good effect when dealing with persons whose mother tongue is not English.

Many are the occasions when dealing commercially with visitors from other companies, knowledge of their language (without making this known), at the start of negotiations is potentially useful. One can listen to any 'cross talk' between the delegates, as well to judge their reaction to what has been said, before the 'official line' is put forward.

My departure from Algiers and Secondment to Ghana Airways

The time arrived when the repairs to the airfield at **Wheelus Field**, near Tripoli in Libya, were complete, and the technical stop in Algiers was no longer necessary.

The route to West Africa was flown by *Stratocruisers,* which had been taken off the North Atlantic route. The Stratocruiser was built by the Boeing aircraft company, and operated to West Africa in an 'all first class' configuration.

The aircraft was not at its most efficient on this route, due to the high ambient temperatures encountered during landing and takeoff and this in itself led to a significant reduction in payload.

One by one, the staff under me at Algiers had departed back to base, until I was left alone to formally shut down our BOAC operations in Algiers. This shutdown required me to carry out an inventory of all BOAC assets, including Catering and Engineering equipment, and arrange transportation back to Tripoli.

In order for this to be done, London (at my suggestion) agreed that we should charter an Air France aircraft based in Algiers, to carry this load to Tripoli rather than send an empty aircraft from the UK for a short journey from Algiers to Tripoli.

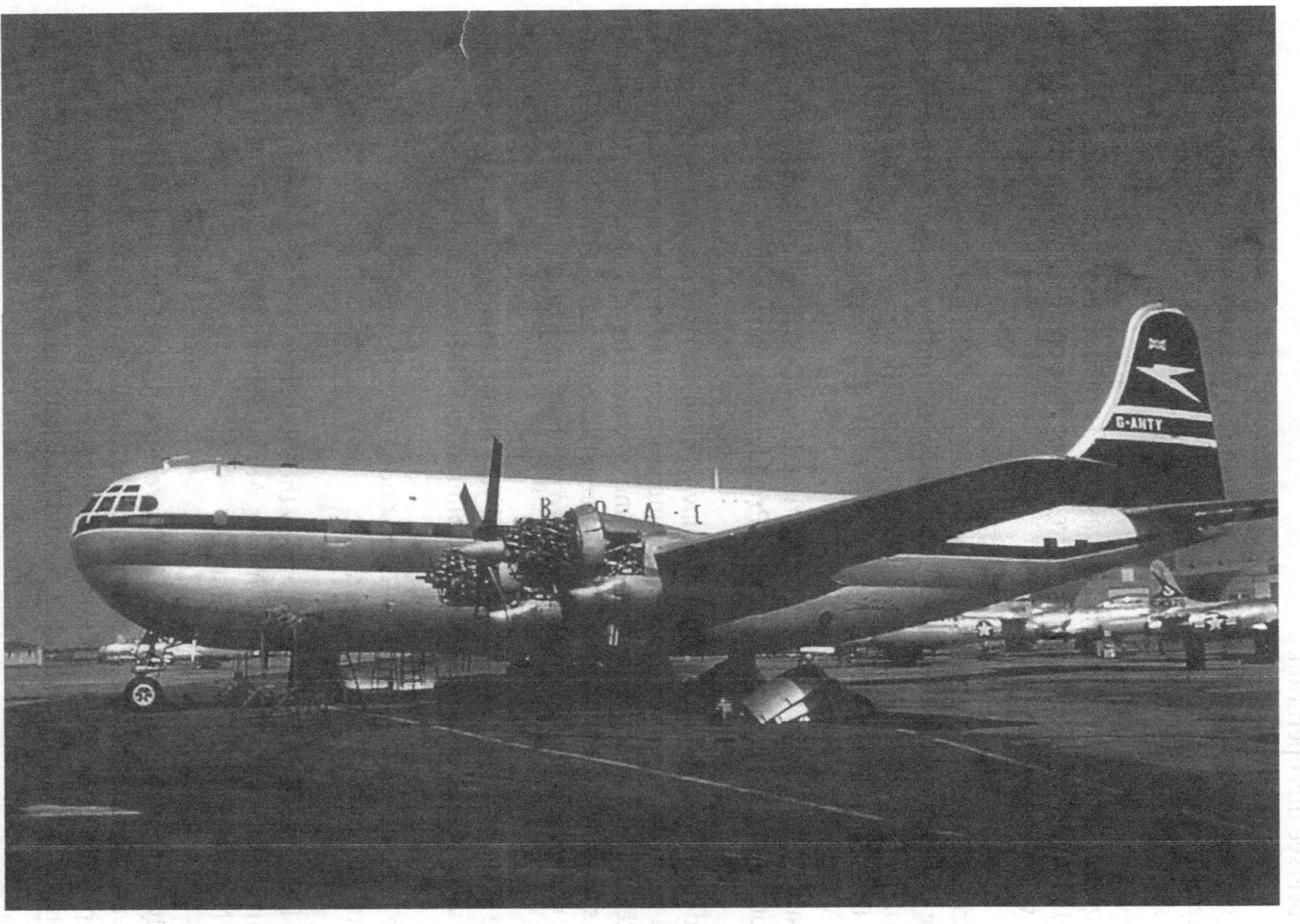

Boeing Stratocruiser BOAC Stratocruiser (G ANTY: engine farings stripped for engineering work (photo courtesy of Mel Lawrence)

The charter costs agreed with Air France were far less than the operating cost of a suitable aircraft from the UK. Air France also agreed that they would undertake the loading of this charter aircraft, so none of the Engineering staff needed to remain in Algiers to oversee this operation.

Once the charter had been loaded and left for Tripoli, I was able to return to the UK, via Paris. I travelled in an Air France *Lockheed Constellation* as far as Paris, and then by BEA *Viscoun*t to London.

When I reported back to Head Office, I was advised to take some leave, which I duly did as my family were still in Rome. They had remained there whilst I was away in Algiers and now I was able to rejoin them.

While in London, I was also advised that I would be seconded to Ghana Airways **to join a number of other expatriates from BOAC**, all of whom were also on secondment. The head of the BOAC detachment was an ex BOAC captain who was soon to become the Managing Director of Ghana Airways.

The formation of Ghana Airways, an Airline that did not exist before the arrival of the BOAC seconded staff, was set up during the Presidency of *Nkrumah.*

This President of Ghana was an Anglophobe, having been imprisoned by the British during the period when Ghana was the Gold Coast, and still a colony within the British Empire. His Minister of Transport, a person by the name of *Krobo Edusei*, ('He of the Golden Bed fame'), was the minister to whom the BOAC delegation reported via the Chairman of the Airline, a gentleman by the name of *James Mercer*, also a true Ghanaian.

The whole 'Nkrumah' regime at the time had very leftist leanings, but they were quite prepared, nonetheless, to use the expertise offered by BOAC, to set up this new airline.

After leave in Rome, my family and I left for London, then on to Accra, the capital city of Ghana, to take up my new appointment.

On arrival I was interviewed at the airport by the local press, and questioned about my brief, regarding the future of Ghana Airways. My comments were published the next day in the National English paper of Ghana.

Fortunately although taken by surprise at my reception, I had not said anything out of place so peace reigned. The rest of the same paper was filled with hate articles about the British Imperialists draining Ghana dry, and extracting all its wealth for its purposes, and that one day soon British blood . . . 'would flow in the gutters of Accra'.

I later had occasion to question the selfsame reporter who had met me on arrival, about the contents of the newspaper articles. His answer was that he only printed articles to represent the views held by the readership of the paper and the government he served. He asked me to ignore the tenor of these articles, as they were not truly representative of the views of the educated masses in Ghana as my later association with these people proved him right.

During my whole stay in Ghana, no one showed or demonstrated any animosity to my family or myself. In fact I worked in close harmony with all the Ghanaians I met during my stay, including the Chairman of Ghana Airways, James Mercer.

I was astonished to discover when I started work that although Ghana Airways was a recognised airline, it operated no planes of its own. Aircraft belonging to West African Airways flew the few daily flights which did operate a service.

Until the independence of Ghana, **West African Airways**, based in *Lagos* was the dominant airline serving that part of West Africa. It appeared to operate on behalf of the British Government, with the responsibility of meeting the needs of all the countries in that part of Africa.

Ghana Airways had formed a Ground Handling agency at Accra, and had the rights at the airport to handle all flights except **Pan American Airways**. I reported to a station manager also from BOAC, and as the Senior Station Officer was responsible for all the ground handling staff and ground operations.

The Ghanaian staff reporting to me consisted of about twenty five persons, from senior officers, receptionists and loading staff. My brief was also to set up a cargo operation in Ghana.

Work at Accra usually started at about 6am and apart from a short break around lunchtime, would be complete once the last local operation (inbound) had taken place just before dark.

Once the staff had been re-organised into shifts, and the seniority and pay structure of the more senior members had been established, I was able to reduce my evening commitment to leave the late shift, to cope with the arrival and dispersal of passengers from the late arrivals.

The main part of my brief from BOAC was to ensure that the local staff met the BOAC handling standards, before BOAC would hand over the handling of its aircraft to this newly formed ground-handling agency.

During the period of my tenure of about six months, Ghana Airways grew from about four daily flights (using West African Airways aircraft), into an airline operating around fourteen daily flights, but now with its own aircraft (which were mainly DC 3 *Dakotas*, and De Havilland *Rapides.*)

All the daily flights had a consistently high load factor. This varied between 85% and 100% in both directions. A considerable amount of cargo was also carried, both local and international.

GHANA – regional locations

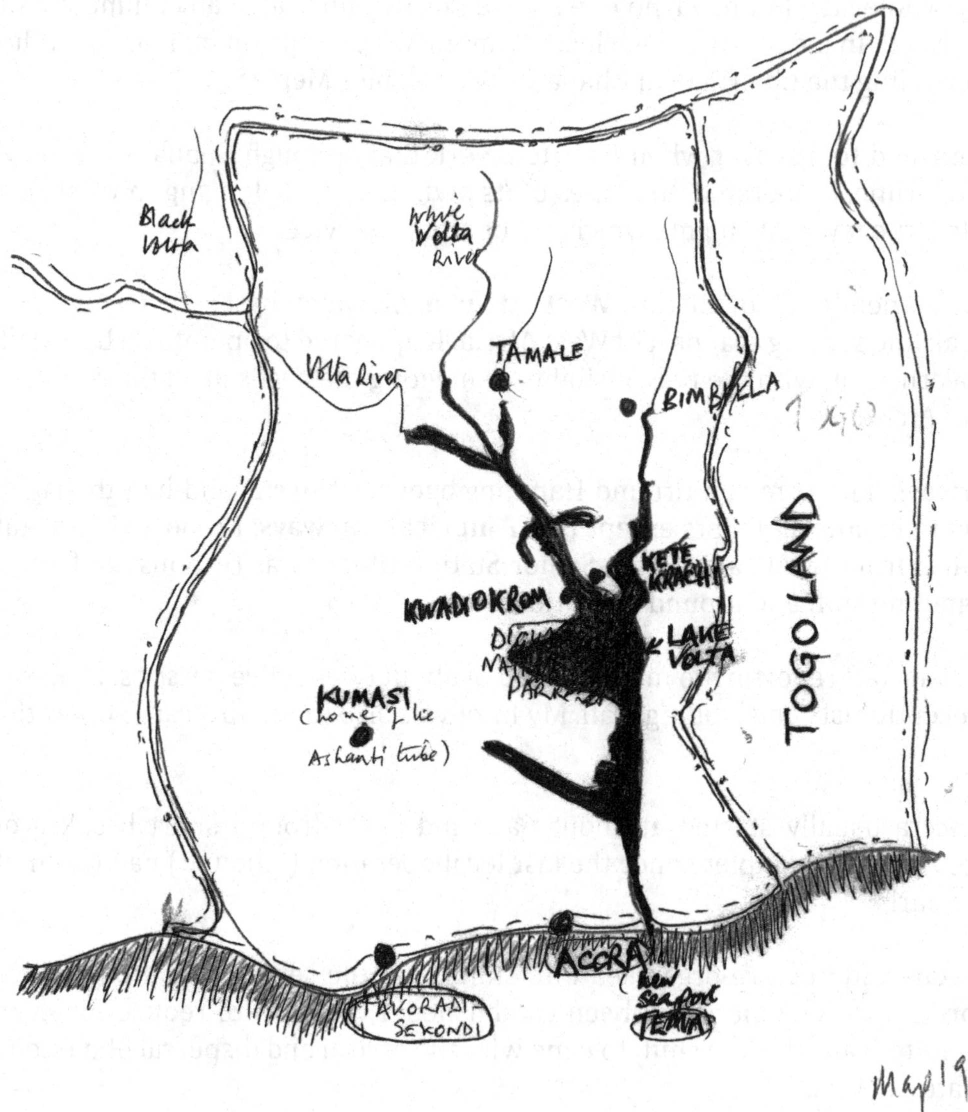

Western Region of Beckwai District – an export source of BAUXITE* (an Aluminium ore)

*Bauxite is a mixture of Iron & Aluminium, and oxides and hydroxides.

map of Ghana – File: map19 ghana tribal and trade centres

The schedules introduced, covered the main cities in Ghana such as *Kumasi,* the capital of the Ashanti tribe, and *Takoradi* the main seaport of Ghana at the time, and *Tamale* much further inland and to the North of Lake Volta. The seaport at *Tema* had not yet been completed but when complete would serve the capital Accra, and was to be situated about ten miles to the east of the city in the direction of Togoland. Around Lake Volta and the Volta River, there was a plentiful supply of the mineral Bauxite. This was needed for the manufacture of Aluminium, and this new seaport would facilitate in the export of this mineral in large quantities around the world.

Although Ghana had gained its independence as a Colony, there were still a considerable number of British and European expatriates living in Ghana, both in Accra, and also in the towns mentioned above. All the expatriates residing in Ghana had very frequent home leave.

The once a day BOAC aircraft, would disembark its passengers on arrival, many of which would want to travel on the day of arrival to the above towns. Transient accommodation at the airport was very restricted and of poor quality. Passengers connecting with the local flights did not want to overnight in Accra. Similarly those arriving in Accra from the outlying districts expected to depart for the UK on the day of their arrival in Accra. This dictated the schedules for the local flights: both outward bound from Accra and inbound to Accra times were to serve the daily UK flight.

Initially the BOAC aircraft were Boeing *Stratocruisers*, but later before I left, these were replaced by the prop jet *Britannia 102*. This was the short haul version with limited operating range. The Britannia 312, with the longer range was reserved by BOAC for the North Atlantic route. A *'prop-jet'*, (or more properly, a propeller jet), is a jet engine that uses some of the thrust generated (passing through rear turbines) to power the forward mounted propellers.

A Ghanaian Interlude

In the six months in which I was in Ghana, five episodes are worth recording.

These are:

—the attitude to life of some Ghanaians;

—my experience with the Unions in Ghana;

—the search for an Engine;

—the Death of a BOAC Pilot;

—my final departure from Ghana.

Each of the above warrants a separate description.

a)The attitude to life by some Ghanaians.

I was at home with my family, when I was advised that one of my senior local staff had been pulled out of the sea by one of his colleagues. He had attempted suicide and had very nearly drowned.

When he had been discharged from hospital, and returned to work, I questioned him about the reason for his suicide attempt. His response to my enquiry really shocked me.

It seems that all his family and relatives, had contributed to his schooling costs, and thus by local custom once employed, he had a duty to maintain from his earnings, both his family and the relatives who had contributed towards his schooling.

It would appear to be a local custom at this time in Ghana, that family groups would select a youngster from among them who could benefit from a good education and would pool resources to get this person through his schooldays.

While he was earning a pittance there was no demand on him, but once he had improved his station in life, they would demand that he should meet his obligations towards them. This burden on him became so great that he could see no way out except to commit suicide.

I asked my senior Ghanaian officer, and a close friend of the Minister of Transport, to talk to this man's parents and relatives to explain this man's dilemma. They agreed to limit their demands on him. He became a very loyal member of my staff from then on.

b) My Experience with the Trade Unions in Ghana.

When I arrived in Ghana, the 'trades-unions' at the airport were very powerful, mainly through the efforts of one person. Although very educated he had been ignored in all promotions because he was regarded as a troublemaker.

After a long talk with him, and establishing the cause of his grievance, he was appointed to a senior position with the airline which he merited. From that day on, all union problems stopped, and he fought my battles for me. Peace and harmony reigned for the remaining four months of my stay in Ghana.

This man became a very able member of the Ghanaian senior staff on my establishment, and provided much help in my brief to make Ghana Airways staff self-supporting. He never let me down so I must have made the correct decision.

There must be a moral to this story.

I guess the old motto with a new spin seems the most appropriate:

'If you can't beat them, get them to join you'

c)The Search for an Engine

In the early days of my stay in Ghana, *Stratocruiser* type aircraft served the station.

These aircraft would arrive from London in the morning and leave in the early afternoon to return to the UK, the same day.

On this day the aircraft duly left, but after about twenty minutes the control tower notified us of an emergency informing us that the aircraft had lost an engine shortly after takeoff and was returning to Accra immediately.

Now the expression ***'lost an engine',*** in aviation terms usually means that one of the engines had been shut down, and the aircraft was returning on the remaining three engines.

In this case the aircraft had truly lost an engine! It had really come apart and fallen somewhere in Ghana, while still climbing to an operational altitude.

The aircraft on its return landed safely, but the area around the missing engine was smoking and fluid of some sort was dripping on to the tarmac. While a full emergency evacuation of passengers was taking place, the local airport fire services were dowsing the engine area with extinguisher fluid to prevent the high-octane fuel from catching alight.

Incidentally the aircraft was also carrying a large consignment of *gold bullion worth many hundreds of thousands of pounds.*

The staff on the ground without hesitation, and without permission, from either the fire services or *myself,* went directly to the aircraft hold to offload this gold, and return its to the Airport strong room.

My concern was that in the confusion of the moment, some of this gold could easily have been taken. Instead every ingot was safely accounted for when checked later in the strong room.

This tale goes to show that in most cases people are honest, and should be trusted.

This is only part of the story. The next day, London requested that we should try to locate the engine, and if found return it to the UK so that engineers at base could identify the cause as to why this engine had separated from the aircraft during its take off climb

The request was so urgent, that all means of communication was used including the local press,(offering a reward to members of the public), if they could help find this engine.

I well recall one Sunday afternoon about a fortnight later, while everybody else in the compound were away at remote beaches, that one of my staff came to see me at home and stated that a teacher from a remote village had come to him at the airport indicating that he had discovered the whereabouts of the missing engine.

The engine was some thirty miles inland from Accra, and that it was located in rough countryside away from any natural road.

I asked the member of my staff to gather up about five of his staff,(plus two engineers), find a suitable lorry to transport the engine back, and meet me at my house in the compound near the airport. The time was around one o'clock in the afternoon, just after lunch.

At the time we drove a *Peugeot 402,* so my wife and children (three in all) and myself set off in this car in calm pursuit of an engine, following the lorry. The village teacher was in the lorry directing us to the scene.

After about thirty minutes travelling on a reasonable road surface we left the marked route and proceeded across country. The surface was not ideal for a private car, but fortunately this was not the rainy season, and the going was over dry brush, and earth.

Along the way we passed many villages, at each of which we were obliged to stop and ask the chief of that village for his permission to pass through. This we did, village upon village . . .

As a reward was being offered for the return of the lost engine each village *en route* gave us permission provided we could take ten of their active young men to assist!

When we finally arrived at the spot where the engine rested, we had two vehicles, and about forty more men than when we started. We only needed about ten able bodied men to lift the engine by hand, all the rest were superfluous to our needs, but still had to be paid for their trouble. The surplus men were merely onlookers. Normally spectators have to pay for viewing, but in this case ***we had to pay the spectators*** *to view the operation . . .*

There is little more to be said about this other than the engine was safely returned to the airport and all the supporters and workers duly paid and dropped off at their villages along the way. By the time we finally returned home it was late evening and we had passed an adventurous day out in the wilds of West Africa, well off the beaten track having successfully gained our quarry.

The Managing Director, to whom I reported on my return, congratulated me on the action taken, but was a little concerned at the recovery cost, until the reason was fully explained.

Shortly after this incident, the short range *Britannia 102* replaced the *Stratocruiser* aircraft clearly not the ideal aircraft for this West African route.

The Britannia for the first time offered a two class service, whereas previously this route was served by an *'all first class'* configuration. This is yet another element of the West African saga.

d) The death of a BOAC Pilot.

The *Britannia 102* started operation to Accra during the mid-part of my stay in Ghana.

The two class configuration was highly acclaimed by the local expatriates when taking their leave in the UK. The reason for this was that their overseas contracts entitled them to first class travel in both directions, whenever they went on holiday which they were able to do for up to between six and eight weeks a year.

Many of these so called 'ex-pats' arranged to make their own travel arrangements, they would obtain the cash for their travel and would use this to purchase economy class tickets. They would then use the cash difference between first and economy class fares, as a supplement to their holiday money.

The above is a slight background digression from the seriousness of what follows.

The *Britannia* services to Accra operated with the arrival, and departure scheduled on the same day. This required a spare crew to be in position for the return flight. The incoming crew, **'by law'**, were not deemed fit to return until they had been sufficiently rested. As this was a daily service between London and Accra, the crew from the previous day's operation would take out the afternoon flight, due out at around three o'clock in the afternoon.

There was a similar but more frequent operation to and from *Lagos* in Nigeria, which is about one hour's flight by DC 3 *'Dakota'* from Accra. This additional frequency in Nigeria required the presence of more than one spare crew. As the extra service out of Lagos was not daily, this meant that on some days, the extra crew was fully rested.

As indicated earlier, passengers for the afternoon departure to London would start gathering in from around ten in the morning with the last arriving just after lunch around one 'clock. As these would come from the remote towns in Ghana, they would be carried in on the Ghana Airways feeder flights.

Accommodation in Ghana was at a premium, and there was insufficient hotel space to accommodate such passengers in the event of a long delay to the long haul flight. An efficient turn around was essential.

On this particular day, at around twelve noon we were about to sit down to lunch at home when a car arrived from the airport, and my senior agent advised me that the Captain due to take out the afternoon aircraft had been taken to hospital and that his condition was serious.

He never recovered fully and was subsequently repatriated to the UK where he died.

The over-riding decision that day was whether to delay the flight, until the inbound captain had been rested sufficiently, or find an alternative solution immediately.

Since delay would have taken the departure into the next day then that day's inbound aircraft would have to carry an extra pilot, to replace the sick pilot who would normally have been rested by then, and ready for a home flight.

The alternative was to try to get the spare pilot, located in *Lagos,* over to Accra in time for the afternoon departure out of Accra.

As it happened the afternoon flight out of Accra was fully booked. Tension was mounting.

I made my way to the Control Tower at Accra airport, and with permission from the Air Traffic Control Centre was allowed to communicate directly through the Lagos ATC to the *BOAC Operations Centre,* in Lagos.

Ground to ground communications was unsuitable for what was planned.

Having explained the situation to the BOAC Operations Office, it was proposed that the spare captain in Lagos, by this time fully rested, should come to Accra to take out the three o'clock afternoon flight to London.

However in order to do so, firstly it was necessary to locate, and then ask him if he was ready to take out this flight.

It transpired that he was at the beach in Lagos, and a car had to be taken out to speak to him there. According to the timetable there was scheduled, a West African Airways aircraft due to leave Lagos and crucially arriving in Accra for about two-thirty, half an hour before the return flight was due to leave Accra. It was essential, for this plan to work, that the pilot would agree and that he could get on the West African Airways flight and connect with the outgoing, fully booked UK bound aircraft.

While all this was going on no attempt had been made to stop the passengers at Accra from checking in for the flight.

The pilot was contacted and agreed to fly to Accra.

Meanwhile, all operational decisions for the afternoon flight were agreed with the First Officer and all fuel and flight plan details completed by myself, in agreement with the First Officer.

At 'two thirty in the afternoon' passengers started boarding the flight. At about 'quarter to three'(14.45hrs) the connecting West African DC 3 *Dakota* landed at Accra airport whereupon the Captain stepped off the aircraft parked next to the *Britannia,* brushed down his uniform, signed the necessary documentation, and boarded the UK bound aircraft as principal pilot.

The aircraft started engines, and taxied off blocks at three o'clock exactly. The passengers aboard who were never the wiser at the efforts made to get this aircraft away on time were nevertheless pleased to be returning to the UK on time.

There are not many jobs in this world, where such major decisions are made on the spot, which involve travel over some hundreds of miles, in order to make a plan come together.

The outgoing pilot did report this effort to London, and the effort duly commended.

However, this was nothing to the personal satisfaction of a job well done.

And a story worth telling . . .

e)My Departure from Ghana.

Even my departure from Ghana was not as easy as it appears.

It so happens that it also coincides with the end of my saga of overseas service with BOAC.

The remainder of this narrative is no longer a series of overseas adventures with the airline, but rather in both a Development, and Computer role in the Airline. How this came about is described in the next and final parts of this book.

My departure from Ghana was not so straightforward because I was not asked to leave but felt that I should do so, once the future of all the BOAC secondees except myself (was made known to me before any of the others were aware of their destiny). I was thus placed in an invidious position, not of my own making.

On the morning this all took place, I was preparing to meet the inbound arrival from the UK. I received a summons to proceed immediately to the home of the Chairman of Ghana Airways. The request was a command, which could not be ignored due to the status of the person who had issued it.

When I arrived at the Chairman's home I was offered a seat and Tea, and advised by *Mr James Mercer*, that very shortly all the expatriate staff were to have their contracts terminated, and that I was to be an exception, since he and Ghana Airways wished me to stay on. This put me in somewhat of a quandary, having been made privy to information about the fate of my superiors, before they were aware of this themselves.

This included both the Managing Director and his Deputy.

My immediate reaction to this was to play for time, and left the Chairman with some excuse that I wished to discuss his offer with my wife.

When I returned to the airport, I immediately sent a private telegram to my boss in the UK, explaining what had taken place and that I wished to be replaced.

The offer made by the Chairman, would meant that I would have leave BOAC, and be employed directly by Ghana Airways. My loyalty remained with BOAC and I did not desire to be 'head hunted'.

I discussed this proposal with my senior duty officer, who was also the friend of the Minister of Transport, and asked his advice. He was very fair in his assessment, and indicated that in his opinion, although not happy to see me leave, he suggested that to accept the offer was not in my best interests. Ghana Airways eventually would become totally nationalised and no expatriate staff would remain employed by them. I would have left the umbrella of my BOAC employment, and after about two years would be released back to the UK with no job.

He confirmed the conclusions I had already reached, and could not wait to see the back of Ghana, although my stay had not been unpleasant and fully rewarding from an experience viewpoint. I had finally grown up in the Airline business having played a focal part in the creation of this new Airline.

While waiting for my next posting to get me out of Ghana with my pride intact, I had applied for a Head Office appointment in the Development branch of the Customer Service Department of BOAC. At the time this was the Traffic Department whose chief was a General Manager.

Almost simultaneously and without an interview I was accepted for this post while at the same time I was offered a posting to Cairo as Senior Station Officer. An SSO appointment to such a large and important a station as Cairo, was just short of a Managerial type of appointment.

Egypt at this time was under presidency of *Gamal Abdel Nasser*, another Anglophobe just like *President Nkrumah* of **Ghana.** It seems that my life at this time was dogged by postings to countries which disliked Britain or any persons from that country.

Only a couple of years had passed since the Suez debacle and Britain and Britons were still not 'flavour of the month' in Egypt.

Additionally this was a single person posting and my family would not be allowed to accompany me until social conditions had improved. On the strength of this I decided to take up the UK posting so that we could stay together as a family, even though we had no homebase in the UK to which we could return. This meant that the family would again be separated until suitable accommodation could be found in the UK.

My wife and three children had by this time left Ghana, and had returned to Rome to visit her parents. I joined them on my way back from Ghana, and after a short holiday returned to the UK to take up my new post.

For the first few months I was like a fish out of water. From a big fish in a small sea, I had become a small fish in a very big sea. The constant references to my overseas service irked my new colleagues. Many of these had been overseas and resented my attitude.

It was very difficult to settle into a conventional '9 to 5' job. Initially very little initiative was needed on my part to just coast along without pulling my weight and I could easily have vegetated. My previous experience and energy did not allow this and so I continued to question not only my job but also the tasks required of me . . .

But then this is another story.

The next part of this book shows how my overseas experience and front line duties provided an excellent basis for the 'apogee' of my career and the events, which were to follow.

On reflection in the long term, my contribution in service to the airline from my home base in London was more valuable than all my overseas service 'learning to fly'.

Chapter 5

Back in the 'High Life . . .' (and Higher Service)

Setting up Base in the UK

This part of the book has to be more biographical. The intention is to describe the part BOAC has played in my life and also in the development of the of the post war civil aviation scene.

I believe the part played by the department I joined, and in this also by myself, have contributed significantly, to the respect in which the Airline was held by other world airlines throughout the forties, fifties, sixties, and seventies of the last century.

In many fields BOAC and later British Airways had been regarded by other major airlines as a world leader and innovator. In this context it only required for BOAC to introduce a new feature for this to be quickly adopted by others. Unfortunately today this is no longer the case.

We follow the thread again on my return to London to take up the new appointment at head office. This followed my holiday in Rome.

For the first time in my career I had joined the 'nine to five brigade'. No longer was I at the mercy of aircraft and their schedules. All I had to do was go to the office, do what I was told and think beautiful thoughts.

My future from then on was mine to do with as I wanted. I could either submerge myself in the daytime drudgery, or fight my way to the surface, and on the way move into a brave new world.

I elected to follow the second path.

This is the story of my efforts to extricate myself.

London Airport 1959 Lockheed Constellation

On our return to the UK we had no home to go to. I had made no provision whilst overseas to obtain a home in this country. Whilst overseas the airline had always provided suitable accommodation, and a return home at the age of thirty-seven was never part of my plans for the future.

Additionally our finances when we returned were at rock bottom, and I certainly had not saved enough to put down an advance to obtain any sort of mortgage at all, let alone the level of housing we had enjoyed elsewhere.

Even though at that time house prices were very low compared to today, a good solid semi would cost about three to four and a half thousand pounds sterling. This compares with the same house in a good state of repair worth at the very minimum one hundred and fifty to two hundred and fifty thousand pounds sterling because it is within commuting distance from the airport.

Our first priority then was to find some suitable affordable accommodation and at the lower end of the market. Until then our children could not join us in the UK, as they were comfortably settled in Italy with my wife's family. Long term **'B and B'** was not a fit way to raise three children under the age of twelve. (**B and B** refers to 'Bed and Breakfast' which implies only lodging and only the one meal specified).

The extent of our family unit at the time was just three children. Later the family unit was to be increased by a further son and daughter.

I had started work even though my wife and I were living in 'Bed and Breakfast' and not yet in permanent accommodation. During the day, my wife made the rounds of the local estate agencies, while in the evenings we looked at properties dining out wherever we could afford.

Life was hard and these were stressful times, and in these conditions I found it difficult to adapt to the new way of working, where my days were mapped out for me by others.

I was no longer in control of my life. The tasks given to me were not always to my liking. I suppose I was being tested in these few months for suitability, and adaptability to my new job.

Eventually we found a house, a *'semi'*,(semi-detached),which though not altogether suitable, *was* within our price range, and well within walking distance of my employer; close enough that I needed no transport to get to and from my place of work.

The car we owned in Rome was still garaged in Italy. A new car was out of the question as all our finances were directed towards the purchase of the house.

Eventually we were able to drive the car from Rome to the UK under its original registration,(MGC326). The journey back was uneventful. The first part from Rome to Nice had become second nature due to the need to renew the car's *'carnet'* whilst in Rome. Although introduced in this part of the narrative, this did not take place until a year or more had passed in our new home.

As soon as a mortgage had been arranged, and our offer for the house accepted, we arranged for our children to join us in London. Even so we all lived in **'B and B'** in Lampton Road near Hounslow central tube for about three weeks, while vacant possession was arranged, and eventually we moved in, *'en famille'.*

I was now able to concentrate fully on my work and my UK working life with BOAC started effectively from this point. As far as I was concerned the first few months at work after my return from overseas service was wasted time.

'The Job'

My appointment in the UK was as the ***Traffic Standards Officer.*** It appears this post was unique, as I was the only person in BOAC with that title.

The responsibilities for the job were partly within BOAC (to ensure that Customer Service standards were set and adhered to), and partly to ensure that standards set by **IATA**, (*the International Air Transport Association*), were introduced as required into the airline working reference.

IATA was and still is to this day the organisation, which sets out the standards by which most of the World's airlines have to comply. Its purpose is to lay down the rules that govern the operation of aircraft and ground handling procedures worldwide. It is not a government organisation, but responds and complies with any edicts issued by **ICAO** *(the International Civil Aviation Organisation)*, a part of the United Nations.

IATA also issues its own rules. These are published in the form of *'Regulations and Recommended Practices'*. All member airlines have to comply with these rules.

The Development Group,(within which I worked), comprised firstly my Manager one of whose responsibilities aside from managing the staff, was to interpret and introduce the ordnances issued by **ICAO**. By his attendance at the **ICAO** committee meetings he would attempt to put forward the case *for* the airlines within this government framework. His role then was to attempt to modulate and amend the bald edicts issued, *to* the advantage of BOAC and other member airlines. Hence he was an active member of *the Facilitation Group* sub-committee, charged with the long term task of the *simplification* of cross border travel.

The second person in our group was responsible for the introduction of **IATA** procedures into BOAC; whilst mine was to promote purely BOAC rules within the above two functions.

To this end this second member of our team had to prove, and have approved, new standards, and produce these in written form for distribution to, and compliance of, all stations worldwide.

A fourth person also had links with this group. He was responsible for the introduction of new aircraft, and to provide suitable equipment both inside the aircraft and on the ground to allow such aircraft to be handled wherever in the world this aircraft was to operate. This meant developing and ordering new devices *prior* to the introduction of such aircraft.

This was the period of time when straight winged aircraft were giving way to those with swept back wings,. The introduction to the civil aviation scene of jet aircraft, involved changes to the wing format of such aircraft.

In my experience most new aircraft cannot be automatically introduced into service. Even today, all the worlds' airports have boarding and loading devices, which have to be assessed against the design criteria of these aircraft. The same applies to existing ground equipment.

The change from *piston to jet aircraft presented a whole new set of problems,* mainly due to the new loading heights, and accessibility to the rearmost cargo holds, due mainly to the sweep of the rear wing sections.

In the immediate post war years, ground-handling agencies were the exception rather than the rule. The introduction of a new aircraft required the stations through which the aircraft would pass to be equipped by the airline with suitable equipment. This was a costly and uneconomic feature of airline operations in that period. In many cases the equipment belonged to the airline, not the station authorities.

The title held by this fourth person responsible for this whole aspect of the airline operation, both in London and overseas was known as the ***GTO,(General Traffic Officer)***. His position was senior to that held by this writer as a mere ***TSO, (Traffic Standard Officer).***

This sets the scenario for what is to follow.

Gradually as I became accustomed to my new chair borne role, I was able to outline personal views and in fact encouraged to do so by my manager. These views had to be designed to improve the operation of the Airline, and not mere fanciful unsubstantiated thoughts. For this overseas experience would be drawn upon, and many battles had to be fought to get such views accepted.

London Airport was the dominant station on the BOAC network, and always had first say in any new techniques and procedures. This became an ongoing battle throughout the years, which follow.

The procedures in force at London Airport in 1959 were archaic, and sadly in need of modernisation. The senior operational staff fiercely resisted all efforts for change. I likened the organisation to an amorphous mass, which would change its shape to absorb any new function, without ever applying it. The more one pushed at one end, so the other end increased. In the end the mass never fully changed its overall size.

The station would only pay lip service to any changes directed from outside the Heathrow airport environment,(i.e. international bodies of authority).

Their motto appeared to be:

'Not Invented Here?... *Not very good'* **(a *paraphrase*)**: abbreviated to **'NIH'.**

As new procedure and systems could not be changed from outside, I was seconded by my boss to the Airport so that suggestions for change were made from inside that organisation, and therefore more likely to be acceptable to the 'powers that be' that appeared to rule BOAC at Heathrow.

Fortunately the two most senior managers at the airport were those I had met while on overseas duty. They also recognised these difficulties and agreed this appointment within the organisation. My brief was to report directly to them and not to any one below their level.

It was the lower level of management who felt most threatened by new ideas, and therefore showed more inertia to change.

When seconded to Heathrow airport, its main operation was still in conjoined huts on the north side of the main 'East-West' runway.

My attachment was to the 'Airport Development Branch' within the airport's infrastructure. As it happens, the manager was the younger brother of ***Alan Mowbray, the Hollywood film star of that era.***

'Alan Mowbray' became a favourite topic in many of our discussions. He still kept in touch with his younger brother, and frequently visited him when on location in the UK. The 'Mowbray family' were of Scottish descent, and George, his younger brother could not wait to return to the land of his birth.

The planning of the new airport buildings in the centre of the runway design was still in the process of development. Unfortunately the site and access to it had already been finalised before, and this was too far advanced to suggest any change. It was necessary to work within the confines of the space allotted for the ground operation.

The airline **BEA** was allotted the 'Terminal 1' and 'Terminal 2' sites, while **BOAC** allocated Terminal 3. My 'brief' was only to affect the procedures and facilities applicable to the 'Terminal 3' site.

At the time, only three Airport Terminal Buildings were planned for the central site: these were to be imaginatively renamed as Terminals 1,2, and 3,(originally terminal 2 was known as the *Europa Building* when completed in 1960 and terminal 3 as the *Oceanic Building*, prior to the opening of terminal 1 in 1969). In addition to these three terminals, a Control Tower, and other administrative office blocks were planned.

One other building was also to be built. It was to separate, (or join, *depending on your viewpoint*) the two Terminals 1, and 2, and was to be the 'centrepiece' of the new central area, and aptly named *the Queen's Building.*

The intercontinental Terminal 3 was to be bounded by two office buildings one on each side of the entrance to the terminal. All the BOAC administrative staff was to be accommodated in the North wing offices, and the other wing was leased to foreign airlines, licensed to use this terminal. These were mainly transatlantic, long-haul operators and those which had an affinity with BOAC.

All the European and short haul operators were to be accommodated within the Terminal 1 and 2 buildings. Terminal 2 was designated to provide facilities for BEA to act as a ground-handling organisation, to handle airlines other than BEA. It also allowed for those Airlines such as Air France and KLM, to provide their own handling facilities.

Terminal 1 was allocated for the *exclusive use of BEA*. The Queen's Building, which lay between Terminals 1 and 2, was to provide BEA and the airport authorities with additional office accommodation, in addition to a visitors viewing platform. It also housed the catering and medical facilities for the users of the two adjoining buildings.

The first major decision before the airport was opened was to allow free movement of passengers between Terminal buildings 1 and 2. This would enable passengers transferring between different short haul carriers to walk without hindrance between each building.

Movement between Terminal 3 and the other two buildings was to be by *'airside transfer buses'*. This would allow quick transfer to and from 'short-haul' and 'long-haul' operations.

Some of the expressions used may be incomprehensible to non-airline readers as they consist of 'Airline Speak' but to those initiated in this language, the expressions are quite rich and meaningful.

The term *'airside'* signifies that there are no further Customs or Immigration barriers between themselves and the aircraft,'(not yet having passed through them *'landside'* into the UK from the aircraft on the runway). Because of the nature of their jobs engineering and technical staff routinely by-pass the main checks between 'landside and airside' with their high security passes without queuing through the landside terminals).

The term **short and long haul** is used to differentiate *Inter*-continental, (Long Haul), from the Short -haul of *Intra*—continental travel, (i.e. entirely within Europe.)

At this time the BEA operation was concentrated at *Northolt* airport some seven miles to the north of Heathrow. All passengers transferring between the two airports had to clear the authorities at both airports before they could travel to their final destination.

I moved into offices on the North Side, used by the *Airport Development Manager* to whom I was now attached.

Various committees consisting of both Airport and Airline staff had been set up to finalise the internal workings of the three proposed passenger terminal buildings.

My brief was to attach myself to the *'Terminal Three Committee'*, which I did through the BOAC Station Manager. In effect my role was to replace, and or advise him on these working groups.

The brief was wide ranging, but the full extent of these only took effect after the move from the North Side to the new site had taken place.

Many changes involved the use of new equipment which not only required time to implement but also to win over some of the doubters at middle manager level.

The full extent of the changes will be described in the later parts of this narrative.

Many of the changes were minor in nature and not worth a description. However, even though only minor in nature, these did allow the airline to move more and more into the technological future associated with airline operations.

Members of the London Airport organisation made many of the suggestions, and the fact that these were espoused by me, and introduced stood me in good stead with both the staff and the middle management whom I still had to win over.

The success of these innovations allowed me to be accepted as a true member of the airport 'organisation' (precursor to the BAA which was formed in 1966), and was thus able to introduce other changes at a later date, even after I had returned to my base at Headquarters.

During my secondment I was involved also with the redesign and development of the new Cargo Warehouse at the airport.

For the first time I discovered all the difficulties associated with the reception and despatch of Air Cargo to all parts of the world.

To carry out these duties it was essential to employ the art of *logical analysis* which was needed to solve the problems as they appeared, when planning for the movement of cargo and passengers within the airport and cargo terminals, and between the buildings and the aircraft.

The experience gained from secondment to the London Airport organisation stood me in good stead when two years later the time came to move on, and I was transferred to the *Information Handling Department* (**IHD**) of BOAC, to design and introduce new systems for the Airline.

The cargo flow systems introduced at this time (1959/60) have not changed to this day, only the control, which by now is computer driven, has undergone any change. The same applies to the acceptance and control of passengers at check in.

Don Hill

The Work of the Facilitation Group within BOAC

The *simplification of cross border travel* was also part of the remit of the organisation in which I worked. This enabled the techniques and methodologies of the sixties to have been refined into those current in the era of the 'Schengen' agreement. Those procedures employed. in the early sixties were necessary because restrictions on cross border travel even within Europe were very onerous indeed

The problems were attacked from two directions: the first solution was to minimise '*departure and arrival formalities*' for both passengers and cargo; the second solution was to explore the worldwide passenger equipment market for *anything* that would hasten the speedy movement of passengers(and their baggage) through the Departure Buildings and onto aircraft.

My manager taught me to think backwards to arrive at the correct path to follow. For example before designing the 'innards' of a terminal building, I was to consider the simplest form of boarding and work back from there. I should therefore ask myself the following two questions:

- *Why should passengers travelling by air not have the same facility as passengers travelling by bus or rail?*
- *Why is not possible for a passenger travelling on a flight to turn up at the aircraft side and board the aircraft directly?*
- *(The latter is the ultimate goal in the facilitation of air travel and many airlines have striven to this aim in the past, including Laker Airways as well as 'Go'-British Airways' own version—prior to the 'facilities' offered by the current exponents of this concept).*

Working back from the aircraft, it is possible to think of all the stop points between this second question and the design of the building. The design then must avoid cross flows in passenger movement, and provide sufficient queuing space whenever any checkpoints involve a slow clearance rate.

Provided these rules are applied to each airport around the world, the design for passenger movement within such airports becomes a relatively simple task.

Many such airports are developed in countries, which are slower to espouse the **ICAO** facilitation concepts. In these cases the additional stops and delays had to be taken into consideration during the individual design.

The design still had to be bear in mind that eventually such airports would fall into line with the global facilitation advances. Any structures developed to house these differences should only be designed around their eventual removal.

The acceptance and removal of baggage for loading also plays an important part in such a design. Baggage from acceptance to loading should follow the principles of minimum movement, and in the main, always be accessible when being moved by automatic means.

The easing of cross border travel restrictions initiated by BOAC, has served the new low cost airlines well. When they entered the market, travel restrictions were practically non-existent for the routes along which they operate. They have BOAC to thank for their current profitable operations.

Instead of using BOAC as the whipping boy with the media, they should accept that they would not be in business today, but for the activities in *the fifties and sixties* by BOAC and other major airlines to simplify cross border travel.

By now I was fully integrated into the Head Office role, and beginning to think like a nine to five 'cog', However, I had not lost any flexibility of mind and continued to search for alternative ways of doing things.

With the experience gained from the London Airport secondment I travelled extensively around the world to advise various airport authorities that at the time were replacing old terminals with new ones. I would be sent drawings for inspection and counsel and report back on desirable changes.

In 1962 I was given the post of **General Traffic Officer** replacing the previous incumbent.

Although still directly under my previous manager I had a floating brief, and became a free agent again. This allowed me to develop new thoughts and concepts unhindered by instructions from above.

Strangely enough, during the whole of my overseas life, I had only visited Africa north of the equator, and Europe. In my new appointment and until I eventually retired I travelled around the world, and touched every continent sometimes for a very brief spell, and other times for extended periods.

Committees On Which I Served (*My Life as a 'Cog'*)

a) Baggage Standards

My new post now allowed me a free hand to investigate, identify problems, and provide solutions to the airline's ground handling needs. In addition to these I was to represent the Airline, on two National Committees introduced by the *British Standards Institute*, **(BSI)**.

Meetings of each committee took place about every two or three months in the BSI offices situated just behind Park Lane in London.

The committees to which I was appointed were the development of construction standards for baggage to be carried by air, and the development of Pallets to carry large loads on both Cargo and Passenger aircraft.

The Standard for airline baggage required baggage to be as light as possible, yet strong enough to withstand the heavy handling during the loading and unloading and delivery process. Potential drops of around six feet from aircraft hold, to the ground had to be considered when determining the materials to be used.

The attendance at these committee meetings required the involvement of manufacturers, testers, members of the public, and also experts in the field of materials. It also needed the expertise of airline personnel where such baggage would be handled in anger. I was the only airline person involved with this committee.

Most of the luggage on sale today has been designed around the standards, which emanated from this committee. The **BSI** issued these standards around the mid-sixties allowing their 'Kite Mark '(of approval) to be displayed only on baggage which conformed to the standards set out by this committee.

b) The development of Standards for Pallets to be carried on Civil Aircraft

The development of standards for the loading and unloading of large heavy loads was a more difficult committee on which I served. There was a good deal of infighting before the BOAC suggestions were agreed and became the industry standard.

When first attending this committee, much discussion and agreement had already taken place. The sole airline representative was from BEA,(the short haul airline) at a timee time when larger(long haul) aircraft were being developed (such as the B747 'Jumbo', the DC10, Airbus and others of that ilk).

To load large amounts of baggage and cargo in a normal forty-five minutes transit time, required the development of new ways of preparing bulk-loads in the Cargo warehouses and Baggage assembly points. These would then be delivered in standard bulk units at the aircraft side. Each of these units was then to be introduced to the aircraft as a single item of load weighing, in some instances, up to five tons.

The concepts were already in place but the aircraft types were still not in service. The Ministry of Defence dominated the committee at the time. Their view was based on the way they saw this need, completely ignoring any commercial considerations. The design and needs were based on the concept that such pallets should be strong enough to be self-supporting. This was definitely a military rather than a civilian concept.

The BEA representative in the absence of a stronger presence by more than one airline was overruled, and had reluctantly agreed with the MOD concept, As a result the loading of aircraft such as the Armstrong Whitworth *Argosy* became very time consuming and uneconomic due to the weight penalty of these pallets.

Each pallet was self-supporting, took an eternity to load and tie down. It used bolts and wing nuts to ensure that the pallets when loaded would be part of the aircraft structure.

My boss told me that this was a *No! No! No!* Situation, and that I should 'do a Molotov' at the next meeting to get any previous agreement rescinded.

Civil aircraft could not carry this excess weight around the world. The payload loss would be prohibitive, as well as the time loss in introducing each item of bulk to the aircraft.

When this point was made at the next meeting the general committee agreed (including the BEA representative). Objections were still raised by the military personnel on the committee, who would not accept the views of the civil air representatives; however the airline view prevailed and is valid to this day.

The airline view was that the development of pallet standards would require these never to be hoisted from above. Any lifting would be from a vehicle *supporting* such load, and lifted up to the loading sill of aircraft from a low level. Movement of these pallet loads from vehicle to aircraft and within the aircraft would be by rollers and turntable.

Nets or covers sufficient to prevent in-flight movement, in an upward and down ward direction, need only cover the load on each unit. The base unit would be attached to the aircraft by simple locking devices. This made the design of the base unit much lighter. The weight penalty would be less restrictive on overall payload, whilst maintaining the advantage of fast loading.

From the above **'pallet'** concept the *scissor-lift loading vehicle* was born. The design has since become an international standard for the loading of pallets on to and off aircraft.

The *scissor lift concept* of loading derived from the existing vehicles used to load catering in bulk on to aircraft at a high level to the aircraft Galleys. The design obviously had to be stronger to allow loads up to **ten tons** to be lifted by this means.

This **BSI standard** set for the pallet was agreed and became accepted worldwide and adopted by **IATA**. Special vehicles were designed based on these standards.

Airline manufacturers requested to include attachments to the cargo holds to allow such unit loads to be fully stressed for all in-flight conditions, by simple locking devices,. These were to be an integral part of the aircraft structure.

*There is now a manual produced by **IATA**, which identifies floor, and height dimensions for each design of pallet, and their compatibility with the aircraft types which can carry these. All manufacturers must now conform to these rules, no deviation is allowed.*

The results of these decisions in the early sixties are valid today with no one giving a second thought to the earlier development but which the UK airlines fought hard for before they were finally accepted.

c) Secretary of the Ground Handling Committee within BOAC.

As **GTO**, the other committee on which I had to serve was that set up to manage the provision of equipment needed to handle aircraft, and to develop new equipment as and when required.

Very senior managers in BOAC attended this committee; attendees in the main were persons of *General Manager* Status or just below. The reports emanating from this body, were invariably presented up to the Executive Board, and normally be approved without question. The Executive Board would only get involved *when the cost to the airline exceeded the financial authority of this committee.*

As Secretary to this committee I had to investigate, research and propose solutions to problems raised by this Ground Handling body. All this was dealt with in a formal way, with the minutes of each meeting, being reported at subsequent meetings. Each item in these minutes had to be identified with some member of the committee, usually me, and progress reported at subsequent meetings.

Doing the 'spadework' through attendance at these meetings served me well, as I became known to the gentlemen on this committee, any of whom may have been potentially useful to the furtherance of my career. This will be referred to later.

The committee did not initiate the developments identified below, but the solutions and implementations had to be passed through them for approval.

The next three developments, with which I was connected while in office, were:

> the introduction of **'Self-Service' trolleys** for use by passengers, to transport baggage within airports;
>
> the introduction *of fully stressed* **overhead baggage racks** on aircraft;
>
> and the introduction of **Computers** to assist in the control of Passenger acceptance, and the loading and distribution of load to the aircraft.

(i) Airport Trolleys

The first of these started with a suggestion from a private individual who lived in Prestwick in Scotland. He sent us a design based on a *supermarket trolley*, that he had adapted to allow baggage to be transported around airport terminals by passengers, rather than have them rely on the costly baggage handlers employed by each airport authority.

The design appeared eminently suitable. It was foreseen that the baggage handlers would resist the implementation, as it was the handlers' incomes that would be threatened.

The chances were such that without the cooperation of the airport authorities, these trolleys would be conveniently kept out of sight of those passengers who may wish to use them. In fact travel around the world today, does suggest that at some airports this is still the case.

It was decided that *BOAC* would buy a limited number and introduce these on a trial basis at 'Terminal 3' in London Airport, for use by all, not just BOAC passengers travelling through the terminal. This was a sales *'gimmick*' and each baggage trolley would carry the statement,

'Provided by BOAC
For your Use
FLY BOAC'

These became very popular and have now become another global standard for all airports, but are provided by the authorities and not the airlines. The general design has undergone change and refinements as time passed but the original concept was still a *BOAC first.*

Obviously the Sales *'gimmick'* has disappeared, but other advertisements appear which help to cover the introduction costs. Additionally some main railway stations around the world have also introduced these as an aid to passengers.

(ii) Stressed Overhead Racks on Aircraft.

Until the advent of the VC 10 into service by BOAC, all aircraft had railway style overhead racks running along the aircraft above window height. These consisted of a frame, with a cord mesh in between to allow passengers to store only hats and coats. No other objects were allowed due to the danger of these falling on passengers in turbulent flight conditions. There was no safe method by which heavy items could be secured on these racks.

The inability to load small items of cabin load to these overhead racks meant that seated passengers were required to stow such items under the seats for safety in case of turbulence. Getting in and out of seats in flight was a difficult task not to be undertaken too frequently, unless one was seated in an aisle seat.

As **General Traffic Officer**, my brief was to freewheel my thinking around problems to find suitable solutions.

These briefs required frequent access to the Engineering Development team in BOAC, providing them with thoughts and ideas expressed to them to respond with suitable design drawings.

In the case of the overhead rack problem, my thoughts on this were expressed to one of the design team in that department, a gentleman by the name of *Tony Roberts*.

He promised that he would think about this and hopefully come up with a solution to this problem. At the time he was also working on a similar problem to increase the amount of cargo space on the VC 10, when the aircraft was not fully booked. These holds would have to be fully stressed to avoid endangering passengers seated in front of these mobile fully enclosed holds. They would be fitted in the rear passenger cabin, and conform to the cabin décor,

About ten days later I went to see him in his office. He showed me a design of an overhead rack fully stressed, with doors opening upwards to allow free access by passengers. These doors would be shut prior to departure, and remain shut in flight to allow heavier loads such as cabin baggage and duty free packs to be safely stowed.

The provision of such racks would free the floors around passenger seats from unnecessary clutter, also allowing passengers to utilise fully the space under the seats to stretch their legs.

I discussed this development with my manager who became enthusiastic and passed this on to ***his*** General Manager. Following this it was necessary to obtain the approval of the Commercial Director before he would present this design to the **Executive Board of Directors** of the airline. The installation of this type of rack was an expensive business and could only be set up with Board approval.

A swift agreement was reached within BOAC to apply these to the *VC 10* aircraft, which at this time was the pride of the BOAC fleet. A prototype trial fitting was introduced to one of these aircraft, to ensure that the design could be converted into the real thing, without losing any of the benefits expected from this practical development.

The trial proved very effective and all *VC 10* aircraft were fitted with these overhead racks. Historical Research will show that the *VC10* was the *very first* aircraft to have fully stressed overhead racks, now a n industry standard.

All aircraft these days have variations on these designs, and for the largest aircraft, the design has been augmented with overhead racks for seats located in the centre between the two aisles.

It seems that BOAC is having a very bad press these days, and little acknowledgement is given to the world wide innovations developed by them, and introduced for the betterment of the industry as a whole. Even the ***Aircraft Manufacturers*** *and* ***Airports,*** *who have taken up these developments, fail to recognise where these originated, and take it as a matter of course that they thought of it first.*

(iii),The Road to Computer Usage (and other stories) via

-'Easing of Cross Border Travel Restrictions' *and some Curious Episodes of the Humane Handling and Transport of Animals-(the Monkey story, Topical Fish story and the tale of the King Penguins and many others just so)...*

-Advances to Easing of Cross Border Travel Restrictions

When I first returned from abroad, passengers travelling overseas were subject to many restrictions before they could leave, but also when entering into a country. Among these restrictions was the need for *Entry Visas,* and in some cases *Transit Visas,* in order for passengers to reach their destination. All baggage was inspected, both outgoing and inbound by Customs Officers, including a 'spot check' on the amount of foreign currency being taken in or out of the country.

Passengers arriving into a country had to undergo an inspection of *Vaccination,* and *Inoculation certificates,* and in some cases such as Ghana, even passengers departing were checked that they had the necessary certificates for the countries **over** which they would be flying, but not landing.

These rules perhaps were introduced by some back room official who had perhaps never even flown, and had misinterpreted the actual needs for these checks.

It was at their behest however the airport authorities had to comply with these ludicrous restrictions.

Passengers travelling to *South America* had to obtain clearance for travel by the Embassy of that nation, before these could be added to the passenger list. This entailed a trip to the various *South American Embassies* the day before departure, to present to them a list of passengers complete with details of their *nationality, visa identity, date of birth,* and finally *their addresses* both at *home* and at their *intended destination.*

All this had also to be included on the *passenger manifest* for such flights and *stamped* by the *appropriate embassy authority.* Obviously the airline was required to pay **a tax** to **the embassy** for this clearance.

All passengers to other destinations had to be listed on a passenger manifest, *even if only in transit,* and not '*deplaning*' at these stations.

By the time I left the department to transfer to the **Computer Organisation**, these *restrictions had almost all disappeared* as much through my own efforts as those of others.

Firstly *passenger lists for all flights were abolished*, secondly the *numbe*r of *visas needed* was *reduced to only a few* countries, and in some cases *travel documentation* itself, particularly within Europe, was minimalised.

Although a **passport** remained a desirable requirement, it was not necessary as a permission to cross borders. An *identification document* available at Post Offices would suffice for intra-European travel.

These goals were achieved, but recent events around the world, have caused many of the travel restrictions to be reintroduced but this time for passenger safety reasons.

Handling and Carriage of Animals in a Humane way by Air:

During the period as **General Traffic Officer**, another of my duties was to ensure that no animals were accepted for travel by *BOAC,* unless a recognised veterinary authority had previously approved this.

By this time all aircraft in *BOAC* were either *jet driven*, (flying at heights over

25,000 feet), or *pressurised* and flying at heights which could still affect the health of such animals.

BOAC had retained the services of a recognised **Veterinary Officer**, who would advise on such matters, and in special circumstances, advice would be sought from the *Royal Zoological Society*, based at the Zoological Gardens in London's Regent's Park.

A few episodes in the 'Safe and Humane' carriage of animals by air, spring readily to mind.

Amongst these are the following highlighted here, including: the **carriage of monkeys** story; the c**arriage of Tropical Fish** tail; the anecdote of the **carriage and transport of King Penguins** and many other remarkable instances involving miscellaneous other live species . . .

—Monkey story.

During my period of office, the 'Sabin' Polio vaccine had been developed, to protect children in particular from this dreadful, paralyzing, disease. In order to produce this vaccine, it was necessary to transport a large number of Rhesus monkeys from India, where this species was to be found in abundance.

Although these monkeys were cute they had some nasty habits, the main one was their desire to urinate frequently in flight. Their urine was evil smelling and the smell was difficult to eradicate even after these had disembarked.

The air-conditioning systems on aircraft were all embracing. The same system covered both the passenger cabin, and the cargo holds. Any smells, which were introduced into the holds, would pass through the filters, and spread into the passenger cabin. At first sight this would preclude the carriage of these monkeys on passenger aircraft, unless the smells could be eradicated before this was passed into the passenger cabin. Any hold used for the carriage of such cargo would have to be isolated from other cargo or passenger baggage.

The transport of such cargo was for the benefit of the nation, and a solution to this problem had to be found quickly. At this time there were insufficient all cargo aircraft to meet the demand for the numbers of such animals to be transported.

The first thing was to ensure that the number of monkeys which could be carried was sufficient for the airflow in the compartment in which these were to be flown. Our resident '***vet***' was involved in the research which followed.

Ventilation Engineers in *BOAC* were requested to measure the number of air changes, which took place each minute in the cargo compartments. Special measuring devices were set up to monitor this in flight. Initial findings indicated that the air movement in these compartments was significantly less than that which applied to the passenger cabin.

Armed with this essential data, the veterinary officer would give an estimate of the numbers, which could safely be transported without distress to the animals on a long haul twelve hour flight. Figures were established based on the weight of such animals and the amount of air they would need to breathe comfortably.

The next part of the exercise was to test the carriage of such animals, without affecting the air breathed by passengers in flight. Any smells created in the hold had to be prevented from escaping without affecting the well-being of any of the monkeys.

Various in flight tests were carried out with monkeys but without passengers other than ourselves, to establish the most suitable remedies to this problem. Only once the right sprays and solutions were found, was the carriage of these monkeys allowed to take place.

Later, the demand for these monkeys became so great, that special cargo aircraft were introduced, and the carriage on passenger aircraft became a thing of the past. However, these earlier tests had established the criteria by which the numbers could be calculated. Quite frequently the numbers that were transported on one all cargo aircraft were in excess of eight hundred!

This required the presence of an attendant to watch over their needs in flight, and to make sure that none of them suffered. This was an unenviable but highly paid job.

On the aircraft the monkeys would be stacked high on each side of the aircraft, with a gangway between the stacks. The attendant was required to walk along this gangway at regular intervals.

I was reliably informed that no walk down this gangway would be completed without some of the monkeys urinating on them. After any twelve hour flight the aircraft and the attendant would both stink to high heaven!

The aircraft itself could be swabbed and hosed down with plenty of deodorant and disinfectant, until the odours had all but evaporated. But pity the poor attendant and his family when he returned home.

No wonder the job paid well, but the applications for this task were very few. The same people continued to apply for these runs. Most of them were unmarried . . .

They never fully lost the stench from these monkeys even after numerous baths and showers. Once used on such a journey, the overalls and the clothes they wore could never again be used except for subsequent 'monkey runs', as these became known.

So much for monkeys, even though their carriage to the UK was to benefit not just the nation but the world as a whole.

—Tropical Fish Tail

In the late fifties and early sixties, there was a craze to find tropical fish not only for the National but also for 'home aquaria'.

These fish would be present in places far from the UK shores. Such fish had to be transported from their place of origin to the UK which in some cases was over twenty four hours flight time away.

The fish had to be carried in water temperatures that equated to their natural environment and they had to be maintained at this temperature until delivered to the consignee.

This required the manufacture of special bags with heat retention properties for the twenty four hours of their journey. Suitable bags were developed and tested and this trade flourished.

With aircraft now operating nonstop and ever more speedily the specific problems of yesteryear are not quite so acute today . . .

—King Penguin anecdote

King Penguins are to be found in the south Atlantic, near *Antarctica.*

The expansion of the air cargo industry in the early sixties, allowed many more animals to be shipped by air than previously. At the time **BOAC** operated *Comet* aircraft to *Buenos Aires*, on a twice-weekly basis. The journey involved at least four stops before reaching the UK from Argentina.

The Comet-holds, in the belly of the fuselage, were pressurised, and had a height clearance of only around thirty two inches. The skin temperatures on the floor of the cargo hold whilst in flight was *around minus 20 to minus 30 degrees CELSIUS*, with the temperature at the ceiling of the hold much higher. At first sight this might seem a daunting temperature differential for any living creature. So when a request came from *Buenos Aires* for BOAC to take up a contract to move many such animals to the Zoos, both in the UK and Europe we were anxious to seek expert advice.

Our enquiries with the appropriate people at the **London Zoo** established that the height of these animals (and despite their aquatic, flightless nature they are classified as *Birds*) was around twenty eight inches.

This meant that to transport these to the UK they would have to travel within the extremes of temperatures which applied to the compartments in which they would be carried.

When this was explained to the Zoological authorities in London, their response was quite enlightening. It seems that King Penguins do not mind *'cold bottoms'* (even at—20 to—40 degrees) as long as the temperature of the air they breathe is suitable. The higher temperatures at penguin head height of thirty inches or so were okay and the temperature differential was actually ideally suited!

The Penguins would be carried in crates so their backsides would never be directly in contact with the external fuselage temperatures otherwise it would be very difficult to unstick them from the compartment floor on arrival.

The only other requirement during the long flight was to ensure that at each ground stop the penguins would have to be hosed down to keep their skin moist.

Having explained this to *Buenos Aires* and the other stations along which these would land, the movement of the Penguins went ahead with little or no trouble until the contract was concluded.

—Carriage of Other Miscellaneous Animals

From time to time the request came to us to investigate the carriage of other animal *species*. Each of these had to be cleared with our resident 'vet' before permission could be given.

For example, even today it is forbidden to carry Dogs in the same cargo compartment with 'Human Remains'. A dog quickly becomes aware of their presence and becomes distressed, howling consistently. Such are the lessons learnt from experience.

The current day UK television program ***'Airport'*** frequently shows scenes of the carriage of animals, and their treatment and condition when these arrive at the airport in London. Some are clearly the worse for wear for their experiences whilst other remarkably unscathed. Clearly the transport regulations are intended for the sake of the animals. Most of **today's** *procedures, and rules and regulations* described were arrived at in those early days, by the major carriers such as BOAC working alongside the 'Animal Welfare Organizations' (present even then). At the time this organisation only had a series of conjoined 'Temporary Huts' in which to operate. Today it housed in buildings specially designed for its purpose, where computers control local micro environments for the sake of the animals and their welfare.

Television shows this quantum leap from ram shackle hut to the state of the art housing quite clearly.

Dawn of the Computer Age

While carrying out all the duties outlined above, in my spare time I read up on the development of computers, and together with someone I came to know well in the *Information Handling* organisation, we visited many of the computer manufacturers of the day, to establish what was available and how this developing technology could be used in my job. It was also useful for these contacts to be aware of the type of problems which had to be resolved.

I was given a free hand by my boss to explore this new area, and began to analyse the functions in the airport organisations which would be suitable for the application of computers. **Gradually a coherent unified total solution to** *the airport problem began to take shape.*

In the sixties when these ideas began to formulate, computers were not as powerful as they are today. Our vision was somewhat limited but nevertheless it was decided that we should set down an operational specification of the objectives we had in mind.

My colleague and I produced the *operational specification* and objectives to my manager who passed them through his 'line manager'.

It was agreed by all that '***this was the way forward***' and were asked to visit other airlines to establish the direction being pursued by them.

With this brief, we visited *Air France, BEA*, and *SAS,* to evaluate what they were doing in this field. None of these at the time were considering their development along the lines of our proposals.

Around this time the department's General Manager had changed, and the incumbent was someone I had served with while overseas and was fortunate therefore to be able to communicate with him directly.

He eagerly espoused our cause, and stated he would:

'***Hang his hat on this way forward***' (which to us, was encouraging).

From then on we received the maximum cooperation to proceed along the lines that we had proposed.

Our visits to the 'rival' airlines indicated that the solutions proposed by them were not suitable for the long haul operator. Their systems would be dealing with '*number crunching*' only, and not with *individual passengers and their needs*. We decided to take our developments one stage further and provide **a full passenger service element** to the number crunching, and with this take into account any requests made at time of booking.

Another design feature in our proposals was that the computer should do the 'thinking' according to inherent logic programmed into it and only request assistance when it could not decide which one of two directions had to be taken. This meant that in all cases 'check-in agents' would introduce the minimum of data, in a simple sequence for all and only respond when asked to do so by the computer. The computer would request further information in clear and unambiguous statements directly to the agent at the keyboard whence came the original request.

This concept is as valid today as it was then.

Chapter 6

KISMET (+ Faith)

Kismet

I am a firm believer that all our future steps along the route of life have been preordained. To my mind the sequences, which follow, show this quite clearly.

Others may argue that it is the decisions taken at any one time that will cause the direction of one's life to change.

In either case as things turned out this is the way I would have wished my life to evolve. The decisions made at the time appeared to be inconsistent with any real advancement to my career prospects. On the whole I was content despite the occasional dips in my progress.

It was about this time that I came to another crossroad in my career.

One of my sons-in-law,(when I told him about the following scenario), remarked that fate and my decision at this time conspired to bring him and my daughter together. If I had taken the alternative path they would never had met. It must have been my Guiding Angel (*not* Guardian Angel), who made my decision for me: ***Kismet***?

This is the way it happened.

Two things occurred almost simultaneously, both of which involved my future. The first of these was the appointment of a very *Senior Information Handling Manager*, (at a level just below *Company Director)*. The gentleman in question had obtained a double first at Oxford, and was highly respected and knowledgeable in the ways of the computer.

When he took office, he was presented with our document '***On the way forward***.' This document recommended the *computerisation* of the ground handling aspects of the airline initially at London Airport, perhaps followed later by New York(depending on the strength of the London conversion).

I still *have in my possession the original documents*, typed on foolscap size paper and dated ***26 October 1966***, together with an account of the original implementation of the system described later.

At the same time, because of my previous station experience, the ground-handling manager of Western Routes had asked me if I would like to take charge of the new **BOAC Terminal Building,** which was being built at *JF Kennedy Airport* in New York.

To this end he and I went to New York and were both accommodated in luxury at the *Waldorf Astoria, on Park Avenue*. The BOAC North American Headquarters at that time was located about one hundred yards from this hotel also at 245 Park Avenue.

The day following our arrival, the General Manager North America, interviewed me in the presence of the person who had proposed my appointment. I was accepted on the spot and the final words from the General Manager on leaving him were:

"Welcome Aboard, see you after your vacation."

On my return to the UK, I advised my wife, and started dreaming of life in the USA, as we departed for Rome and a well-earned holiday.

Meanwhile the ***Information Handling Manager (Director)*** advised my General Traffic Manager that he had read my proposal, and that he would like to borrow me for about six months, so that these could be explored further with a view to early development and implementation.

On my return from Rome I was presented with this dilemma, take up my New York post with promotion to ***full managerial status,*** or *be seconded to the Information Handling Department* without immediate promotion; He tendered the advice that I should seriously consider 'Information Handling' offer as this was the way into the future.

His advice was taken and I moved into a new world, filled with a language I could barely understand. This language was *'Computer Speak'*. It was a language, with which computer users around the world would use to communicate.

Eventually I began to get to grips with it and could apply it over and above my own preferred language. Today even adolescent youngsters are brought up with *Computer Speak* as a second language, as they '***surf the Internet***'.

The six-month secondment started in 1966. I retired formally in 1981, **after 40 years' service** (*plus an extra 4 years due to my earlier overseas service*). At the time of my retirement I was still an active member of the 'Information Handling Department'. The six ***month*** secondment lasted from 1966 to 1981, (a mere 15 **years**) . . . :)

By the time I retired I had achieved my goal of becoming a full Manager, on the senior staff list of the Airline. However this had been achieved in the Computer, not the Ground Handling, Organisation where my initial ambitions had been aimed . . .

After four years on the sidelines following my retirement I was approached by British Airways to return as a Consultant for about six months, this was in 1986. This consultancy task continued on a six-monthly renewal basis until **June 2002**. *It was at my wish and at the age of 79 that I decided that I had had enough and stopped.*

On my 'second' retirement from the Aviation scene, I decided to put down in writing the direction my life took after my initial induction into the airline scene. It appears to me that not many persons are aware of the early pioneering days, and this would be a good way to start the book.

The next part of this story describes my life in the computer-working environment and my travels around the world helping to implement the system developed with my help. This system was sold to many of the world's major airlines including some of those in the USA. The system has become the standard against which all alternative developments are judged.

My Transfer to Information Handling, and the Future

At first my move into the world of computers was as strange as my first posting overseas. Everyone I spoke to talked in a language which I barely recognised as English. I had not yet learned *'computer speak',*

I was surrounded by young graduates, and at the age of 37 was considered an old man. I had to prove myself in this new environment before I would be accepted.

There was little airline expertise around in this new field. This meant that our original proposals were presented to IBM the US Computer Giant. They came up with a specification suitable for the power of the computers of that day. The IBM 360 was at the time the most powerful in the IBM armoury.

As IBM were to be involved it was only natural that they would not suggest any other computer to drive their system proposal . . .

IBM had just designed the first reservation system for airline use, and had designed a control program to drive this system. Based on the knowledge of their recent development which made no provision for the differences and variations incurred during the booking of a passenger any time up to *twelve months* before departure, and the check in of that passenger up to *twelve hours* immediately prior their intended departure, their potential system was considered at a senior level. When the IBM development proposal was submitted to the Senior Customer Services management, they recognised that it lacked the thoroughness to meet all the check in requirements, and rejected it. **Although not playing any part in this rejection, I did agree with the decision to do so.**

*It will be noted that in the foregoing summary I have already introduced statements in 'Computer Speak.' Some terms, which are commonplace today, have been used such as **Control Programs, Computer power,** etc.*

More such expressions will appear later.

As a result of this rejection the Information Management Department was asked to set up a team to manage, direct and specify in greater detail, (naturally using *computer speak*), how such a system would function within the control program used for the reservations system.

Up to three other station personnel from London Airport were brought in to join me. They would provide the necessary 'London' expertise to apply to the development of the London operation.

As it turned out later, only one of these lasted the course. The others fell by the wayside and became the followers, not the leaders of this development. Some were used to assist in the implementation at London, but did not assist in providing the analysts and programmers with the required information on which the technical people would depend.

Experts from *Arthur Andersen*, of recent, (i.e. 2002) accountancy ill repute were brought in to enable both the BOAC line management as *potential users,* and the programmers employed from outside, each with different levels of experience, to define and complete a very complex system of *design according to potential usage.* ***Probably this was the first of its kind in the world.***

The Arthur Andersen advisers, with whom we worked, were an excellent team, and without their help the current systems in use by many of the world's airlines would not have been developed. They helped us to channel our ideas and concepts in the right direction, and always provided clear courses of action on the paths to follow, without ever imposing their views on how the end product was to perform.

This is all I need state about the above subject.

After the original definition, my next task was to set up a team to present **'test data'** at all stages of development. This data would be used to test the programs as they developed.

The final test was to cover the whole system, and we had to act as *'Devil's Advocate'*

(a 'Critique of Pure Reason') when presenting data to 'programs'. The intention in our test program *was to break the logic,* not to see if it worked. Seeing how to make the programs work was the job of the **programmer**.

Another of the tasks passed on to me was to help the Arthur Andersen group to define the **Data Base**. This would be needed to store both **permanent and transient data.** Without an established data base the programmers and analysts could not define the programs, which would drive the project.

At the time all **data, programs**, and **test data**, had to be introduced by **punch cards**. This was a laborious and tedious process. Woe betides anyone who tripped up whilst carrying this data from the office to the computer!

All the cards once punched, had to remain strictly in the sequence in which these had been punched. Any change to that sequence would render all the cards useless until the offending cards had been replaced in their correct sequence.

Eighteen months passed, and the development continued apace, until all programs had been tested and cleared. While this **testing** process was under way, three other factors had to be fully considered.

The first of these was to be the ordering of equipment, and deciding the *location* of all this equipment around the airports. This also required the introduction of *high speed message lines* to link the equipment located at London Heathrow, with the mainframe computer, housed some distance from the front line equipment. In the case of the New York installation, the link at this time was via the *transatlantic undersea cable.*

The second consideration was to be the training of non-computer staff at the airport who were to use the system when introduced 'live'.

Thirdly, there was the task of providing suitable written procedures to allow the system training to be started. These manuals would also serve in the future as ready references to the system for the users. These would **not** be written in *'computer speak'* but had to be in **plain English.**

The programmers had provided ample documentation but it was all in the new language. Much of this had to be simplified and translated into everyday expressions at a level of English, which could be interpreted by non-technical persons

The day came to switch in the system to flights departing London. All was ready, equipment in place, procedures written, and the staff to be involved with the cut over, fully trained.

Preparations were made to run the system in tandem with the old procedures, until the new had functioned normally, and the computer and program logic shown to be stable. The dual run was planned for a week, but as it turned out after the first forty eight hours, the staff themselves elected to stop the manual procedures, as these were too complex and demanding of staff time. The new system was so much smoother and quicker, and provided a far greater degree of accuracy.

Other airlines at the airport quickly focussed in to the new system introduced by BOAC, and passed the message back to their Head Offices. It took very little sales effort to put the system up for sale. BOAC were inundated with requests from other airlines, to install this system into their own home bases.

BOAC *Information Handling* was awarded the **Queen's Award to Industry** for its ***technological innovation*** in the provision of the *Departure Control System.* I still have the tie produced by the airline to mark this historic occasion. It was only given to those **directly involved in the development of the system,** not its users.

The system developed in the late sixties and implemented in the seventies, and sold too, to many other airlines, has also become the **IATA Standard** for *Departure Control Systems.*

The introduction of the system at other stations on the BOAC network, and its sale to other airlines enabled me to visit many countries around the world, at some of which I enjoyed extended periods of residence.

I continued to be involved in the evolution of this system to provide more and more automation.

Queens Award image.

Left:

The Queen's Building,

Heathrow Airport,

(circa 'late sixties')

Below:

'Almost like a Whale'...

the characteristic whale- fin

Vickers VC10 tail,

(early seventies)

Implementation at Prestwick in Scotland.

It is not my intention here to dwell on the system, but to describe in some detail the places, which were visited in the furtherance of its development, and implementation.

At the time ***Prestwick*** was one of the link stations on the North Atlantic route, and it was in great need of such a system as the transatlantic flights started in Manchester, barely thirty minutes flight time from Prestwick. Passenger loads were evenly distributed across these two stations.

This fact placed a lot of pressure on the staff at Prestwick who had barely one hour to accept and accommodate its passenger load before the flight had even left Manchester.

I stayed at the 'Links Hotel' on the shores of the mouth of the River Clyde, with the *Isle of Arran,* visible across the river mouth.

The isle was frequently bathed in mist.

In the early morning after breakfast, I would walk across the Prestwick Golf Course, towards the Airport Buildings. The mornings were crisp and fine in the most part, and to walk across the course to my place of work was a pleasure. I have seldom in my life found a similar environment of such enchantment, with the waters of the Clyde to the left of me, and the undulating green of the Golf Course, ahead of me. This scenario continued until I was barely one hundred yards from the Terminal Building.

In the late afternoon after all airport activity ceased, I returned to the Hotel, and as long as it was daylight I would explore the shores of the river-mouth walking towards the town of ***Ayr***.

The waters rippled on the sandy shore. The sand was littered with small and large multi-coloured pebbles, many of which I picked during these wanderings. Some of these were so beautiful that they appeared to have a jewel-like sheen to them.

When the weather was bad, Ayr was a short 'ten-pence' bus ride away from the town of Prestwick. (!)

After a week in this idyllic part of the British Isles, I returned to London and the family.

My next venture overseas was to the *old BOAC Terminal* in *the International Building at John F Kennedy Airport* in ***New York***. The Airport previously had been named *'Idlewild',* but had its name changed after President Kennedy was assassinated in 1963.

The story of this implementation is described later.

'Computers', and the New World.

Once the new Computer system had bedded down at both ***London*** and ***Prestwick*** the next expansion involved the use of the same facilities at ***New York*** airport, all driven by the London based computer. *This was to be another world first.*

The planned operation involved the installation at each passenger 'check-in' station, with equipment similar to those installed at the other two stations. This time, however, each transaction would cross the Atlantic to the main computer in London.

The agent in ***New York*** making the request to the computer would receive a response at the **same *set*** *in less than five seconds.* The response would be sufficient to allow the agent to complete the check-in process. (*'Set'* is again computer speak for an origin of communication with the *mainframe*).

I could describe in technical terms how this was to be achieved, but this would be of little interest to the great majority of readers and would definitely 'include lots of computer speak!'

Once the success of this new venture was assured, the BOAC operations worldwide could be covered from the same London based Computer. All that would be needed was to provide a Computer powerful enough to meet the demands placed on it. Even if this ideal was being approached by the late seventies, by 1985 this objective had definitely been achieved.

Computer power is judged on *the speed of communication* between it and the many outposts interrogating the same machine, the ability to receive many messages at the same time, *processing* these same through its *programs*, and return the responses directly to the *'sets'* where each interrogation was made. This ability('speed') is defined as the *number* of messages, which can be *handled per minute*, coupled with the ability to *store and process* each message in a given sequence, both through 'real time'(priority) and 'batch time' processing(queued up secondary requests).

It would utilise pauses in each message, in order to retrieve files, by initiating the processing of other messages(*batch processing*). It would be necessary to prioritise activity, know when to pick up on previous messages as and when these were ready for processing to continue. This would be an ongoing process, '24/7' as is the saying, (twenty four hours a day and seven days a week), and would require a very sophisticated control program, to receive process and issue responses in a strictly controlled sequence, without ever losing its direction.

The main frame computer in *London,* would be dealing simultaneously with messages from *New York, London,* and *Prestwick,* and at the same time the control program, would be dealing with ***Reservations***(enquiries and bookings), received either directly from other agents on the network, or by teletype messages from other systems but always *'live'* or *'online'* i.e. *'real-time'*.

I believe it is essential to state the complexity of the BOAC installation with which I was involved, so that any reader will understand the ***pride***, which I felt at being part of this new enterprise.

There is so much more one can describe about this brave new world of computers.

Today, much of this is commonplace and taken for granted, but in those days in the early seventies, it opened up a brand new chapter in one's life. It was as exciting as the feelings I felt when I first joined the airline, and was sent to my first overseas posting to *Malakal.*

The system introduced at this time, sent a ripple of interest throughout the aviation industry, such that within eighteen months of its introduction the whole system was sold many times over to airlines worldwide.

Evolution not Revolution

The initial system was in a constant state of evolution to allow more functionality and for more activity at station level to be automated. These developments became known, unsurprisingly as Phases 2 and 3 of the original system's development.

I have always been an advocate of '*evolution not revolution*' in the development of computer systems. The risk factors in revolution are too great. Revolution requires a change to the main structure of the system, whereas evolution only requires that new items be added piecemeal, to both the data structure, and to integrate new programs into the ongoing and proven system.

Just as an aircraft or motor vehicle already in service undergoes changes to improve its performance, so the same applies to Computer Systems. This is what I regard as evolution. Revolution is when a new model is introduced in which design and parts are changed wholesale, and not yet tested in a true functional environment. Financially it is a far bigger gamble.

The original system design was made for *a BOAC type long haul operation*. However, many short haul airlines such as *Swissair* and *KLM*, were showing interest in using this system as a base on which to build a more sophisticated system for use by the *high density, short haul operators.*

Their initial assessment was that the system structure was sound, but more automation was needed to reduce staff levels and still meet the schedule demands of the *high-density, short haul operators.*

Together with *Aer Lingus* and *South African Airways*, who had already purchased and introduced the new system, it was proposed to specify a further development, subsequently identified as Phases 4 and 5.

Swissair asked me, to analyse their current method of operation at **Zurich**, and propose how this could be substantially improved by a more advanced development of the current system.

From my report to the Management of *Swissair* they gave BOAC a letter of intent to purchase, provided certain modifications were undertaken to modify it to meet the needs of the short haul operator.

KLM, the Dutch airline did the same, and work started on the specification of this new advanced system.

SR (as *Swissair* was then), and *BOAC* undertook to provide a detailed specification, and from this the five airlines would work together to produce a joint system based on the original base.

Each airline was apportioned a part of the specification, and would develop this at their home base. All were required to use the database developed jointly by BOAC and SwissaiR. There would be frequent consultations between the partners, when overlaps had to be identified and common paths evolved and followed, with any variations to the theme providing fresh data fields.

Target dates were set and achieved without difficulty, and the fully revised system implemented without a hitch.

All the program and *user testing* was carried out on *the SR* system **in Zurich**, at ***Kloten*** to be exact. All five airlines sent programmers and users to **Zurich**. BOAC were asked to coordinate this joint venture, and I was placed in charge of the combined *airways testing* group,('multi airline' function assessment).

'Front line' user and program testing was an ongoing continuous feature, and lasted *from early November until late March of the following year,* with implementation due in **April or May** of that year, firstly in *Zurich then London.*

The success of this new system increased the level of interest by many more airlines, and the system development costs were repaid after the next six sales. This was far exceeded, before the next development phase was started.

Each development phase resulted in considerable staff reductions which in themselves would have justified its development, without the profit from subsequent sales.

By the time these phases were developed and introduced, the application of *Computer Science in my Society* became a part of my life, and I would *think, dream, and breathe* computers! So called *'Computer Speak'* became second nature, and I could converse and confound others, ('tit4tat'), when using this new language, far more effectively than the days when others would confound me with this new 'lingo' . . . *'computer speak'*.

For the time being, I will continue with the implementation of the system in New York, as this was a world first and needs to be described more fully.

Implementation in New York.

I left London for New York immediately after Christmas (1969) of the year the system was first introduced in London. This was at the request of the US Management who required my expertise to support the staff at the airport.

Strangely enough on my arrival, the new BOAC Terminal Building was now under construction, and could be seen from my place of work at the International Terminal Building close to the Airport Control Tower. I could have been in charge of this had I accepted my other appointment...

The original planning that went into the implementation at London was applied to the plan for New York, including the dual operation.

By the time I had arrived all equipment and training had been completed, and all that was required of me was to ensure that when the operation started, I was around to help out and show both front and back room staff the intricacies of the operation not explained to them during their training.

My presence was also designed to provide confidence in the system. This was the first time the operation of aircraft check in and aircraft control in the US had changed from a purely manual, but 'labour-intensive', role, to a fully automated, efficient computerised control of departure activities. The name given to this total system became known as *The Departure Control System*, **DCS** for short.

All systems worldwide whether based on this DCS or others are now identified by the term **DCS.**

No problems were experienced with the introduction of the new system in New York; however it is worth remarking on the attitude of the staff using this totally new system. Later experience with other airlines showed this to be identical.

Despite all the training which they had undergone, front line staff were all very nervous and lacked confidence in this new toy.

When the first passenger approached them, they made the initial entry and to their amazement the responses they received in the prescribed time, enabled them to conclude their dealings with the passenger far quicker than they would have been able to before. *It was a pleasure to see the relief on their faces.*

After about twenty four hours, similar to London, all the manual back up procedures were abandoned by the staff.

Two things stand out in my mind about New York, *one* was the weather in late February, and *the other* relates to an incident on the subway.

New York Weather

My duty days in New York in the five months I was there, started at around 0800hrs and finished around 2300hrs once the last London bound flight had departed.

Due to these long days, I was accommodated at a very good hotel within ten minutes' drive of the airport. However the location of this hotel was in a rather insalubrious part of New York, near to the Jamaica precinct on Long Island, close to Rockaway Boulevard. Travel to and from the hotel was by hotel car, which operated on a regular run from the hotel to the airport and back, and at night on request.

I well recall one evening after the last departure, when I went outside the heated terminal building into the icy cold atmosphere. There was strong wind blowing. I thought I was hardy and could withstand that sort of weather, but not so.

The hotel vehicle always pulled up at the same spot on one of the centre islands outside the terminal building, about thirty yards away.

I was suitably dressed for the winter conditions expected wearing a very heavy *'Cromby'* overcoat, a 'heavy-duty, roll-neck, thick-wool' jumper, scarf, woolly hat and gloves. Even so while waiting for the transport to return to my hotel, I had to take refuge in the heated building every five minutes. If I had not done so I am sure that I would have become frozen solid on the spot where I stood!

Never again in my life have I experienced such cold. The wind chill factor must have been similar to those met by the explorers of the North Pole . . .

While taking refuge inside the building I was concerned that the vehicle would arrive and depart if the driver could not see me. It was late at night, and the ground was icy with packed frozen snow. The driver once having returned to the hotel would not venture out again that night.

New York Subway Experience.

Occasionally when I had a day off I would go to the City. To do so, there were two routes I could take. One of these was by local bus into Jamaica town at the end of Rockaway Boulevard, and then on the subway into the city. This route was not recommended because at the time New York City was not a safe place to visit and the Jamaica precinct even less so.

The other route was by hotel car to the airport, then from there on the **Q10** bus to 'Kew *Gardens, Richmond'*, and then by the *6th or 8th Avenue Independent* Subway into the city. This was the preferred route.

On this particular day after a visit to the city, I was returning on the subway from downtown to my destination, which was 'Kew Gardens' subway station. I noted a gentleman in his early thirties and of unkempt appearance, staring at me intently. He made me feel very uncomfortable.

In New York, after the offices shut and most people had returned home, the subway continued to operate, but most carriages were almost empty.

I felt concern that I was being targeted by this person, and considered how I should avoid his attention.

Firstly, I moved my seat to the other end of the compartment. Shortly after I noted that he also moved to my new location across the aisle.

By now I was really getting alarmed, as it became obvious that I was the centre of his attention. At the next stop I exited the compartment and moved to another. Hey presto, he did the same, obviously 'to keep an eye' on me! He did not look like a member of the New York police to me.

I now had to think fast as to how I could elude this man's attention.

The station at which I was due to leave the train was large, ill lit and not very active at this time of the day. That station would be an ideal spot at which I could be attacked.

The next station at which the train stopped was Queen's Plaza, a major transfer point on the New York subway. There would always be a crowd at this station at any time of the day.

When the train arrived, I got up and exited the train. He did the same, but from a different exit door of the same carriage.

I stood on the platform and as soon as the doors started to shut, and just before they were fully shut, I jumped back in to the same train. To my relief, this man was left standing on the platform. Thus I came away, unscathed from this experience.

I discussed this experience with my American colleagues. From them I was advised that when travelling by the subway in the late evening or at night, to travel always in the last carriage.

A guard is always present in the last carriage. Not only is he armed, but also has radio contact with the control room. This allows him to radio ahead, so that police can be sent to meet the train in the event of a disturbance of this kind.

On all subsequent trips into town I followed this advice, and was amazed to discover how many passengers travelled in this compartment, on what appeared to be an empty train.

My next extended stay in New York happened after we sold the Departure Control System to United Airlines. The first targeted implementation was at their Terminal building in the John F Kennedy airport complex.

For this stay I was accommodated at a Hotel overlooking Central Park. This involved further travel on the New York subways. I always followed the advice given to me when boarding late trains, and was never again threatened in the same way. So the advice was obviously sound.

I have not used the subway in New York since then, although a frequent visitor to that city. I do not know if subway travel on late night trains is any safer now, but am given to understand that New York as a whole is a much safer city these days.

Throughout my stay in New York I never visited Central Park. At the time I was told it was not a safe place to visit at night and I always worked during the day.

I am given to understand that any visit to New York, without savouring the flavour of the Park in daylight hours is a delightful pleasure missed.

The number of daylight activities which take place in the Park, could well fill a day, and provide a far better view of New York, than a visit to the 'Macy' complex, or a walk through the seedy central part of the city around Broadway, and Times Square.

The Helicopter Ride from the Airport to Central New York

The last exciting episode, worth recounting experienced during my visits to New York, is the journey that I undertook by Huey Helicopter from the Pan American Terminal Building at JFK airport, to the Helipad, situated on the roof of the Pan Am building. This was located at the top end of the Avenue of the Americas in New York City.

This journey took place a short time before the operation was suspended permanently after a particularly nasty accident. This was when one of the scheduled helicopters was blown over the edge of the Helipad on the roof of the building to the road below in very strong and gusty wind conditions.

Debris from this incident rained down on the persons below going about their normal daily business. There were casualties both on the landing site, and in the street below.

Strong winds were part of the landing scenario in New York at this very high level. The force of these winds themselves were increased and made more turbulent by 'the funnel effect' as these blew and eddied down the streets and avenues of that city. When 'de-planing' out of the helicopter, it was very difficult to remain upright, due to the strength of such winds. A quick dash to the building entrance was necessary to avoid being blown over by the combined effects of winds and helicopter down draughts.

On this particular day, I had been visiting the PANAM terminal at the airport as part of the plan to sell our system to this airline. Eventually they bought the system and installed it in New York and other Eastern seaboard states from which that airline operated.

Two Japanese gentlemen and I were the only passengers to board this flight destined for the PANAM Building in the centre of the city.

There was a strong wind blowing at the time in New York City, and the departure of the flight could have been aborted at any time. As it turned out the flight did depart, and apart from some turbulence en route the view of the city from the air was tremendous.

Although the winds were strong, the sky was blue and only a few puffy white clouds impeded our view of the city from such an altitude.

The approach and landing is altogether a different story.

The journey across the city showed off New York in all its glory, and although I boarded the flight with some trepidation, this being my very first Helicopter journey. The view was so breathtaking that I completely forgot that we were due to land on top of a very high building, in the middle of the city.

We approached the landing site and noted the presence of a large gold domed top building close to our landing site. Two other buildings of approximately the same height as the landing site were also close by.

The pilot made his first approach by flying past the Gold Topped building then turned towards the landing site. Below down each of the streets and avenues, could be seen people moving about, just like a plague of ants in one's garden.

The first approach failed as the wind force affected the landing and took it off centre, towards the edge of the building. The aircraft took off again and circled around the gold topped building again. By this time the other two passengers, and myself, had become alarmed at the dangers involved in the second landing attempt.

However the second approach was successful and we landed safely. Outside I could see the Engineers and ground staff scurrying around buffeted by the strong winds.

We disembarked hastily and ran to the shelter of the reception area, from which an elevator took us to the street level. Only then did I feel safe enough to relax.

I have never again flown in a Helicopter, nor do I have any further wish to do so!

More about 'System Evolution'—and its application to Short Haul Operations.

By now, the reader should have digested the earlier perspective of *'Evolution not Revolution'*. This section expounds further on this theme.

The original system had been developed for BOAC, and its type of operation. Other European Airlines operated similar type flights, but in the main, (like BEA), also operated a large number of daily flights to and from other European cities. Nearly all these flights were of less than three hours duration, and in many cases under an hour.

The above types of flights represented about eighty per cent of the operations for these airlines and specifically in the case of BEA, the entirety,(one hundred per cent), of its operations.

The high frequencies and fast turnaround time, required a more sophisticated approach in the development of the existing system.

The short haul airlines up to this point were using number crunching systems with little or no Passenger Service element. They wished to retain the benefits offered by the BOAC facility while at the same time introducing more automation.

What developed from this and 'the fruits' of the next development was to introduce a facility that could potentially monitor each flight's progress up to and including departure.

The development is not as simple as it sounds. It had to provide station variations on the level of activity and the times at which these would be carried out. Each flight at each station around the world would be at a different stage of its departure, and different activities had to be scheduled in the local time zones at which these would have to be triggered.

At the same time that the automatic triggers were functioning to complete certain essential preflight functions automatically, each flight had to be monitored and report to the appropriate flight control centre around the world.

If a flight was reaching a critical point (because of load or fuel shortages, or the over acceptance of passengers),this information would need to be conveyed centrally as these were situations which only a Controller could make a judgement on, and advise appropriately a course of action.

The facility was designed so that it could identify the right person to notify at the correct station on the worldwide network, and take the appropriate action to the response from the individual making this judgement.

At stations with a high frequency of operation, more than one controller was on duty, each controlling a given number of flights identified by their flight number.

In today's *British Airways* **DCS** facility, more than thousand flights daily are monitored, and controlled automatically, many without any intervention from Control agents. Individual actions for one flight within these activities take place simultaneously around the world, and are activated on a local time base.

All the activity takes place in a *multiprocessing environment*, and is not on a message-by-message sequence but whole problems are dismantled and processed in parallel simultaneously, hence being a more powerful generation of computers still and are known as ***'5th Generation Parallel Processors'***. Many messages are processed simultaneously, so whatever the activity rate the agents do not notice any delay in the response to their enquiries.

The facility developed in the late seventies is as valid today as it was then. No new purchaser of the system has so far attempted to replace the logic which went into this development, so it remains to this day the 'definitive article'...

New phases have been introduced since, but the *Auto Control feature* remain as a focal point to their development.

The introduction of the newly evolved system, when introduced to the BEA operation, resulted in a saving in staff numbers in one department of around one hundred persons that potentially could be redeployed more efficiently. This department was operating on a twenty four hour, seven day a week rotation, three hundred and sixty five days a year.

This development generated even more interest by the world's airlines. The five airlines involved in this were inundated with requests to sell the system, both to ground handling agencies working on behalf of airport authorities, and airlines who wished to introduce the facilities to suit their own operations.

Sales activity now took on a new impetus, and resulted in my travel to many other countries to support the sales, and assist with its implementation.

My further travels took me to:

Korea,
Omaha, (USA),
Singapore,
Sydney
Tel-Aviv
Lisbon,
Vancouver,
Toronto (Quebec),

Miami,
Auckland,
Amsterdam,
Zurich,
Japan(via the polar route,)
Taipei (Taiwan),
Hong Kong,
Bangkok,
Helsinki, and
Johannesburg

I believe today if one asks any of the Computer personnel in those countries, if they know who I am, they will readily recognise my role in the technological advances made, and implemented around the world, for the benefit of the airline industry.

The stations and airlines described above are not set out in any particular order. I may perhaps be able to produce a cameo write up about some of these places, all of which I visited in the course of my days. I had now become an integral part of the Computer Department both as a senior development officer and subsequently as manager of the system.

So far the experiences described in the first part of this book, have tended more towards the episodic. Unfortunately and perhaps to the detriment of the book, the latter part(UK-based)has in the main elaborated upon my personal development, and '*self-aggrandisement*'.I hope that the readers, if they get this far, will bear with the writer.

I am naturally very proud of the part I played in the growth of both BOAC and British Airways as a world leaders in the airline industry, and the recognition of this in the **Queen's Award to Industry**. This award was given for the technological advances made and its use of modern day technology, with particular emphasis on the advanced use of computers, to solve current day problems.

Since the seventies and eighties computer technology has advanced considerably, but I no longer have a part to play in these advances.

I only hope that readers with an interest in this part of the book will recognise that it is only 'on site' experience, integrated closely with technical expertise, which can provide true solutions to problems.

There is a tendency for the technical experts to ride roughshod over the views of other experts in the belief that they know better. My experience indicates that this is not so. Each member of a development team has to work closely with other members and draw on their knowledge. No one group should dominate the other merely because they believe they know better. ***'Look, Listen and Learn' is the watchword***.

Furthermore, when choosing persons with the required expertise to contribute to a development, the persons have to be of a *calibre* to think beyond the level of their current expertise, and have sufficient confidence in these beliefs that they will stand up and be counted when arguments develop between these two opposing expert viewpoints.

Such people must have minds which are flexible such as to allow them to think beyond the levels of knowledge they have gained from their work experiences . . .

Concorde

Concorde -now on permanent display and storage at Heathrow and elsewhere, was an iconic *'Speedbird'* of her own time, the seventies. An early symbol of European co-operation she was technologically advanced, beautiful and fast (regularly breaking the sound barrier to achieve speeds of Mach 2.2). With her enigmatic, mathematically derived wing shape, Concorde was clearly identifiable in the sky both lunch time and 6.30pm in the evening, as she flew over West London to the glee of her many admirers. Flying regularly out to New York and Dubai and Sydney, Concorde was for many years, British Airways' flagship. .

3-View: Aerospatiale Concord
Aerospatiale Concord.

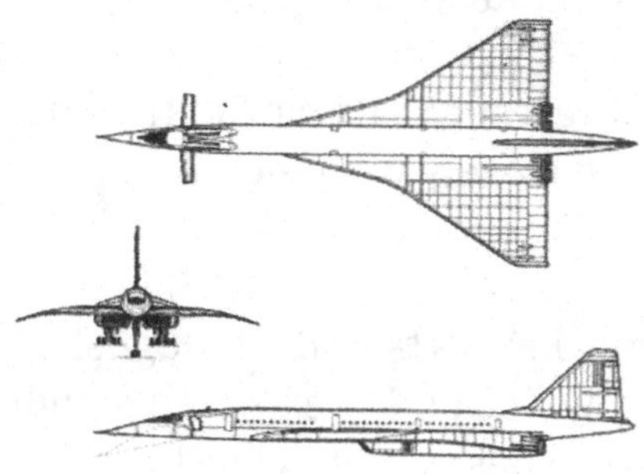

Chapter 7

The 'The DCS Ambassador Reports'

"Cameos, travel snapshots and word sketches from around the world in eighty ways"

Incl.

Seoul,
Hong Kong,
Tel Aviv,
Lisbon,
Sydney,
Omaha,
Singapore,
Copenhagen,
Bangkok,
Sao Paulo

Where the author known as Mr.'DCS(the DCS Ambassador' had managed sales of the DCS(DEPARTURE CONTROL SYSTEM) system on behalf of BOAC for the greater good of the UK Economy . . .

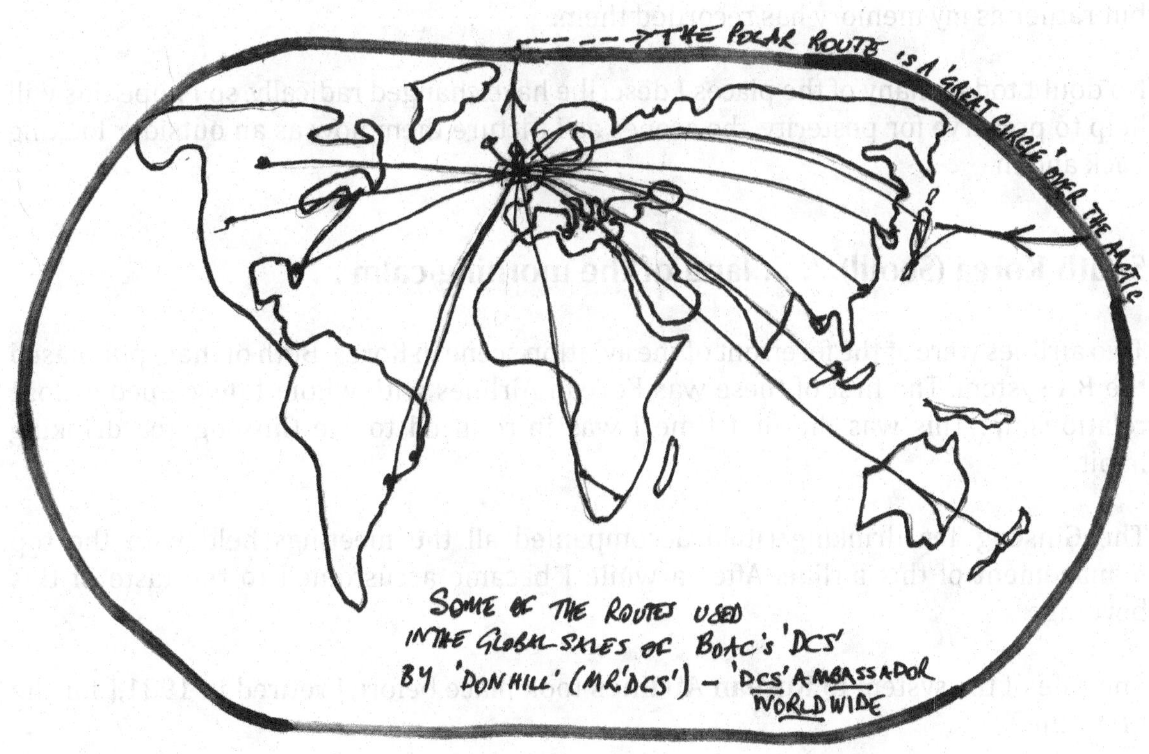

global world map in remaining page space—this map showing routes out of London to cities named

Cameos Sketches of City Life (in the places visited)

The cameos of the various countries described in this section, are only my own views after short visits. Some of the descriptions are based on stopovers of only of two or three days, others as a result of an extended stay of over ten days, but always only ever 'snapshots' of the cultures visited, even though like my first few chapters the longer visits which were more in depth.

Naturally for those short stays I was no more than a tourist, but for the longer visits I became for a short while, integrated with the local inhabitants. I came to know the places of interests and the 'character of the people' perhaps better than the regular tourist.

For the longer periods of stay my associations with that airline or station enabled me to mix with both the very top echelons, and also those at the other end of the spectrum who were at the heart of the front line operation.

After such a long time and without the benefit of a diary or notes, the cameos describe my lasting impressions of those places visited. These may not be exactly as they were but rather as my memory has recorded them.

No doubt today, many of the places I describe have changed radically, so I hope this will help to preserve for posterity, the scenes as I picture them now as an outsider looking back and in.

South Korea (Seoul), '. . . land of the morning calm . . .'

Two airlines were at the forefront of the aviation scene in Korea. Both of them purchased the BA system. The first of these was Korean Airlines with whom I developed a close relationship. This was the first time I was introduced to the Ginseng Tea drinking habit.

The Ginseng Tea drinking ritual accompanied all the meetings held with the top management of this airline. After a while I became accustomed to the taste of this beverage.

The sale of the system to **Korean Airlines** took place before I retired in 1981,(for the first time.)

The sale to **Asiana**, the second airline in Korea, took place after my readmission to the BA scene as a Consultant in 1987.

The introduction of the system to Korean Airlines at *Kimpoh(now Gimpoh)* airport was a difficult operation. Spoken English was not the easiest of languages to the Koreans, and all communication between the management and staff had to be confirmed in writing from the very outset. This was very time consuming but essential.

I discovered later that whenever discussions took place in English. The Koreans themselves always made copious notes almost on a word for word level. They would nod their heads as though they had fully appreciated everything that had been said. Whether this is the case is a matter for debate.

The language differences prevented them from long complicated conversations in English. However, it became apparent the next day that they had fully understood all the discussions even at the highest technical level, and would come up with very pertinent questions about the previous day's discussions.

When they eventually received the very technical manuals, which accompanied the delivery of the system, the Koreans read these with great understanding, even more so than the persons of pure British extraction in the UK, and would discuss in great detail various items in the text, which required clarification.

Knowledge of these attributes made the sale of the second system much easier, as their ability to understand the written word was taken into account to promote this sale. We obtained this second sale against stiff opposition from our competitors who by this time were offering *derivatives* of our original system!

At the time of the first sale, BA was not operating any direct flights to Seoul. Travel to Korea, would take us either via Hong Kong, or Tokyo. I travelled both routes, the first time via the Polar route stopping at Anchorage in Alaska to Tokyo, then by Korean Airlines to Seoul. The other occasion was by way of Hong Kong then also on to Korean Airlines to Seoul.

The security for entry and departure to and from Seoul was very strict and lengthy, both for their own citizens, and foreigners visiting that land. It seems apparent that they felt threatened by their northern neighbours' and had to prevent entry by any North Koreans into South Korea at all costs.

It was against this background that the first system was installed.

Hong Kong.

Jardine Matheson, the general sales agents for BA in Hong Kong, wished to avail themselves of the system to handle both BA and other airlines' flights operating into and out of Hong Kong.

The BA General Manager for the eastern Routes, asked us to investigate the extension of the existing system in London for use in Hong Kong.

With this objective in mind, a senior communications manager and myself went to Hong Kong to appraise the situation, before we could give '*Jardines*' the necessary assurances.

There were already the necessary communications high-speed links in place to serve the Reservations Booking Office in that city, but it would be necessary to test response times and the effects on the line capacity, which could result from the addition of a large number of additional transactions to the link.

At the time, (pre 1981) no commercial satellites were in orbit, and all communications were by a combination of land, and undersea cable links.

In order to ensure reliability, alternative routings were necessary as a fallback measure. The communications manager discussed this with the local Cable and Wireless managers. They assured him after the requirements were discussed that the existing link via Australia would carry the extra traffic without loss of performance, and that an alternative routing via Tokyo would soon be available.

Armed with these assurances, the discussions with Jardines were concluded subject to satisfactory 'on line' tests and subsequently the DCS link, once activated, became the first dynamic link halfway across the world.

From this single link, and the advent of satellites, today all the world's airlines

(including British Airways),operate their check-in systems from their mainframe home-based computers. This again became another first for *British Airways*, the son of the merger of BOAC and BEA.

Apart from this, there was little time to visit the delights of Hong Kong. The General Manager of *Jardine Matheson*, with whom we dealt for this project, invited us to dinner on the Harbour Cruiser, which *Jardines* used to entertain their guests.

Jardine Matheson had put us up at the Mandarin Hotel, a hotel partly owned by this group. This hotel was situated a short distance from the pier at.which were to embark for dinner on their harbour yacht.

We all met up at the pier, boarded the vessel and sailed out into the dark of the harbour.

Hong Kong viewed at night from the middle of the harbour, was a sight never to be forgotten. One sees photographs and film clips of this, but to view it for real, far surpasses the images one derives from the other two pictures.

Both sides of the harbour, towards the island, and also in the direction of Kowloon on the mainland of China, were ablaze with the lights from the city streets and skyscrapers, and also the road traffic moving along the highways on both sides of the harbour. Imagine the view from space.

The harbour itself was full of moving traffic of all kinds including the regular Star Ferry, which plied between the Island and the mainland at fifteen-minute intervals. All these were silhouetted against the dark background and the lights from the city. One could distinguish these vessels by the lights they carried, and also as they moved, the obliteration of the city lights covered by their silhouette.

The scene was not only in black and white, but also emblazoned with the range of colours from the advertising lights, and the multi colours overhanging the Chinese Shops visible from the shore, mainly on the Kowloon side.

At midnight we were still out in the harbour, but Hong Kong was still alive, very much along the lines of New York. It appears to be a city that never sleeps.

One last memory before I leave the Hong Kong saga, relates to *Kai Tak,* the old airport used by all airlines before the present airport was built. I record this for history as in time the memory of this airport will fade.

The approach to this airport was either over some housing development around the airport, or directly from the sea. The inland approach was necessary because of the presence of a mountain range in China too close for a direct approach. Unfortunately this approach was the one used more frequently.

The approach required a very sharp turn on to the runway after passing over the high apartment blocks very close to the runway threshold.

On the side of the mountain was a large sign indicating when the sharp turn should take place to approach and land. If visibility was bad this sign became the only criteria by which a safe landing could take place. Miss it and the aircraft would plough into the hills.

The approach over the apartment blocks was so low that one could observe the washing hanging on the lines on the roofs of the buildings. Even the colour of some of these could be clearly identified.

One day a colleague and I had checked in early, and proceeded to the far end of the terminal to watch the aircraft coming in to land. Visibility was not good and the mountain sign was in constant use as a checkpoint.

It became obvious to us that aircraft belonging to foreign airlines would see the sign and turn immediately, thus bringing the aircraft slightly off centre to the runway necessitating final adjustment immediately prior to touchdown.

The local airlines, especially Cathay Pacific, would continue their approach for a few more seconds before the sharp turn, and would be aligned correctly on their final approach.

I presume the reason for this is that foreign pilots would only fly to Hong Kong infrequently and would play it safe, whereas the pilots based in Hong Kong would meet these conditions more frequently and be more confident during the landing manoeuvre.

We left **Hong Kong**, and returned to the UK in a VC10 using the long way around, via **Brunei, Colombo and Dubai**. First class seats on the direct route were at a premium, and we chose the indirect route for the comfort of First class for the long journey home after such an exhausting stay.

Israel (Tel Aviv)

El Al, the Airline of Israel also introduced the same system.

What is worth reporting about this visit, was my journey to **Masada,** the mountain kingdom in Israel, famous for the stand made there by the Israelites in years gone by, when the Romans occupied this land.

The journey to Masada took us through Jerusalem, past Jericho, (whose City Wall Joshua famously razed to the ground to the hullabaloo of trumpet and horn), through to the shores of the Dead Sea, thence to the base of this mountain fortress. Access to the top was by cable car; although we were assured that there was another way to get to the top on foot.

The Israelites, had escaped to this fortress to avoid the rule of the Romans, and would use this path to harass, waylay and pillage the logistical stores supporting the Roman Legions that were besieging the mountain top.

A visit to the top is well worth the expedition as much of the fortress is still as it was in Roman times. This includes the massive ramps built by the Roman soldiers in their attempts to scale the sheer cliff faces that acted as a natural protection for the Israelite inhabitants living high above them.

The residents of the **Masada** fortress were well equipped with all 'mod. coms.', which were available to them even then, including drinking water. This they collected and stored from the occasional rain, which fell. I believe the original location was built as a refuge for the use of one of the Kings who ruled Israel at this time.

Many books have been written about **Masada.** Anyone who wants more information about the history of this site should refer to these. I am not writing a precise historical novel but only giving my impressions of the sites of interest, which have been visited.

The return from **Masada** was via the **Dead Sea resort**, whose name escapes me, where we were offered the opportunity for a swim. Others did, but I declined after seeing the way that people would be floating above the water line rather than in it!

The return to **Tel Aviv** continued after this break following the southern route **via Bath-Sheba**, where we stopped for refreshments, then on to the coast and north back to **Tel Aviv.**

I was very surprised at the modern aspects of the town of **Beer-Sheba.** It was so different to the biblical references about this desert town, the so-called town where the Queen of that name lived. The town was so lively and vibrant and despite its location in the desert it was very green and lush.

One thing of interest I noted was that the Israelis had provided a water pipeline through the ***Negev desert region***. Many Bedouins or desert nomad enclaves had gathered around this pipeline.

Where these enclaves occurred the Israelis released the water so that the nomads could grow their own crops to feed both themselves and water their livestock.

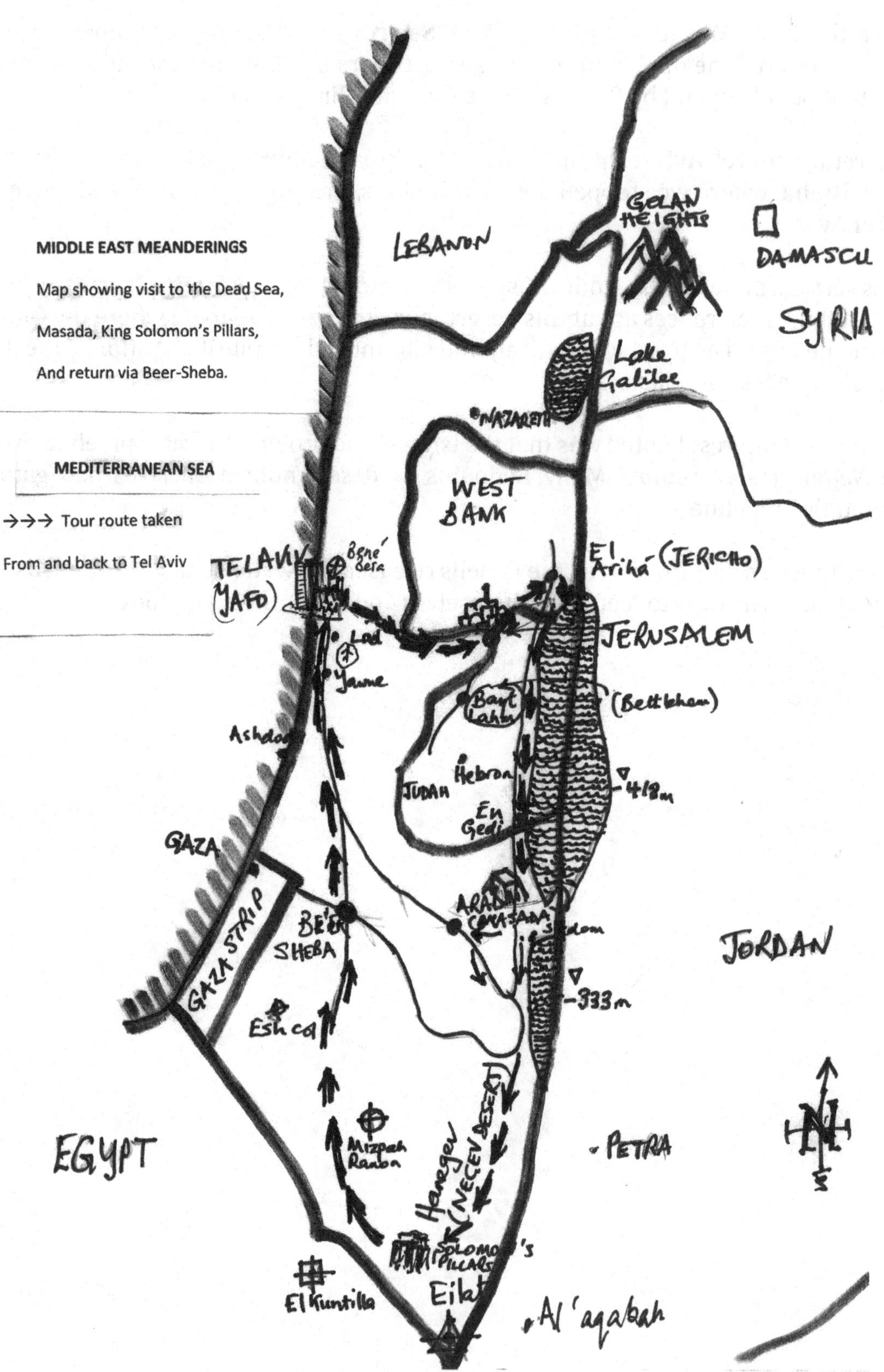

map of Israel showing path of Journey taken via Jericho and Masada

A Slice of Homespun Philosophy on the Above Observation . . .

I find it difficult to understand that there should be so much animosity between the two peoples who inhabit the territory, the land called Palestine.

Water is the lifeblood of desert inhabitants, and this free supply, which was not available before, indicates to me that given peace the two nations should be able to work together to provide a better future for the families of both nations. They both have a common heritage and despite their religious differences, both to the untrained ear have a common basic understanding of each other's language

The word in Hebrew for greetings is 'Shalom' and in Arabic, it is 'Salaam' the 'Aleikum' element is the Islamic adjunct for God or Allah. As an outsider I see very little difference. Both are peoples of the Book: it is not for nothing that the nomadic tribes are known as 'sons of Abra'am'.

People who live and work together in harmony are far more productive both for themselves and humanity as a whole. What does it matter whose land it is? Possession is titular,('in name') only. Land is for the people who use it to derive a living, not for the politicians for their own self-aggrandizement or hidden agenda.

It is politicians who initially create disharmony. They are past masters in the art of inflaming people with the necessary passion to follow their edicts. They engender tribalism either in the name of religion, or political doctrine, leading to bloody conflicts. If they left well alone, people themselves would learn in time to live in harmony with their ***neighbours*** *for the betterment of both nations. Why interfere with the natural course of events, even though this may take many years, even decades, of peace to achieve.*

History only becomes so after many years of existence. Give it time and events will sort themselves out. No one person is better than the next at the start. Given the same education and conditions some will make more of the opportunities afforded; others may wish to lead a more contented existence without the wealth others accrue in their walk through life.

Who is to say that in the terms of real life, one is better than the other?

As long as all are given the same chances, they should then live without jealously for those who have made more of their life, sometimes at a greater cost to their personal happiness.

Enough of moralising, it only came to mind because of the area to which I have referred and the current conflict which besets the two nations involved as the father of a large family.

Lisbon (Portugal)

My stay in Portugal was just after the liberalisation of that country from the Dictator ***Salazar.***

Until this time the whole country had been a police state. Although Portugal had always been on the side of the Allies during the war, the conditions under which the population lived were no different to Italy or Germany of that time. We, (the West) paid lip service to the regime merely because it sided with the Allies.

After the overthrow of the dictator, a great sense of freedom swept the country, all restrictive laws abandoned, including that of censorship.

The people I met when I was sent to introduce the system in **Lisbon**, for *TAP* the national airline of Portugal, were euphoric about their newly won freedom of expression.

In that atmosphere one could have sold a donkey to the head of a racing stable, and convinced him that it would win a classic race.

No advantage was taken at this state of mind, although we sold and introduced the system in very quick time, and with the enthusiastic help of both front line staff and programmers of that airline.

I was full of admiration for Portugal and its people, and how quickly they had adapted to a new way of life, without the aid of *'Big Brother'*. The country is very beautiful, and its people so charming that the visit although short was a pleasure throughout.

The main memory I brought back with me was the meal I had at a restaurant on the banks of ***the River Tagus***, just beneath the large bridge over our heads that spanned the water. The fish courses offered were superb, with large helpings of highly seasoned shellfish in between each course. Wine was plentiful both during and in between courses.

Sydney, (the Trials and Tribulations of my Visit, 1980)

I had to go to **Sydney** to attend a meeting of all DCS users.

These meetings were arranged so that all users of the same system both at the technical and user level could exchange views and notify changes, which had been made.

The method of exchange saved development costs for the introduction of new facilities. All attendees from other airlines worked on systems, which had the same database, so the integration of changes was a relatively simple matter

The common nature of the systems enabled the airlines to establish a way forward. Major developments could be shared, because all staff that had been trained in the new system could share in such a development.

Programming staff not involved in their company's system maintenance program could be allocated to any new common project. This helped the system to evolve at very little cost to all participants.

Unfortunately during this visit, one of my sons who had been studying for a Chemical Engineering degree at Surrey University and had been sent to South Africa, (for his third year attached to Mobil Oil) had had an accident while out there.

He was located in **Durban** and during this spell he had purchased a Beach Buggy, to allow him freedom explore that very beautiful country. On the second day of my visit I had a phone call from the UK to state that my son had been involved in a serious road accident and was in hospital in awaiting an operation.

Fortunately one of the representatives at this meeting in Sydney came from South African Airways and was a great help. He phoned his office in Johannesburg, who put us in contact direct with the hospital, and I was able to establish that although very serious at the time, his condition was stable and improving by the hour.

My wife and one of my other sons went to Durban (assisted by my colleagues in the UK who arranged all the travel details). My SAA colleague arranged to look after them in Johannesburg and arrange their onward travel to Durban.

The hospital indicated later the same night that it was no longer necessary for me to proceed from Sydney direct to South Africa as my son's life was no longer in danger and my wife and son would keep me informed of progress.

I was greatly relieved and thankful for the assistance given to me during this period of worry by all those around me.

By the time I arrived back in the UK, my wife and son were also on their way back, and about a week later my hospitalised son also returned from South Africa, a little the worse for wear. He had not completed his full year of this course, but the university authorities agreed to let him finish the year in a location closer to the University in Surrey.

United Airlines, and Omaha.

I stated earlier that *British Airways* had sold the system to *United Airlines* (UAL).

After the implementation at **New York**, it was to be introduced next to their station in **Omaha, Nebraska**. I was asked to cover this implementation together with some of their headquarters staff who by now had got to grips with the system, and would soon support its introduction on their own.

Omaha was the last station at which *BA* had contracted to cover. Once established there it would be left to *UAL* to cover its introduction across the rest of its network, including **San Francisco.**

San Francisco was the station at which the original development of *UAL's* own system had been introduced and found wanting. After twenty eight days the *UAL* system had to be abandoned.

This was the reason why *UAL* had to scour the market for a system, which could be purchased off the shelf. The *BA system* came out top of its shopping list after all US and European systems had been investigated.

The *BOAC Sales Manager* and I had to visit **Denver, Colorado**, to discuss the bones of our system to the *UAL* computer staff based at ***Englewood*** to the south of **Denver**. The visit lasted ten days, during which time we visited the beauties of the Rocky Mountains.

Because of the distances involved in getting to and from our place of work, we were allowed to hire a car while out in Denver.

During this stay we were able to visit **Lake Dillon, Mount Evans**, and the ski centre of **Aspen**, as well as **Central City.**

Aspen is a very well-known ski resort to all Americans. The town located in the Rocky Mountains was a town similar in style to a smallish Swiss ski resort town. It is most unlike any other US city, built on a scale in keeping with any ski resort in Europe. Even the chalets were most un-American in style.

On the other hand our visit to Central City, a typical town of the west was a disappointment but nevertheless picturesque. Our approach to this 'Cowboy' town, took us past a *number of prospectors still panning for gold by the side of the stream* flowing down from the mountainous regions above the valley.

In the townlet called Central City we found a saloon which purported to be the original type of bar present in the late eighteen hundreds. I found it surprisingly small, no more than the size of a good-sized living room in a semi back home.

Hollywood has certainly used its 'Texas' imagination to get into that space, the dance hall elements of the western scene together with a large bar and gaming tables.

Now back to my visit to Omaha. This town at the time was the centre for the **Strategic Air Command** of the **US Air Force**. Many of the passengers travelling from Omaha appeared to be Air Force Personnel.

It was there that I tasted the tenderest of mammoth-like steaks. The restaurant was just beside the stockyards, and we had been assured that the meat we were eating had been taken from cows fed mainly on corn. The steak, although an inch thick, could be cut with a fork: it was even tenderer than a fillet steak.

Another strange thing about any visit to the American Mid-West is the fact that although I hailed from Europe, local residents appeared to have little knowledge about life outside the US and within the US, of the Mid-West itself. They could not envisage another part of the world outside the US with a population greater than their enclave in the US. England to them was no more than a town in another country. How often have visitors to this part of the USA been asked if they knew a 'Mr. Smith from England,' for example?

People in that part of the USA are so insular that the world only revolves around their own small environment.

At the Airport in Omaha, I came across an Englishwoman who hailed from Manchester in the UK, and when she heard that someone from the UK was on the station, she made a beeline to meet me.

Even though I have never visited Manchester in my life we had a lot in common to talk about, if only to talk our own form of English. We talked for about thirty minutes and she returned to her insular world of the ***'Omahans'***, never again to be seen by me for the rest of my stay.

The journey back to **New York** and the arms of *British Airways* took about two and a half hours, during which time I was plied with unending in-flight drinks, all served in miniatures at the same time. This was presumably so that the *UAL* Hostess would not have to be disturbed unduly for the rest of the flight.

I heard later that the **San Francisco** had 'cut over' after **Omaha,** went very well and then **Chicago,** (the main station on the *UAL* network), was cut over shortly after. We heard no more from UAL after that, so presumably they were satisfied with the system we had sold them.

The system currently in use by UAL has evolved from the original one sold to them. I *recently had occasion to test the links between these two systems and found that the methods of entries and responses had changed very little over the years.*

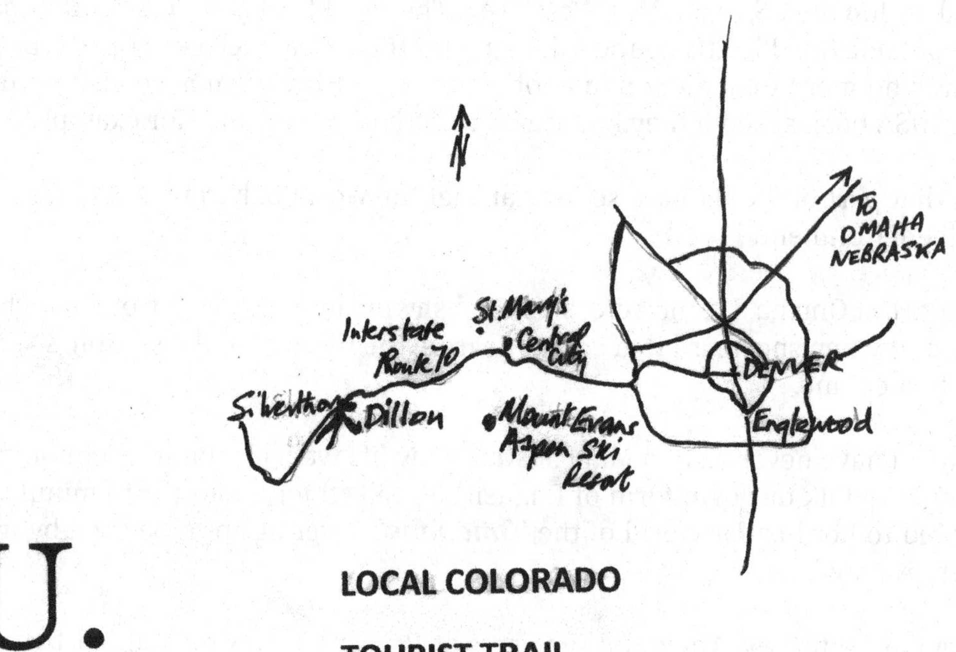

LOCAL COLORADO

TOURIST TRAIL

U. S. A.

insert map showing locality of Denver /Aspen ski resort Plus Colorado/Nebraska border

Singapore and Singapore Airlines

Another airline that purchased our system was *Singapore Airlines*. This airline had recently split from the original airline, which encompassed both Malaysian and Singapore Airlines. Both had decided to go it alone, and each developed in subsequent years into second stage world airlines.

I could understand how *Malaysian Airlines* could develop on its own, because it had a large country behind it. On the other hand **Singapore** was no more than a large city on an island linked to Malaysia by a causeway. Its population size was perhaps less than Hong Kong.

As it transpired later, Singapore became the larger of these two airlines, and for many years operated at a profit. Today, it is buying into other airlines which are in financial trouble, and has a great deal of influence in the World Airline scene.

In its post war history, Singapore has had three airports, the first of which was situated almost within walking distance of the old town centre. It was the scene of an accident to a BOAC aircraft many years before I arrived there. In the centre of this derelict complex was a fine restaurant, no doubt constructed around the old Terminal building.

On completion of our mission to install the system the SIA management royally entertained us to a full Chinese Meal exquisitely cooked and presented. I am not normally partial to Chinese cooking, but in this case I really did enjoy the meal.

The airport at which the system was introduced was named *Payar-Lebar* and was located well outside the city boundaries.

The design of this new building was very simplistic, with the aircraft parked within thirty yards of the 'check-in' desks. This allowed baggage to pass directly through the building on a moving belt to waiting trolleys, to be transported the short distance to the aircraft waiting nearby. The aircraft were so close that the trolleys could have been wheeled there instead of being pulled by tractors.

However, the 'check-in' areas were not air conditioned and became steamy hot in the morning, unlike the offices situated immediately behind, (and all the passenger waiting and boarding areas) which were fully air conditioned.

After the first two days I stayed in the air-conditioned rooms behind, to await any calls from the front desk. At the time I had the build and features, which were similar to the chair-bound detective '***Ironside***', portrayed by the actor Perry Mason. In this story, the detective despite having been shot and crippled in pursuit of his quarry was able to continue his investigative work with the assistance of a small retinue and 'specially' converted van. This was long before the 'disability lobby' was fully vocal in society. As I passed my time in the most comfortable seat in that room, a wheel chair, I fulfilled the illusion and became known to the staff as '***Mr Ironside***'.

As stated at the beginning of this part, I can only put down on paper that which I can recollect from these travels. The rest was so routinely hum-drum and unremarkable that it did not constitute part of my *'memory bank'*.

More Singapore: The 'Oberoi Imperial', and a 'Nasi Goreng' Recipe

While in Singapore I stayed at the *'Oberoi Imperial Hotel'* situated outside the city limits, but close to the other major hotels, and the principal major shopping stores in Orchard Avenue. The Hotel was located at the top of a small hill, and had a very imposing appearance as its architectural style was Indian, both in colour and building design.

Below the hotel was a Japanese garden, with a restaurant in the centre at which I ate occasionally. Behind and above were some 'pleasures gardens', which were frequently used by the indigenous population for social and family outings.

Two things stand out in my mind about this stay. The first was the excessive heat and humidity, throughout the twenty four hours of each day. The regular afternoon downpours, which did nothing to reduce this heat just added to the humidity and made living even less tolerable.

Each day around 0060hrs (ante meridian), I would leave the hotel for the airport. Travel would be by air-conditioned taxi. The heat and humidity hit me each time I left the air-conditioned atmosphere of the hotel lobby to the waiting taxi, a matter of some twenty feet away. The atmosphere was almost suffocating.

The same feeling occurred when I left the taxi to enter the 'check-in' area of the airport. Adjustment to the ambient conditions came slowly, but after about thirty minutes my body adjusted to the heat and humidity.

My other lasting memory of my stay in Singapore was the delicious *'Nasi Goreng'* dishes prepared and served by the Hotel kitchen. I ate very little else whenever I dined at the Hotel in the evenings.

I have tasted this dish in many other countries and restaurants, and have even tried to emulate this dish at home. None of these attempts either by chefs at other famous restaurants, or myself have ever come close to the flavours and exquisiteness of this dish served at this hotel. But then, Singapore is very near to the home of this dish from Indonesia.

Any book of recipes will provide the basic ingredients for this dish, but I challenge anyone to produce a dish of equivalent stature to that served by the *Chef at the Oberoi Imperial in Singapore.*

Singapore has grown rapidly since the 1970s, with hotels being pulled down and new ones reconstructed at a great pace. I only hope that this hotel and the quality of its service still remain.

Oberoi hotels can be found throughout Asia, and can only hope that this one is still standing. I have retained fond memories of the Oberoi Imperial in the Singapore of the late seventies. 'Please, *'Let it be, Let it be'* as was the Beatles' Song's Evocation.

I understand that today the *Payar Lebar* airport has given way to the new one built in ***Changi***. Presumably the site of this new airport is the same as that which housed many of the British Prisoners of war after the fall of Singapore.

I only hope, if this is the case that passengers passing through this airport will say a silent prayer for those who lost their lives on this site.

Copenhagen

My visit to this city was very brief. It took place before the BOAC departure control system was introduced.

It was an exploratory visit to establish what the *Scandinavian Airlines System,(SAS)*, was developing, and whether anything could be learnt from their development. As it turned out very little was learnt.

Two things surface from what remains in my memory, the first of which was the landing in Copenhagen, on *a Trident 3* operated by ***BEA.***

The airport for **Copenhagen** was *Kastrup* and the approach to this airport was from the sea. On this day with clear skies and visibility, the Trident aircraft made its approach testing out its 'auto land features'. I watched out of the window as the aircraft came into land. All that could be seen was water, when suddenly all the engines appeared to go into *'reverse mode'* with a loud roar; and while I was still in *'panic mode'*, the aircraft cleared the runway threshold, and landed safely . . .

Subsequently I found out that this was just a *normal* landing without cause for alarm. Mind you, I do feel that passengers should have been warned about this.

The other incident of note was getting hopelessly lost while walking around the centre of that city. I was reliably informed by others who had visited this city, that nearly everyone could either speak or understand English, but as I discovered this is not so.

I left the town centre, and got hopelessly lost in the streets around the centre. I had not walked more than a mile, but the area became more residential, and no longer a shopping district. As it turned out I was not too far away from the famous *Tivoli Gardens.*

When I asked for directions to return to the city centre in English, no one I spoke to could understand my request. I spoke to more than three people but all to no avail.

Even when I hailed a passing taxi, the taxi driver himself did not understand where I wished to go. Only by touring round the city did I finally find the city centre, and asked the driver to stop.

My view after this episode is that *there is no truth in the saying that everyone in Denmark can either speak or understand English.*

The 'Bangkok Experience'.

The system was sold to *Thai Airways*. This required a visit by a technical expert and myself to talk to the appropriate Thai Airways personnel. The *Bangkok* experience was no different to the others I encountered *in Korea*, *Hong Kong*, and *Singapore :* multiple lane road traffic congestion, smoky unhealthy atmosphere, and unseasonable weather.

By this time system implementation or new sales of the system had become just second nature, and no longer a task which stretched my abilities. So there is little to report on the work side of this visit.

This visit was to sell the latest version of our system to Thai Airways. I was only one of a group of three. We were accommodated at a HOTEL EREWON, a short walking distance from the British Airways offices, in downtown Bangkok. This was close to the shops trading mainly in silks of all kinds. Outside the hotel was a six-lane highway with all six lanes always fully occupied, by stationary cars going nowhere, 'very fast'. This scene was no different to that which I had experienced in Korea.

At peak times both in **Korea** and **Bangkok**, it would take about an hour to complete any journey of less than seven miles. The fumes, which were emitted from these stationary vehicles, was quite overpowering whether walking to the shops or travelling in a taxi whose windows had to be kept open due to the heat and humidity. It was almost impossible in Bangkok to find an air-conditioned taxi, and when it was possible the excess cost would be almost prohibitive.

The hotel rooms at the hotel, an old fashioned placel similar to the '*Raffles*' in Singapore, were not luxurious. Although deemed to be a first class hotel, the air-conditioning was poor; the rooms were ill equipped with modern features, which was very unlike the other more modern hotels in the same town.

The main lobby and rest rooms were very much more pleasant, with a swimming pool, around which were set a number of tables, at which one could dine in the open air to the sound of splashing water, as guests dived in to the water. In the background from the bar, a piano played mainly western type music. This was all very relaxing and I had no great desire to return to the loneliness and discomfort of the bedroom. The whole atmosphere encouraged one to either eat or drink, or both.

At one corner of the hotel outside the front entrance, there were ongoing religious ceremonies around a makeshift open air Temple. I was advised that it was used mainly by Thai to praise or pray to their God. The prayers were either to give thanks or pray for a 'something specific to appear' . . .

This place of prayer was adorned with much gold trappings and statues. Thai religious dancers robed also in fine gold silks with elaborate headdresses would always be present to inspire the locals to pray.

But for the high temperature and smoke from the road traffic, one could spend a good hour or more just watching the ever-changing scene at this place of worship. The atmosphere was so unlike those to which I had become accustomed within our own religious environment.

It was possible to stand and watch proceedings at this shrine in a state of peace and relaxation, amidst the sound of cars, horns and the noise of the crowds walking past.

The impression I gained of Bangkok was not that usually associated with that city by the tourists. We never had time to savour the more notorious aspects of that well-known city. A working two days is no way to get to know a city.

The route to and from the airport, once outside the city had deep wide ditches on either side of the road with people standing in these water filled trenches up to their waists, either collecting or planting vegetation

There is nothing more to be said about my visit there.

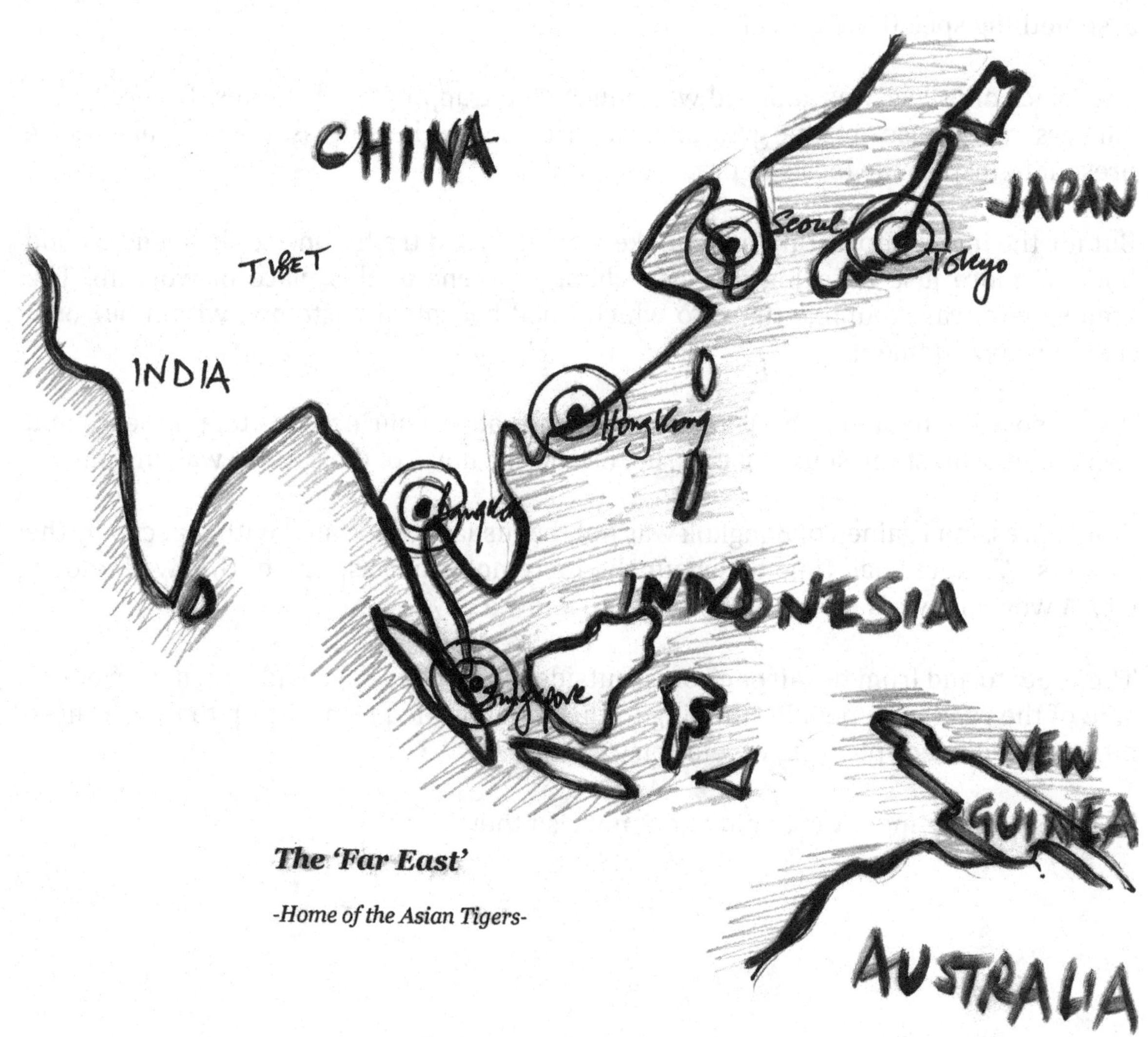

The 'Far East'

-Home of the Asian Tigers-

map of Far East enclosed herein

My visit to San Paulo in Brazil

A colleague and myself were asked to visit Sao Paolo to advise the airport authorities on the construction features required for a new airport.

The contract for the construction had been given to a major Brazilian Construction company, with offices throughout all the major cities in Brazil, including **Rio de Janeiro**. This company traded under the name of *'Hydroservices, of Brazil'*.

Another gentleman from a computer consultancy firm which at the time came under the name of 'LEASCO' formed part of our group. We were required to submit a report after some ten days of discussion with the architects. This was to include the features required of a new airport, and the type of computer, which could drive the required elements.

For this task the company agreed to finance our stay, and also pay out a large amount in consultancy fees all of which would accrue to BOAC.

We were accommodated in a very nice hotel, whose name I forget but in which, each of us had a full suite, with a bedroom and en-suite bathroom, a 'walk-in' dressing room, and a fully fitted lounge with mini kitchen, separate from the bedroom. This was luxury indeed.

On the last evening before our return we were entertained to a banquet by the director of the project. He indicated how grateful he was at the contents of the report he had received.

During the meal I was seated about three places removed from the Director. About ten minutes after we had sat down, the person sitting next to me gave me a nudge and passed to me under the table, a note from this director asking me personally if I wished to join his firm at a salary, which at the time was to me quite exorbitant.

Although flattered by this offer, I declined, as my future rested with the airline not some company who could not guarantee me any long-term security.

With my growing family, a jump into the dark was the last thing I needed, especially as I did not speak Portuguese and would find working in that environment very difficult.

My experiences in Ghana, where a similar offer was made, taught me to tread carefully before taking such a step.

The next day just before departure, we were handed a large sum of *Cruzeiros* for the work done. The sum was as agreed in the contract signed with BOAC. What we were not told was that due to the currency restrictions in force we would not be allowed to take this amount of money outside Brazil!

So the all the money earned in respect of our consultancy fees had been paid directly to us as coinage! Unable to export any such large sums the money was handed over to the BOAC Manager to be banked in the airline's account in Brazil. Many were the visiting 'firemen' that visited this country after our departure, who would draw on these funds deposited by us in the local bank without recognising their source and genesis in our original contribution.

My next visit to Brazil was at **Rio de Janeiro**, where I was involved in a similar venture, but this time fully on *BOAC's* behalf, again for a new airport to be built to serve that city. The national airline *VARIG* had invited us to participate in the discussions they were having with the architects.

I cannot state that I was very impressed with **'Rio'** as a city. Apart from the area around the *city centre*, the *Copacabana* beach, and *Ipanema,* the rest of the city to me appeared to be dirty and ill kept. Much could have been done to improve the lot of the majority of its citizens.

The difference between the living standards of the rich and poor was too marked to be acceptable. *Why must so much wealth in a country be owned by such a small percentage of the population? Why is there not a fairer distribution of wealth in such countries?*

I do not suggest that there should be equality, but at least a raising of the minimum living standards to allow all people to live in dignity.

The more countries I visited on my travels, the more it became apparent, that the living standards of the poorest had to be raised to make life on earth at least bearable for the vast majority who inhabit this earth.

The differences in living standards at the poorest level in Europe, is far higher than their equivalents in Asia, Africa, and South America.

Until this problem is resolved universally, there will continue to be both religious and tribal jealousies, and consequential conflicts.

A content population is far more likely to resist the pressures imposed on them by their politicians. Do 'politicians' breed tribalism and faction for their own selfish aims? If they did ***not,*** *I wonder whether they would find it so much harder to find people prepared to sacrifice what they have, for something they may never get('by jingo')* . . .

I also have no doubt that it is the lack of a proper education which helps to foster this tribalism. Could it be that this is the master plan by some politicians to retain and expand their influence on their peoples?

On this philosophical note I will end this saga of questioning everything around me . . .

I hope the experiences recounted will strike a chord in others, so that the history of the latter part of the 20th century can be recorded by other participants of these times.

'History is viewed in retrospect but always lived in prospect' it has been said.

I think modern history has to be seen from more than one viewpoint.

Research is one thing, but presenting the atmosphere of the times through the eyes of a single person, can add considerably to a reader's knowledge and perspective of the quality of these times.

'Synoptic' vision implies a viewpoint from one perspective and is often used to describe the origin of the Gospels as coming from one origin, (St Mark AD 70).

'Synaptic' transmission (a neuroscience phrase) implies the modulation of a signal through a series of cell linkages, rather in the manner a computer is internally connected through tiny transistorized, *'on/off'*, *'andor'* & *'Nandor'* logic gates in its own micro-architectural anatomy . . .

Like all stories, modern history has to be seen from more than one viewpoint . . . otherwise . . .

History will have taught us nothing and we were always **fated** to repeat the mistakes of the past (first as tragedy and then as farce) . . . but then we have a God Given . . . **'free will'.**

"Though I may speak in tongues of angels and of men but have not LOVE,
am nothing but the sound of clashing symbol or the noisomeness of a gong.
Love is all there is . . ."

. . . so said St. Paul to the Corinthians.

'Here endeth the last lesson.'

©DON HILL 07 October 2002 '(with more yet to be written).'

List of S-23 Short Sunderland 'C' Class Empire Flying Boats

(and associated Vessel Name)

G –ADHL	Canopus	**G-ADHM**	Caledonia
G-ADUT	Centaurus	**G-ADUU**	Cavalier
G-ADUV	Cambria	**G-ADUW**	Castor
G-ADUX	Cassiopeia	**G-ADUY**	Capella
G-ADUZ	Cygnus	**G-ADVA**	Capricornus
G-ADVB	Corsair	**G-ADVC**	Courtier
G-ADVD	Challenger	**G-ADVE**	Centurion
VH-ABG *(G-AETV)*	Coriolanus	**G-AETW**	Calpurnia
G-AETX	Ceres	**G-AETY**	Clio
G-AETZ	Circe	**G-AEUC**	Corinna
G-AEUE	Cameronian	**G-AEUF**	Corinthian
G-AFBL *(VH-ABF)*	Cooee	**G-AFCJ**	Champion
G-AFCU	Cabot	**G-AFCV**	Caribou
G-AFCW	Connemara	**G-AFCX**	Clyde
G-AFCY	Captain Cook *(now ZK-AMC Aotearoa)*		
G-AFCZ	Australia	**G-AFDA**	Awarua *(originally Cumberland)*
G-AFKZ	Cathay	**G-AFPZ**	Clifton
G-AFRA	Cleopatra		

A celebration of the life of

DONALD EDWARD HILL

1st June 1923 – 3rd April 2011

MONDAY, 11TH APRIL 2011

ST ERCONWALD'S CATHOLIC CHURCH, WALTON-ON-THAMES
at 10:30am

COMMITTAL SERVICE AT HANWORTH CREMATORIUM
at 12:20pm

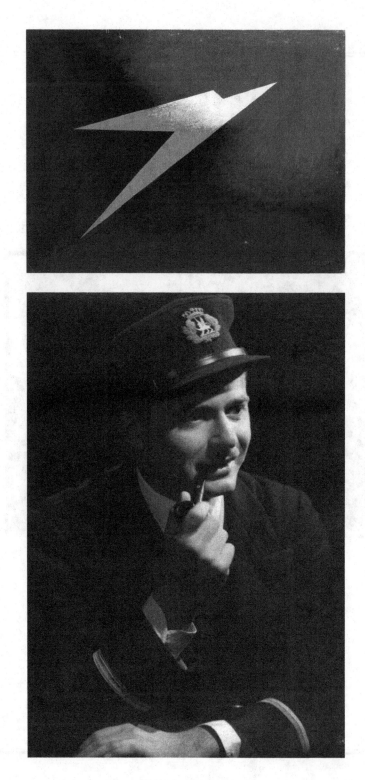

'Pilot Officer 71919 Don Hill'...
'to the ends of the earth'...(W. Golding)

CMR-200 Short S.23 "C-Class" Empire Flying Boat

in "British & Australian Airline" service

[Four-Engined Flying Boat]

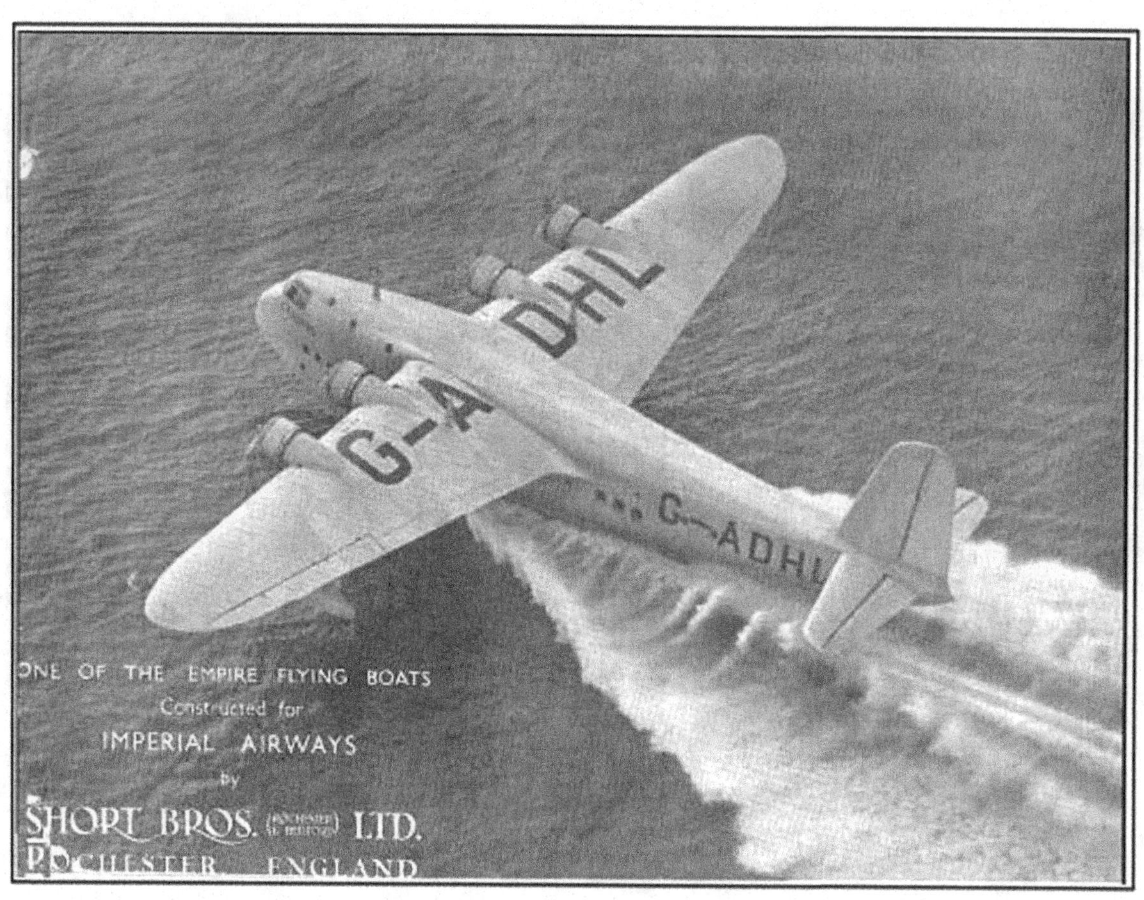

Canopus In Flight

'Speedbird' Bibliography

Philip's Concise Atlas of the World The Royal Geographical Society;

The Second World War Vol.1-6, (esp. Vol. 4 'The Hinge of Fate') Winston S Churchill;

The Seven Pillars of Wisdom, T E Lawrence(Col);

World Aircraft, Robert Hall, (pub. Chapman);

Comets and Concordes,(and those I flew before), Peter Duffey, (pub. Paladwr Press)

Babs, Beacon and Boadicea, Brian Harris(pub. Speedwing Press)